A JOURNEY TO THE SOURCE

OF

THE RIVER OXUS

CAPTAIN JOHN WOOD

EDITED AND INTRODUCED BY

Matthew Schrimpf

NASHVILLE, TENNESSEE

OZYMANDIAN EDITIONS
Nashville, Tennessee
www.ozymandian.xyz

First published in 1841.
Second edition published in 1872.
This edition published in 2024 by Ozymandian Editions LLC.

Introduction © Matthew Schrimpf, 2024.

ISBN: 978-1-966134-00-8

Ozymandian Editions books may be purchased in bulk for business, educational, or promotional use. Special editions can also be created upon request. For more information, please contact the Ozymandian Editions special orders department at special.orders@ozymandian.xyz.

Ozymandian Editions is dedicated to the dusty corners of that greatest of all tutors, the past. We seek to deliver to the curious reader crisp editions of lively titles, both classics and heretofore neglected texts, as well as new works of distinctive interest, all worthy of careful contemplation by the glowing hearth of a manor or the drafty candlelight of a garret.

To learn more about Ozymandian Editions and join our community, we invite you to join us on our website, which you can access at www.ozymandian.xyz or by scanning the QR code below.

Editor's Note

Our guiding principal in this edition has been the faithful preservation of the author's voice, and as such we have made only limited adjustments to the original text. Idiosyncrasies of spelling, punctuation, and style remain unchanged. Place names have also been retained in their original forms (e.g., retaining "Sind" rather than the modern convention of "Sindh"), with the exception that most accent marks on words and names from non-Western languages, recognizing that they provide limited insight into pronunciation to the modern Western reader, have been removed for greater ease of legibility. We have relied on the second edition of the book, edited by his son Alexander and published thirty years after the original, in the creation of this latest release. We are grateful also to Alexander for providing in his edition numerous supplementary biographical details on his father on which we have drawn in introducing the text.

Introduction

Afghanistan has, for the entirety of the twenty-first century, played a starring, and troubled, role in geopolitics. Despite its modest size and distant situation, it has consistently occupied the front pages of American newspapers ever since the September 11th attacks and the outset of the War on Terror, stretching through two decades of armed conflict and nation-building efforts to the heartbreaking images of desperate people crowding Kabul Airport, grasping onto departing airplanes, and tumbling to the ground in August 2021 in their attempts to flee the country before the the U.S. completed its military withdrawal and the Taliban reasserted its full control over the country.

The outsize prominence of Afghanistan in grand strategy, is not, however, only a recent phenomenon. Indeed, the conquests of Babur and Tamerlane reach back to centuries before the country began to figure in European affairs. When western empires started to take a greater interest in this forbidding territory and its people in the early nineteenth century, it was still only roughly known. The development of a more refined understanding of its geography now acquired a greater urgency for diplomats, military men, and traders alike.

In 1836, at the outset of the anabatic journey whose recollection he would set out in the pages to follow, Lieutenant John Wood of the Indian Navy received the instruction from his superior, Sir Alexander Burnes, that "while we perform the duty which has been entrusted to us, it is still to be borne in mind that we have it in our power to combine with the correct discharge of that duty the advancement of general knowledge." With the Russian and British Empires consumed by the Great Game for Central Asian dominance, that duty was for Wood to fill in with practical detail the heretofore only dimly sketched geography of the Indus River and the mountains of Afghanistan above it—to acquire "a more perfect knowledge... as well for the purposes of commerce as of war." It was a perfect mandate for a young officer of burgeoning curiosity.

Wood was one in a long line of Scotsmen to serve on the frontiers of the Empire. Born in Perth in 1813, he had joined the Indian Navy after finishing his schooling. In 1835, he took command of the first steamboat to traffic on the Indus, a vessel owned by a Persian merchant in Bombay, the launch of which was consistent with the British government's objective of increasing commercial activity on the river and in the region. Wood proved himself an effective surveyor with his analysis of the suitability of its channels for navigation and his careful measurements of its rhythms through the seasons, and the skills that he honed during that time would contribute to Burnes' confidence in appointing him to his subsequent mission.

If his recollections of this journey were circumscribed only to the strict fulfillment of his duty, their interest for a general readership, whether in his own time or in ours, would be limited. The enduring charm of his book rests in its ability to provide the nineteenth-century equivalent of a GoPro livestream as Wood traverses a harsh and uncertain terrain, treats with not only local potentates but also holy men, peasants, and bandits, and achieves one of the greatest cartographic feats of his generation in tracing to its rarefied origins a river that had figured in the imaginations of geographers and historians since the days of Alexander's conquests. In

Wood's own words, the book "affords another proof of how often the real events of life exceed in interest the wildest conceptions of fiction."

Wood's journals are, beyond their gripping adventure, also a self-reflective demonstration of how approaching unfamiliar peoples, cultures, places, and, indeed, times with a mind primed for learning and open to empathy can lead to richer understanding and even admiration. In praising the contributions of one of the local members of his traveling party, he observes:

> More intimate acquaintance with Eastern countries has considerably modified my unfavourable opinion of their inhabitants, and taught me to dissent from those wholesale terms of abuse which Europeans too often lavish on the native population. It will generally be found that our opinions of a people rise as our acquaintance with them increases. Vice in every community is sufficiently prominent to be seen without being sought after; but the wise and good shun notoriety, and it is only when we probe society deep that they are discovered.

While he found much to admire, however, his views of the local society were not romantic or sentimental. He was appalled by the active and brutal trade in slaves that he found to be a commonplace reality in this region. He was not shy to confront this injustice when speaking with local leaders, recalling that "I exerted myself to point out, in the most impressive terms I could use, the deep guilt of this degrading traffic, and how contrary it was to every principle of humanity and justice." He was not optimistic that his own words alone would do much to move the hearts of these leaders, but he expressed hope that sustained efforts toward the promotion of education could eventually eradicate the blight:

> For my own part I can perceive one and only one mode, by which the traffic in human beings may be

done away with. It is in the general diffusion of knowledge. The time will come, though it may be still far distant, when the printing press shall perform as great wonders through the whole of Asia as it has done, and is still doing, in Europe. Then, and not till then, will man know what is his duty towards his fellow men. That slavery can continue to exist in any nation where instruction, moral and religious, is generally diffused, I hold to be impossible. Let all those who are anxious for the abolition of slavery, and the conversion of the heathen nations, exert themselves to diffuse education among them.

The reader may undertake his or her own evaluation of Wood's forecasts relative to the current state of affairs in Afghanistan under the government of the Taliban.

Wood may have been a military man bearing the weight of an arduous and extended mission, but he also invites his reader into some of the lighter moments of his journey and indulges in a spark of humor with a charmingly casual, matter-of-fact delivery. We see one of Wood's companions rapt in joy upon his engagement to be married, and we meet a naturally jolly young man who recounts his own rather less happy experience of marriage with a mixture of fear and good humor ("On that ill-fated day she seized me by the throat, and has held fast ever since.") We meet a dueling Frenchman demanding satisfaction when his companions decline to join him for a bottle of wine before breakfast, and we join Wood in treasuring the song of a tea kettle on a fire's red embers on a night of howling wind. We hear of the pleasure that the addition of a dog brings to Wood's company, and we learn of the fearsome consequences of calling an Uzbek a "dog-seller."

The lake that Wood finally identifies as the source of the Oxus would stand for fifty years as the definitive answer to that question, until Lord Curzon would contest his claim and trace its origin to an ice cave in the same mountains. Upon reaching the source of this "celebrated river," consistent with his office, he first fulfills his duty—giving us the specifics of its elevation, latitude, longitude, and water temperature and his methods for ascertaining these facts—and only afterward proceeds to indulge in more poetic description of the terrain ("the hoary summits of the everlasting mountains, where human foot had never trode, and where lay piled the snows of ages") and the commentary thereon left by his predecessor Marco Polo.

After completing his journey up the Oxus, Wood continued to live with an explorer's spirit. He retired from the Indian Navy when the conflicts of the First Anglo-Afghan War fractured his relationships with the Afghans whom he had, during his expedition, assured of his government's goodwill. Wood's subsequent career would take him to Australia, New Zealand, and Europe, but his final mission found him back where he had started—on the Indus river, commanding a flotilla of steam ships, and keeping up the rigorous workload that would eventually fulfill his desire "rather to wear than to rust out." Taking ill amid the fatigue of a hurried journey to Simla in 1871, his body, but not his legacy as an explorer, would finally do so.

M. Schrimpf
October 2024

CHAPTER I

The depressed shore of Sind offers no remarkable object to the mariner's eye. The coast-line is submerged at spring-tides, when the delta of the Indus resembles a low champagne tract of verdure, with tufts of mangrove dotted along its seaward edge; and the approach to the embouchure of this far-famed stream has a dreary and unpromising aspect. Entering by the Hajamari mouth, we wound up its tortuous channel to Bander-Vikkar on Saturday the 17th of December, and there exchanged our sea-going boats for the Sindian dundi, or river craft.

Sind has two ports, Vikkar and Karachi. The former, situated on the river, is used only for the export of rice, the staple of Lower Sind; while in the latter, lying just without the delta, centres the foreign trade of the country. It is plain to all who are conversant with nautical affairs that Karachi is the only safe seaport for the valley of the Indus. When the season is favourable the merchant may indeed send his goods direct to the mouth of the Indus; but everything here is subject to such constant change—the weather, the depth of water, the channels, and the very embouchure itself—that this voyage, even in February, is not without its hazards. As the danger is more in approaching the river than in quitting it, the exports may, in November, December, and January, be sent direct from its mouth: but all imports should go to Karachi, which affords the only safe anchorage during the other nine months of the year.

After a short stay at Vikkar permission arrived from Haiderabad for the mission to ascend the Indus, when, threading the upward portion of the Hajamari, we entered upon the main stream at the village of Siya'han.

In the neighbourhood of Vikkar is the imbedded hull of a Dutch brig-of-war, pierced for fourteen guns, affording proof, if any were wanting, of the ever-changing course of the Indus. It is vain in the delta of such a river to identify existing localities with descriptions handed down to us by the historians of Alexander the Great. The whole country from Kach'h to Karachi is alluvial, and none of its spontaneous productions, the tamarisk tree for instance, exhibit the growth of a century. Higher up the course of the river, where its channels are more permanent, this tree attains to a large size, and this never being the case in the delta, our conclusion would appear legitimate, the soil at both places being the same.

Could the northern apex of the delta be as easily fixed as its triangular sides can be defined, we might then venture to speculate on the probability of Alexander having visited Kach'h or Gujerat. Burnes has, I think, shown that the mouth by which the Grecian fleet left the Indus was the modern Piti. The "dangerous rock" of Nearchus completely identifies the spot; and as it is still in existence, without any other within a circle of many miles, we can wish for no stronger evidence. But I must own that, though both tradition and formation attest the Run of Kach'h as having in former years been an inland sea, I should, considering the short detention of the fleet at Pattala, be more inclined to look for the lake of Alexander's historian within the limits of the modern delta of the Indus than to appropriate the Run for its site. Dunds, or large sheets of stagnant water, formed by the annual rise of the river, still exist on the line of the Pinyari. These abound in fish of a large size; and, though differing from marine species, the Greeks who state their identity may here be supposed, without impugning Arrian's veracity, to have come to this conclusion more from the large size of the fish in the lake than from a very minute examination of their varieties. Supposing then the Pinyari to have been the eastern arm of the delta in the days of the Greeks, we should fix the site of Pattala where now stands the modern town of Jirk. But, as before observed, the absence of tangible localities involves us in a maze of doubt; and hence our deductions are oftener the result of fancy than sound inference.

The old Dutch-built vessel mentioned above affords negative evidence that the mouths of the Indus in her day were not more accessible than at present. She is built for shoal waters, as her sailing draft could never have much exceeded six feet. Her construction, like the "galliot," is round-sided, flat-floored, with little depth of hold—all qualities adapted to shallow seas. Her length is seventy-one feet and her width of beam twenty-five. The port-sills are now about two feet and a half above the ground, and the nearest stream the (Siya'han) is distant 200 yards from the wreck. From 300 to 400 rounds of shot and shell, together with twenty musket-barrels and some pieces of brass and iron ordnance, were disinterred from her after-hold. The shot was of every calibre, from an ounce ball to a 12-pounder; and along with other rusty articles was forwarded to Ha'iderabad for the satisfaction of that court. The Amirs, we may well imagine, were better satisfied with this present than with a somewhat similar one since made them from Karachi, when some 32-pound shot were lodged by H.M. ship "Wellesley" in the walls of its castle.

We have tolerable evidence that the Indus has never been more or less navigable than we now find it to be. Tavernier, nearly two centuries ago, said, "At present the commerce of T'hat'hah, which was formerly great, is much diminished, as the mouth of the river is always getting worse, and the sand, by increasing, scarcely gives room for a passage." Again, Captain Hamilton, who

[13]

speaks very favourably of the Indus, marched, in the year 1699, with a caravan from Lari-bander to T'hat'hah, so that in his time there was a portage the same as at present; and we are thus warranted in concluding that the navigable capabilities of the stream were then not greater than they now are. And lastly, Mr. Crow, a very accurate observer, who, at the close of last century, was the East India Company's agent at T'hat'hah, thus writes: —"The Indus, as a river, has few merits, except its periodical swell; its stream is foul and muddy, and so full of shoals and shifting sands, that flat boats only are safe, and scarcely any others used."

Every one who has written of Sind mentions the gross ignorance and timidity of her people; and last year at this place my introduction to them was marked by an occurrence somewhat confirmatory of this opinion. When the little steamer I then commanded entered the river, she was boarded by a deputation headed by the Nawab of Vikkar. On their taking leave, some of the party would, contrary to advice, persist in crowding into the ship's punt. Pushing off from the vessel, the little boat heeled to one side, on which half a dozen frightened Sindis ran to the other; and the boat, as we all expected, turned keel-up, and swamped the deputation. Fortunately there was little current, and, the firm bank being at hand, no lives were lost.

The deltas of large rivers (the Nile excepted) are usually too monotonous to interest the eye. In the Indus, after passing the belt of mangrove that margins the sea-coast, and ramifies wherever the water is brackish, we meet with the tamarisk and reedy-grass, varied occasionally with a solitary Parkinsonia, which here, like the cocoa-nut palm on the coast of Africa, denotes the near neighbourhood of man.

When opposite to Pir Putta we rode over and visited this ziarat. The hill upon which the buildings stand is of crescent shape, and from its northern brow you look down on a sheet of water in the stagnant Bagar, once a principal branch, but now a deserted bed, of the Indus. A ruin rises from the other horn of the crescent, while the space between contains the tombs of holy men. The elevated site of Pir Putta, and the beautiful white stucco with which its walls are covered, render it a remarkable object amid the dead flats of the delta; and it is discerned from the river long before you come abreast of the shrine. The saint who is here interred is said to have been contemporary with Saadi, the Persian poet, who flourished in the thirteenth century of our era. Pilgrims, while here, are supported by the chief of the district, who has stored up for their consumption large quantities ot grain and ghi. It is customary for strangers to contribute to this fund, and likewise to bestow some gift on the shrine. We gave alms to the poor, but were not permitted to take leave without being reminded that something was due to the tomb itself. Sind abounds in the remains of saints, and her morals are corrupted and her wealth dissipated by their depraved followers. This shrine is, next to that of Lai Shah-baz, at Sihwan, the most revered in the country.

The hills on which Pir Putta stands are of the limestone formation, with which a shelly deposit is largely incorporated. They rise about two miles south of the temple, take a northerly direction, dip under the bed of the Bagar, and reappear on the other side of the Mukali hills, by which name they are known at T'hat'hah. Three and a half miles north-north-west of the town the range terminates; its general direction being about north-by-east, and south-by-west. The hills are tabular, but often disconnected, and their greatest elevation, I should think, under 100 feet. Their surface is barren of vegetation, if we except the milk-bush and pelu tree.

T'hat'hah is a place interesting to modern geographers, from its being the supposed site of the Grecian Pattala; but is better known in Hindustan by the fine productions of her looms. The town lies at the foot of the Mukali hills, in the alluvial valley of the river, and three miles distant from its stream. The mounds of rubbish upon which the houses are piled slightly raise its site above the level of the valley. In the season of inundation its environs abound in swamps, and after heavy rain pools of stagnant water are numerous, both within the city and in its suburbs. Good dwellings are scarce; and, from the very perishable materials of which most of them are constructed, there is considerable trouble in keeping them in repair. A heavy shower of rain, by shedding their mud-plaster, disfigures the outside of a house that may yet be comfortable within, and gives an appearance of poverty where it may not really exist. Still, making a fair deduction for defective architecture, and the squalid habits of Sindis, the present state of T'hat'hah is the reverse of prosperous, while her inhabitants wear that blanched, sickly hue, the faithful index of an unhealthy clime. In the summer of 1836 I had ample reason to denounce this place as an unhealthy locality; an opinion which the sickness of our troops cantoned there during the year 1839 has unhappily verified.

The manufacture for which this town has acquired some commercial celebrity in the East is the lungi, a rich fabrication of silk, cotton, and gold, variegated in pattern and of close texture. The raw silk in most estimation with the weaver is that from the Persian province of Ghilan.

On the bills behind T'hat'hah are the tombs of many a by-gone generation. The ground for a distance of four miles is one burial place. Many of the larger mausoleums, though falling to decay, are yet noble structures. The architecture cannot be referred to any of the legitimate orders, but there is a sombreness and solidity about it that well becomes the grave. Above the entrance door to one small neat enclosure, containing different-sized tombs, apparently those of the several members of one family, was inscribed in Arabic the single word Allah (God). Supposing them to have been struck by "the pestilence that walketh in darkness, or by the destruction that wasteth at noon-day," what word could better express the anguish of the lone survivor?

In the neighbourhood of T'hat'hah are the ruins of Kullan-Kote and Sami-Nuggur, places to which the natives ascribe a high antiquity. The latter is a diminutive earthy mound three miles north-north-west of the town, built over with hovels; its elevation above the valley, and consequent security from inundation, having attracted inhabitants to it. Kullan-Kote, or "the Large Fort," is four miles from T'hat'hah, in a south-west direction. It is a fortified hill three-quarters of a mile in length by about seven hundred paces broad, and at one time was evidently surrounded by water, though the lake is now confined to its north and north-west angles. The outer wall in many parts is standing, but there are no vestiges within from which to conjecture what its internal arrangements may have been. The face of the hill overhanging the lake has a disturbed appearance. The rock is split into deep chasms, and huge blocks of conglomerate lie scattered below. A spot so suited to the Hindu ascetic has not escaped the wandering fakir: their habitations are, however, modern.

From the advantageous site of T'hat'hah for commercial purposes, it is probable that a mart has existed in its neighbourhood from the earliest times. But as the apex of the delta is not a fixed point the site of this city must have varied as the river changed. As a place of traffic it would naturally be situated close to the stream, and exposed to its ravages; nor is it likely that the buildings of the ancient city were more substantial than those of the modern T'hat'hah, which, standing in the valley of the same wayward river, is still liable to similar calamities. Hence we have a series of names, Dewul, T'hat'hah, Brahminabad, Nuggur-T'hat'hah, and Sami-Nuggur, by which this commercial mart was known to successive dynasties, or perhaps bestowed on occasions when the river's encroachments rendered a change of site necessary. Deterred from the erection of any permanent stronghold in the plain, the inhabitants

[17]

would naturally look to the neighbouring hills for refuge. The commanding situation of Kullan-Kote afforded them this, and its name (the large fort) seems to imply its having been a place of refuge in times of danger. The love of building, restrained by natural causes in the valley, found full scope for its indulgence on the Mukali ridge behind the town. Here, neither labour nor expense has been spared, but only for the absurd purpose of giving the dead better accommodation than the living.

Leaving T'hat'hah on the 10th of January, we looked in at Ratti, a little village on the opposite shore; where, in the opinion of one of its fair inhabitants at least, I had been an unwelcome visitor the preceding year. The circumstances were these:—the steamer had moored just below the village, when, at about seven o'clock in the evening, we were startled by a loud continuous noise, like the rush of falling water or the rolling of distant thunder. The up-heaving of the river and quick heavy roll of the vessel told us that part of the bank had given way. Before the water could regain its level another and another mass fell into the stream. We landed and surveyed the scene. Since sunset a great alteration had taken place in the bank of the river. One house had been ingulfed, and its inmates were now busy removing to a place of safety what had been saved from the wreck. Large fires were blazing on the verge of the bank, by help of which, the people were endeavouring to find where the next mass would part. Those whose houses stood nearest the stream were employed conveying their goods and chattels further back, aware that though the river's caprice might grant a respite for a day or two or more, yet its ravages would only be the more destructive when they were renewed: for when the current inclines to a new channel, the opposing bank must continue to be undermined until a shoal is formed, sufficient to give a new direction to the stream. The night was still and dark, save the dull sonorous sound of the plunging mass booming across the turbid waters, on which the beacon fires shed a leaden glare. The people are so accustomed to these visitations, that no screams were heard, nor was there a look of terror on any countenance: but one of the sufferers, the crabbed old lady to whom I have alluded, was uncharitable enough to attribute this disaster to the presence of the firingis (Europeans).

When the waters of the Indus are low, the noise caused by the tumbling in of its banks occurs so frequently as to become a characteristic of this river. During the silence of night the ear is assailed by what at first might be mistaken for the continued discharge of artillery; two, three, and even four reports are often heard within the minute, and even thirteen have been counted in that short space of time. In the angles of the reaches the occurrence is most frequent; but its effects being then mostly confined to worthless sand-banks, are attended with little detriment to the inhabitants.

On the 14th of the month we were abreast of Hilaya, a village on the west bank of the stream, where hearing of a lake not far distant, we went to it. On the road we passed a small venerable looking square enclosure of plain freestone, which our guide informed us was the tomb of Jam Tamatchi, the father of Indus fishermen. It had its legend, which a Sindian gave us, pointing to an individual who, we were informed, was lineally descended from the Jam. Tradition is always worthy of a hearing; but it the Celtic bards of our own land are liable to the charge of having contributed to corrupt the sources of history, the fables current in Sind may be charged with the heavier offence of having directed its stream.

The method of fishing in Kinjor lake, though practised elsewhere in Sind, was new to me. Below that part of the water to be fished a line of nets supported on stakes runs right across the lake. At intervals along this barrier line short circular nets opening inwards are attached, like so many outworks of a fortification. These project considerably above the water, and are formed of double stakes, one perpendicular and level with the surface, the other long and slanting backwards. Between these hangs a bag-net, into which the fish falls when it tries to escape by leaping. The figure represents the position of the stakes.

When the nets are placed, fleet of small boats assemble in the direction A at the head of the lake, and dispersing over its surface bear down on the barrier net. As the object of the fishermen is to frighten their prey,  tom-toms, tambourins, triangles, cooking-pots, and shields, are pressed into use for the occasion, and most discordant are the sounds that ensue. The fish driven before their pursuers, make for the opposite end of the lake at B, and encountering the principal net, are, in their endeavours to double it, piloted into a bastion. Here, their exit opposed on every side, and the noise increasing, they try to leap over what they cannot pass through; but however high they jump, it is only to drop into the trap prepared for them.

We halted next day near a village called Sonda. Hitherto the appearance of the country bordering the river had been monotonous and dreary. Here we had an agreeable change. From the head of the Hilaya reach, on looking south, we could, for twelve miles, trace a noble stream full half a mile wide, and throughout the whole of that distance, as straight as an arrow in its course. The west bank for some distance to the south is lined by a low range of sandstone hills, between which and the river lies a belt of fine babool trees. The opposite bank, though a shorter distance, is clad with similar mimosa, and from among their dark foliage on both sides of the river little white turreted towers occasionally show themselves to the river voyager. The barometer gave 136 feet for the height of the ridge, in climbing which we roused, from under a prickly pear bush, a savage-looking hyena.

At this spot the Indus takes a sharp turn, and in the bend is a projecting rocky ledge, under cover of which, on its south side, alligators love to sun themselves. They are the guryial or long snouted variety, and are harmless, at least I never heard of their being otherwise. It is strange that at Karachi, a place so close to the Indus, fakirs should possess the other species, none of which are met with in the river. Among the outlying hills that skirt the Hala mountains, about nine miles from that town is a hot spring, the temperature of which, where it wells from the earth, is 136° of Fahrenheit. The stream irrigates a small valley and supplies some swamps with water, in which the fakirs keep numbers of tame alligators. The pond where we saw the congregated herd at feeding time was about eighty yards long and perhaps half as many wide. It was shallow and studded with small grass-covered islets, the narrow channels between which would only admit of a single alligator passing through at a time. Two goats were slaughtered for that morning's repast during which operation a dozen scaly monsters rose out of their slimy bed, crawled up the back of the tank, and eyed with evident satisfaction the feast preparing for them. All being ready, a little urchin, not nine years old, stepped without our circle, and calling ow, ow, (come, come) the whole tribe was in motion, and as soon as the amphibious animals had gained terra firma, the meat was distributed. Each anxious to secure a piece at his neighbour's expense, the scene that ensued was ludicrous enough, and not a little disgusting. A hind-quarter of a goat gave rise to a general engagement. One by one the combatants drew off till the prize remained in the grasp of two huge monsters. Their noses all but touching, each did his best to drag the bloody morsel from the jaws of his adversary: and a long struggle ensued, in which, by turning and tossing, twisting and writhing, they strove for the mastery. It was a drawn battle; for the leg was torn asunder, and each retained his mouthful, when, with heads erect, they sought the water, showing as they crawled along considerable tact in avoiding their less successful neighbours.

I should have mentioned before, that for escort duty the mission was provided with a small detachment of Arabs from the Rajcote residency. These men had not yet all joined, and at T'hat'hah twelve Beluches of the Jokiyah tribe were hired to accompany us through Sind. They entered our service with the greatest readiness, and proved by their subsequent conduct that they fully merited the confidence reposed in them.

Late events have unfortunately but too well established the insatiable appetite of the Beluche race for rapine. But let us not forget the wide distinction between the guilt of plundering an invading army's commissariat, and that of robbing the merchant or traveller. Both of these classes may with some confidence appeal to the honour of the tribes, and except being mulct in heavy duties have rarely suffered any loss, even among those natives who were the most active in harassing our troops. There is much to be said for these misguided people. Where clanship prevails, the chief and not his men is responsible for the actions of the tribe. The Khan of Kelat has since paid the penalty of his folly; yet, though disloyal to Shah Shuja, he gave his life to the cause he had espoused,—and who will venture to malign the motives of the man who set such a seal to his principles? During the late campaign across the Indus, it has been customary for some of the Indian journals to brand both Beluche and Afghan as cowards. The first are doubtless a vaunting race, but the storming of Kelat proved them good men and true. At Ghizni, though taken at a disadvantage, the resistance our troops encountered from an unprepared garrison shows of what the Afghans are composed. It is harsh to use such hard words against any nation, especially when we recollect there are pages in the early history of our own country, during the struggles between the English and Scotch for example, when the troops that fought bravely one day, acted like very cowards the next. A disorderly rabble, though composed of men individually brave, can offer no effectual resistance to disciplined battalions; but were the same men brigaded, officered and hedged about with cannon, they would soon become formidable soldiers. We have proved this in India, and Russia has done the same both with the Persian and the Turk. Far be it from me to palliate the many cruel murders of defenceless camp followers of which these men, both Afghan and Beluche, have been guilty. Yet man in his semi-barbarous state is so little given to reflection, and so much the child of impulse, that in judging of his actions where our own interests are at stake, we are apt to be swayed by prejudice and passion where reason only should decide. But to return to the Jokiyahs.

A question had arisen as to whether these mountaineers or the Arabs were the better marksmen, and it was agreed that an hour's practice should decide. A bottle was placed on a sand-bank, about seventy yards off, to hit which entitled the winner to a canister of gunpowder. Round followed round, and still the bottle stood unhurt; at length the Jumti's mirbar detected that the line of fire was direct on Mecca; and this discovery, while it opened the eyes of both parties to the cause of their former failures, had the additional effect of restoring their lost good humour. The bottle was shifted, and confidently this time did the marksmen kneel and take aim; but it was to no better purpose, not one of them could hit the mark, the alteration made having neither steadied the hand, nor improved the visual organs of either party.

A southerly gale springing up, our sails were soon opened before it, and by sunset of the 18th the fleet reached Haïderábád. The preceding day had been passed at anchor, the heavy sand drift rendering it next to impossible for the crews either to track or sail the boats. Jirk was the only place of size which we passed, and in order to obtain some compass bearings I had occasion to visit it. The town is about midway between T'hat'hah and Haiderabad, close to the river, on the summit of a table-hill belonging to the sandstone ridge where the alligators bask. Its houses have stone wind-sails fronting the prevailing wind, by which means a stream of pure air is made to circulate through the several apartments when, out of doors, scarce a breath of wind seems stirring. This method of ventilation is very general in Sind, and none but those who have passed the greater portion of the twenty-four hours in a feverish state of existence, with the thermometer at 100° of Fahrenheit, can duly appreciate its use.

In a turner's shop in Jirk we saw a well-finished article turned off the lathe. It was only a drinking bowl, but the delicacy of touch with which the colours were laid on far exceeded my ideas of Sindian skill. Many of these people have naturally a turn for mechanics; witness the beautiful gun-barrels made all over the country, the much-admired products of the T'hat'hah loom, and a very handsome description of orange-shaped box, manufactured at Haiderabad; which last, when it finds its way into the British provinces, is placed upon the same side-table with the rarities of China and Japan. Timber being scarce in Sind, much ingenuity is often displayed in the patch-work of their boats, and individuals are to be met with who have successfully imitated the construction of musical boxes and other ingenious contrivances, and articles of fancy work.

The mission remained a fortnight at Haiderabad; but as many descriptions of this court and capital are already before the public, I need not dwell upon the subject.

Before quitting the city we visited the tombs in its neighbourhood, and well were we repaid for the trouble. The hill on which the town stands is a mile and a half in length and seven hundred yards broad. Its direction is about north-by-east and south-by-west, whilst its height may be eighty feet. On the north end of this plateau are the tombs, and at its opposite extreme is the fort and town. The tombs of the deceased members of the reigning family are grouped a little apart from those of the preceding dynasty. Of the Talpurs, that of the reigning family Mir Kuram Ali is the only fine structure. Display characterised this chief in life, and a love of pomp seems to have gone down with him to the grave. It is a quadrangular building, with a turret rising from each corner, and a handsome central dome. But the mausoleum of Gholam Shah, of the Kalora dynasty displaced by the Talpurs, is far superior to all the others. Its figure resembles that of Kuram Ali's, but without the corner turrets. The purest parian marble lines the inside of the building, which is highly ornamented with mosaic work and decorated with sentences from the Koran. The tombs of the Kaloras are neglected, but those of the reigning family are kept in tolerable repair.

The chief, Amir Nur Mohamed Khan, was evidently solicitous that his reception of the mission, and the sentiments he professed to entertain for the British government, should make a proper impression. Whilst guests at his capital we had been honourably entertained, and now that we were to resume our journey northwards, we were invited by him to accompany himself and his brother, Mir Nasir Khan, in a visit they were about to make to some Shikargahs (game preserves) at Lakkat, about forty miles north of Haiderabad, and which lay in our line of march.

The attachment of the Sind Amirs to field sports is well known. To gratify this passion, large tracts of land on the banks of the river are set apart for game-preserves, and kept in a state of nature. For so doing the Amirs have been censured, though I am inclined to think with too great severity. Were the population of Sind double its present number, there is ample land for their support without infringing on the ruler's prerogative. The exclusive privileges enjoyed by their Highnesses is not peculiar to Sind, but one that has prevailed in most countries in a similar state of society. The history of our own land more especially offers numerous examples of oppressive forest-laws. Hume tells us, that a king of England possessed sixty-eight

[25]

forests, thirteen chases, and seven hundred and eighty-
one parks. Further, that transgressors in these were, in
Richard the First's reign, punished by mutilation and
the loss of sight. No Sind Amir ever thus sported with
the life of the subject.

Around Lakkat the country is covered with jungle,
among which are the game-preserves. On reaching the
village, the Amirs presented each of us with a suit of
Lincoln green, after receiving which we were warned to
be ready on the morrow. By sunrise next day we were on
the hunting ground. The shikargahs are laid out in the
form of triangles, and so connected that the game, on

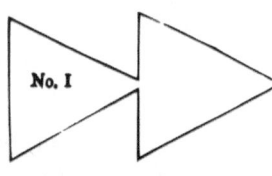

escaping from one enclosure
takes refuge in another.
Thus:—Entering No. 1, we
took our station in a rustic
booth at its apex, and
patiently awaited the game's
approach. The shikárgáh was
a thick forest of young trees, with plenty of underwood
and tolerable herbage. In front of us was an open space
of about ten yards square, and, for double this distance
beyond, the forest was indented by narrow pathways
radiating from the booth. A pack of dogs had been let in
at the opposite end of the enclosure, and we had not sat
long before we heard the noise of their approach. The
jackal early took alarm; but seeming conscious it had
only the dogs to fear, the cunning animal trotted
leisurely across the cleared space into the next
shikargah. Mir Nur Mohamed sat with a couple of guns
before him, watching with a painful earnestness the
jungle in front. At length in one of the lanes, a boar, a
grizzly-looking patriarch, was detected showing his
tushes. The Amir nodded and gave a gun to Captain
Burnes; and had our gallant commander broken a bottle
a hundred yards off, his skill as a marksman could not
have been more highly complimented than for
slaughtering this huge boar at arm's length. A few
minutes more elapsed, when the underwood was seen to

shake, and presently a deer broke cover. He came dashing down the green lanes at a gallant pace, but ere he could clear the break he was despatched by a ball from Nur Mohamed's rifle. It was an excellent shot. We beat up two preserves, but all the game they yielded was a couple of deer and eight hogs.

We next attended their Highnesses on a hawking excursion; but the banks of the Indus were not here sufficiently open for this old English pastime. The Amirs nevertheless expatiated on the pleasure this sport afforded them, and enumerated the variety of birds in their possession, all which, they added, come from Afghanistan. Food was procured for the smaller of these falcons by a kind of archery that I never saw practised elsewhere. There is nothing particular about either the bow or the arrow, but in using the weapons the archer darted the arrow so as to strike the object with its side instead of its head. The larks, which he was shooting, were picked up stunned by the shock, but alive. Partridges are shot in the same manner.

At Lakkat I left my companions, and returned to Haiderabad, from which place my examination of the Indus commenced, the section of the river south of the capital having been accomplished the preceding year. From this time I only met the mission occasionally when it halted at the large marts on the Indus, for the purpose of procuring information on their trade and commerce.

Chapter II

Separated from head-quarters, and by the nature of my employment restricted to the river, our intercourse with the Sindis was now mostly confined to river-lying tribes. The country indeed holds out no temptation to stray inland, and but few of its towns repay the visitant for the trouble he is at in getting to them. Halla and Khodabad we had been informed were exceptions; and on the 21st of February, being abreast of these places, I paid them a visit.

Halla is divided into the old and new town. The last division is much the larger of the two, and is the most considerable place between Haiderabad and Sihwan. Like the last mentioned town, it derives no small degree of importance from the shrine of a Mohamedan saint, that of Pir Mukdum Nu. The land around is highly impregnated with salt, and what little cultivation I noticed is confined to an old bed of the Indus, close to the smaller Halla. The bazar is partially roofed, but however effectual the covering may bve as a defence against the sun, it does not keep out rain, for when we were here the ground beneath it was a perfect puddle. The bustle of its bazar showed that the place was thriving; and if agriculture does not flourish, the mechanical arts apparently do. Halla has been long noted for its excellent earthenware and Sindian caps. The latter being national, are worn by all classes, rich and poor, privileged and oppressed. The prosperity of the cap-maker is evinced by numerous symbols of his craft in the shape of stout round-headed posts, which, standing out in the streets, fronting the shop-door, are more like kerb stones than sign-posts.

The manufacture of earthenware is confined to the new town. Here are two establishments, one employing six furnaces, and the other two. The clay is taken from the bed of the Indus, and the wheel upon which it is worked is evidently the potter's wheel of Scripture. The patterns are various, and such as are intended to contain rose-water, or slabs for the decoration of tombs, are tastefully executed, the latter especially being remarkable for warmth of tone and brilliancy of colour. The metallic oxides used are those of iron, copper, and lead. In the composition of the finer articles, ground flints form a principal ingredient.

An earthy, soap-like substance that the natives term "chunniah" is obtained from lakes not far from Halla. Chunniah is largely eaten by the women of Sind.

The ruins of Khodabad are situated a little to the north-west of Halla, and cover two square miles of ground. It wras a favourite residence of the Talpurs, and here many of their chiefs have been interred. Under one dome, and side by side, lie the founder of the dynasty, Futi Ali Khan, and his brother Mir Gholam Ali; while in an adjoining mausoleum are deposited the remains of Byram, Bejur, and Sobdar, chiefs of the same house, who suffered severely from the tyranny and vindictive spirit of the latter Kaloras. The mausoleum of Futi Ali is small yet neat, built entirely of red freestone, the only marble used being for the prayer-slab that fronts his grave. The other tombs are of a still simpler construction. The three chiefs lie on the same platform, and their graves are protected from the elements by a light canopy supported on pillars.

The tombs just mentioned are the only buildings in Khodabad which are in even tolerable preservation; of the dwelling-houses not one is entire. Little more than thirty years have elapsed since this city rivalled

Haiderabad in size and population. How perishable then must be the architecture of Sind! and, in a region such as this, how apt will the antiquary be to invest, in the ardour of his search, mounds of yesterday's formation with the sanctity of ages! In a mud basin undergoing continual change, such as the valley of the Indus south of the mountains, it is almost vain to look, after the lapse of so many centuries, for indications of the Grecian general's march. The Panjab rivers are similarly circumstanced; it is therefore no matter for surprise that the altars erected by Alexander on the banks of the Hyphases have not been discovered. I do not think the account given by his historians favours the idea of their having been erected in the Alpine regions of the Panjab. Alexander was evidently crossing the plains when the mutiny occurred that necessitated his return. In such a time of ferment the most easterly limit of his line of march would in all probability be the site of his altars, and the chances therefore are that they have long since been swept away by the changing streams of the Beas or the Sutledj.

On the evening of the 22nd of February, as the crew were securing our boat to the bank, they discovered a family of otters, which by their angry cries seemed to consider us intruders. Anxious to obtain one, an attack was forthwith planned, but though no precautions were omitted it was only partially successful. Two were made prisoners, and as many more escaped. The latter refused, however, to quit the neighbourhood, and throughout the night serenaded us with piercing shrieks, which were redoubled whenever the captives replied to their call. The two we had taken were full grown, but evidently the young of those which had escaped. The habitation of these interesting little animals had two entrances, which met before they reached their inner circular burrow, and were elevated four feet above the river, which in this month was at its lowest level. Two days after these otters had been taken I was awoke in the middle of the night by a noise proceeding from the fore-part of the vessel, and on inquiring the cause was told we were boarded by otters from the shore. When I got on deck the assailants were swimming alongside, giving utterance to a sharp peevish whine whilst those on board, after vainly struggling to get free of the bag that held them, grew calm, but still continued a low piteous moan. Whether the visitors were the parents of our captives, or strangers attracted to the boat by their calls, is matter of doubt. In either case the circumstance is remarkable, for since the 22nd we had moved ten miles onward, and crossed from the left to the right bank of the Indus.

When in the delta, the matins of the lark told us when day had dawned; but here the song of this early warbler is often interrupted by the partridge's call. In addition to the common grey partridge, Sind possesses another species of striking beauty. The head, breast, and belly of this bird are of a jetty black. A red ring encircles the neck. The back of the head is speckled white and black, while a large white spot is dotted under each eye. The wing-feathers are spotted yellow on a black ground. Those of the tail are short and downy, marked by delicate white and black bars towards their extremes. This is a heavier and altogether a nobler looking bird than the other. From the predominance of dark feathers in its plumage, it is usually called the black partridge.

On Friday, the 3rd of March, we passed Sihwan, famous in Sind for the shrine at Lai Shah-baz, and equally notorious for its beggars and courtesans. The castle is an object of interest to Europeans, from the bare possibility of its being one of those beleaguered by the Macedonians. Burnes speaks of it thus: "By far the most singular building at Sihwan, and perhaps on the Indus, is the ruined castle overlooking the town, which in all probability is as old as the age of the Greeks. It consists of a mound of earth sixty feet high, and surrounded from the very ground by a brick wall. The shape of the castle is oval, about 1,200 feet long by 750 in diameter. The interior presents a heap of ruins, strewed with broken pieces of pottery and brick. The gateway is on the town side, and has been arched: a section through it proves the whole mound to be artificial." It is mournful to contrast Sihwan as we now see it with that city's once flourishing condition. The Ayen Akbari tells us that Sewistan, of which it was the capital, had forty thousand vessels upon the Indus; and, after making a due allowance for the bold assertions of Eastern authors, we learn from such a statement that it must once have been the centre of commerce and wealth. It is a singular coincidence, that the tonnage now upon this river is very nearly equal to what it was in the time of the Greeks. Two thousand vessels of all sorts, from the galley to the tender, are said to have composed the fleet of Alexander, and of these eight hundred are called by his historians vessels of war and transports. During the late military operations in these quarters, the vessels that would come under the latter designation were found to amount to about seven hundred, and if we include the small craft of the fishermen (the tenders of the Greek fleet) we might easily reach the larger number.

The method of building boats on the Indus is illustrative of another circumstance in Alexander's memorable expedition—that of transporting his vessels by land from the Indus to the Jalum (Hydaspes). In this country the sides and bottom of a boat are completed apart, and then brought together to form the vessel. The labour of carrying the largest boat may thus be much lightened, and is an operation of common occurrence in the present day on the banks of the Indus. The Macedonians had been in the habit of doing the same thing at the Isthmus of Corinth, and it thus becomes a question whether boat-building, as practised there, countenances the idea of Sindian naval architecture having had its origin in Greece.

Proceeding onwards, the bed of the river widened, and its immediate banks, when low, were either covered with pulse or oil plants. These crops require no tending, and whether destroyed by the inundation or swept away by the stream, the farmer's loss is light. But valuable produce—such as sugar, indigo, cotton, and grain—requires greater circumspection; and fields of these are seldom seen exposed to such dangers, except when the waywardness of the river, by eating away the bank, has set at nought the most cautious calculations of the husbandman. When this unfortunately happens, as it often does, the bank for some distance above the fields may be observed fenced with tamarisk branches, which has sometimes the effect of preserving it from further waste should, however, the body of the stream have set in on the farmer's land, he must nerve his mind to witness the labour of a whole season lost in a single day.

These constantly recurring changes in the course of the Indus confuse the rights of property on its banks. We are told that geometry owes its origin to the inundations of the Nile destroying the landmarks in its valley. But the Sindians prefer superstition to science, and have resort to the following primitive mode of settling their differences:—Mir Nur Mohamed Khan we shall suppose to possess the east bank of the Indus, and his brother Mir Nasir Khan the west. On the inundation subsiding a new island rises in the stream, to which both parties lay claim. A boat is ordered, and a confidential servant on the part of each Amir, stepping on board, takes with him half a dozen empty earthen jars. The boat is now placed half a mile up-stream, beyond the island, from which position in mid-channel the twelve pots are committed to the guidance of the current. On whatever side the smaller number of these messengers pass by the island, the new-formed land is thereby decided to belong of right to the proprietors on that bank of the river.

This portion of Sind is populous and well cultivated. Numerous villages are seen from the river, and all of them embosomed in trees. Though the country produces no timber available for ship or house building, every village has its clump of evergreen, reared less for ornament than shade. Near Mitani are a few gigantic peepul-trees, which, standing singly in the fields, have a very agreeable effect. In a country like Sind, where there are no hedges, plantations, copses, or enclosures of any sort, to break the monotony of its level surface, it is good taste to encourage planting. The fakirs, who take a pleasure in gardening, are the great horticulturists of the country. I have known one of them to freight a boat at B'hkur to transport plants to Haiderabad, a distance of near two hundred and fifty miles. These people swarm in Sind, and are the pests of society, for their drain on the working man far more than counterbalances what little good they do; but the fakir here mentioned deserved well of the community, at least in this instance.

The season for taking the pulla-fish had now commenced, and the animated appearance presented by the river's bank was indeed an agreeable change. Until lately the stream rolled silently onwards, whilst here and there the scattered huts of a few miserable fishermen, a boat occasionally dropping down with the current, or perhaps a herd of cattle swimming the river, were the only indications that the country was peopled. But at this time the Mianis, or villages, that remain unoccupied during one half of the year, become suddenly thronged by a busy and cheerful population. Here may be seen a crowd dragging to land a net of more than ordinary dimensions; while, clustered by the water's edge, stand expectant the children, the aged, and the infirm, all equally eager to learn its contents, and to shout their Shahbash should the "haul" exceed their expectation. Passing on, we observe the surface of the river to be dotted with little dark specks, which, on a nearer approach, are discovered to be fishermen supported by earthen jars, or upon dry reeds. Those mounted on the former frail but buoyant bark float much at their ease; not so the poor fellows who ride upon the latter. By degrees the reeds become sodden, and the fisherman's head is then just above water; but to counterbalance this inconvenience, his bark costs him no care, and at the commencement of every trip he launches forth upon a new one. The pulla-fish enters the Indus about the beginning of March, and quits it early in September: that is, they frequent it during the whole time the river is rising or full. In the latter end of May they are caught in the greatest quantity; the drag-net landing sometimes a hundred and fifty at a haul. As we ascend the river the fish is less plentiful. I have met with the pulla as high as Mittun-Kote; but there are no established fisheries north of B'hkur.

The river is portioned out into sections, where the right of fishing is strictly confined to their respective Mianis. The inhabitants of these villages are registered, and, besides giving every third fish to government, a tax in money is levied on the village. The amount was fixed by the Kaloras, and according as the communities have since their time prospered or declined, so is this assessment felt to be light or oppressive; the present government not having as yet made allowance for their altered numbers. The produce of the Mianis is sold by the fishermen on the spot to those who purchase this right of government: for in Sind the revenue is farmed to the highest bidder. The money obtained from these fisheries is part of the Dur-myani, or general revenue of Sind.

I had heard so much of Wulli Mohamed Lagharl, whose memory is deservedly held dear by all classes in Sind, that when abreast of Larkhanah I could not refrain from visiting the place of which he had been so long the governor. It is a rambling-built town, situated in a date-grove, on the banks of a fine canal. The necessaries of life are here exceedingly cheap, and water plentiful, whilst the luxuriant foliage of the mangoe-tree affords a cooling resort in warm weather to the inhabitants, who have thus reason for being attached to the spot, and have a Sind proverb—

"Hoard abroad, but squander in Larkhanah."

It is really cheering to hear of such a character in Sindian annals as that ascribed to the Nawab. Peasant and noble alike applaud his virtues, and the rulers of the land did not refuse to profit by his counsel and advice. Many anecdotes of this chief are told by those who knew him, illustrative of his ready wit, his love of justice, and his deep knowledge of mankind. The following story shows his talents as a keen-sighted politician:—When Mohamed Azim Khan held power in Kabul, he despatched Mudut Khan with 20,000 horsemen to recover the arrears of tribute due by Sind. The Sirdar encamped near Shikarpur, and sent forward an officer to demand the money. It was refused, and the Court of Haiderabad thought of nothing but repelling the Afghans by force of arms. Before proceeding to this last appeal, the Amirs sent to Larkhanah for Wulli Mohamed Khan; and he, on being asked his opinion, counselled peace. On this he was saluted by the chiefs in durbar, by the opprobrious name of Wulli Bam, or the Hindu. Nothing daunted, the Nawab looked round, and inquired of the Amirs how high they estimated the life-blood of a Talpur? "Beyond price," was the reply. "Well then," said the sagacious Wulli Mohamed, "victory is in the hands of God; but should you try the fate of battle, whether vanquished or victorious, many of your relations, now present, will be missed at next durbar." This reasoning produced the desired effect; and Wulli Mohamed was forthwith deputed by their Highnesses to compromise matters with the Afghan Sirdar. The Nawab spoke in a different strain to Mudut Khan: "Are your people mad," said the wily chief, "to enter a country as enemies where there are seventy thousand Beluches, Sahib-i-Shumshir (excellent swordsmen), in arms to receive you. Try the issue if you will; but first listen to the advice of one partial to your countrymen. You are aware that the strength of Kabul is gone, and that the Yuzir has his hands fully occupied in keeping the tribes in check. You are in a country without a single friend; and if defeated, which it is certain you will be, you cannot expect to see Kabul again. To save your honour, I shall endeavour to persuade the Amirs to give you as road expenses (nalbundi) two lacs of rupees." Mudut Khan acceded to the arrangement, received a lac upon the spot, and bills on Kabul for the remainder.

On the 24th we reached Rori, where, learning that Captain Burnes was expected on the morrow from Khyrpur, on his way to Shikarpur, we awaited his arrival. Next day he came in, bringing with him an agreeable addition to our party in the person of Dr. Lord, who had been appointed to the medical charge of the mission when it was first organized; but being at a distance from the Presidency when we left it for the Indus, he had only now been enabled to join us.

The ruins of Arore lie S. 26° E., three miles and a half from Rori. They occupy a rocky ledge, overlooking what appears to be a deserted arm of the Indus. From the existence of a substantial causeway connecting Arore with the Rori side, it would seem that this bed, up to a very late date, was submerged by the waters of the inundation. The soil is of superior quality; and when I visited the spot it was covered, south of the causeway, with crops remarkable for their healthy and luxuriant appearance. The causeway is 480 yards long, fifteen feet wide in the centre, and ten toward the ends. It has a central arch of fifteen feet span, besides five other small ones. The height of the former is ten feet. Arore is also known to the Sindis by the names of Kumun and Jatri. While here, I heard of the ruins of a place called Mulala, on the east bank of the river, fifty miles to the north of Rori.

Returning from Arore, we encountered a party of eighty-three fakirs on march for the shrine of Bhawul Huk at Multan. A heavy club graced the shoulder of each, and from it dangled behind a small lota or drinking-cup. They were a sturdy set, with little of the devotee in their looks. As they passed us I involuntarily gave them the road, while my thoughts reverted to an Irish gang on march to Donnybrook fair. The provoking importunity of these people is past belief. Sometimes they will surround your tent, and, what with their horns and stentorian lungs, almost drive you to desperation. While thus noisy and troublesome, their behaviour is often so truly ludicrous, that, though well inclined to be angry, you are constrained to laugh. The Amirs suffer equally with their subjects. I remember once to have seen a fakir make a most determined set on the charity of Mir Nur Mohamed Khan. The fellow would take no refusal; and on the Mir's sharply observing that "beggars on horseback could scarcely be in want," briskly replied, "that all he required was money to buy a saddle." His impudence did not avail him.

At Rori a low bleak ridge, of limestone and flint formation, crosses the bed of the Indus. On the east bank the rock, crowned by the town of Rori, rises abruptly from the river, and is washed by a current of four miles an hour at one season of the year, and of nearly double that velocity at another. On the west bank, where the town of Sukur stands, the ridge is depressed and is swept by a narrower and more tranquil stream. In the mid-channel are several islets; the tile-stained turrets on one near the east shore giving it more the appearance of a Chinese pagoda than a Mussulman's tomb. Two of these islands are famous in Sindian story: B'hkur for its strength, and Khadja Khizr for sanctity. The banks of the river for some distance below B'hkur are fringed with the date-palm; and its appearance, always pleasing, is here heightened by the character of the neighbouring country. On the west bank stand the ruins of Sukur, with its tall minar towering gracefully above the dark date-groves. Red flinty hillocks form the background on both banks; while between them rolls a broad stream, adding beauty to the whole.

The Indus, throughout the whole of its navigable course, is occasionally swept by terrific blasts, which, while they last, prostrate everthing before them. Fortunately, they give timely warning of their approach, and long before the gathering storm bursts, the careful tracker has moored his boat in security. At this place, on a subsequent occasion, I witnessed one of those short-lived sand-gales, which in strength and in sublimity of appearance I have never, either before or since, seen equalled. We were then on the Sukur side of the river. On looking across the water about four o'clock in the afternoon, gloomy clouds were seen coming along, their heavy masses evidently pregnant with the elements of a storm. Momentarily they deepened their dark hue, and as the waving masses moved and rose above the date-trees on the opposite shore, the grove almost appeared to be on fire, the boiling cauldron of clouds above representing smoke, while the lighter shades of the dense mass looked like flame. The grove was soon veiled in darkness, and an ominous silence hung over the Sukur bank, while the storm in giant strength stalked over the naked surface of the river, as yet unagitated by the smallest ripple. Presently the gust struck the bank where we stood with the blast of a hurricane, and for two minutes blew with a force which it was impossible to face. Cowering with others behind the pillars of a dilapidated house, though sheltered from the fury of the storm, we had yet ample employment to prevent suffocation from the torrents of sand it carried with it.

Sukur is the place where Shah Shujah, now King of Kabul, defeated the Sindian army in 1834. The expedition which the Shah then undertook for the recovery of his throne was, though thus far fortunate, eventually unsuccessful; and his Majesty, after a variety of hardships and adventures, again returned to his asylum in Lodiana. The slaughter at the battle of Sukur is said to have been considerable, and a still greater number of men are believed to have perished in the Indus than by the sword of the Shah's adventurers. One Sindian chief, high in rank and very corpulent, had taken the precaution of anchoring a boat in the stream, as a means of retreat in case of defeat. Exhausted and breathing hard he gained the boat, but no exertion of her crew could lift him on board. Time pressed, and life is precious. Absorbed with this one thought, he forgot both his dignity and the respect due to a Moslem's beard, and

called out to his people, "Rish bagir!" (seize the beard)—
an expression by which, as a sobriquet, he is still known
in Sind.

Chapter III

Shikarpur did not equal my expectations. I knew of its extensive connexions in Central Asia, and had concluded that a place possessing so widely ramified an agency, and the residence of so many rich bankers, would, in proportion to its commercial importance, have surpassed in appearance the less favoured towns of Sind. But the only point in which it seemed to be superior was in the large and comfortable dwelling-houses of its wealthy Hindu merchants. The bazar is large, wider than usual, and, like that of most eastern towns, roofed over; but the covering was in a sad dilapidated state, while the shops were either ill supplied with goods, or their owners shunned display; it was however well frequented, and from its crowded thoroughfares I should conclude Shikarpur a populous place.

While here, a Mala or fair wras held in the dry bed of the Sind canal, to the banks of which I hurried, with a companion, to witness the festival. This rejoicing is held in honour of the periodical rise of the Indus, the blessings of which they partake of by means of this canal. Our way led through the principal bazar, but, except by a few elderly shopkeepers whom the love of gain still kept at their posts, it was deserted. Outside the city-gates numerous vehicles had taken their stand, which, for a mere trifle, were at the service of foot-passengers. They were in constant request, and many a happy group did we pass, comprised of all ages, sexes, and conditions. We had come out for amusement, but the annoying pressure of a dense crowd speedily made us sensible we were to pay for this pleasure. At length we got into the bed of the canal, and, having rode clear of the crowd, dismounted and secured our camels to the bushes on its banks. On foot we were soon lost among the multitude, with many of whom we had much friendly converse, and being in the native garb we enjoyed the scene without being ourselves objects of remark. Walking down the right bank of the canal, our attention was first drawn to a large peepul-tree, from beneath the spreading foliage of which issued the sounds of music and the song. This was a Hindu Nautch, and the singers were men. The audience were ranged in rows, encircling and pressing close upon, but never jostling, the performers. The females present outnumbered the men, but during the time we remained there was no unbecoming levity in the one sex, nor any quarrelling or drunkenness in the other. The rate of remuneration to the performers was left to the liberality of the audience, and here the cold prudence of the sect was as remarkable, though not so commendable, as their quiet and orderly demeanour.

Neither copper nor silver money were to be seen in the fair. Refreshments were paid for in cowrie-shells, of which there are ninety-six to a pice, the smallest copper coin in circulation.

Leaving the Nautch, we walked up to a party of four demure-looking men, who, in the society of their wives, were quietly enjoying a game at Chopper Kallu. They civilly invited us to a seat on their mats. The game is played like chess, but, instead of sixty-four squares, the Shikarpur board has ninety-six. Cowries were used as dice, and cone-shaped pieces of ivory for chessmen. We inquired of several such parties what the stakes were, but received for answer that they never played for money.

Observing a number of people entering a large building, we did the same, but, save some pretty faces and a hideous-looking member of the Hindu Pantheon, nothing was to be seen. It was the residence of a holy man, who, on such an occasion as the present, would not fail to make the most of his credulous visitors.

As the evening drew on the crowd began to disperse, and from our station on the elevated banks of the canal we could see the ladies at parting shake hands with as much cordiality as is customary among Europeans. Many went down into the canal and bent their foreheads to its bottom, blessing the water-course for former gifts, and then for their anticipated continuance; others put a handful of its sand to their lips, then, scattering it in the air, made one or two circular motions with the body, and departed homewards. When men are seen on their knees muttering a manter, or spell, before a paint-besmeared idol in the gloomy recess of some dark and moist cell, it is natural for those blessed with a clearer light to regard with horror this profanation of the commandment, and to stigmatise those who so act as a nation of idolaters. But when we see individuals, in the gratitude of their hearts, prostrating themselves by the banks of a noble river, the agent and immediate cause of the soil's fertility, we are inclined to judge less harshly.

I had often before remarked that a native of Sind never travels without shoes or sandals on his feet; and to-day this was amply verified. In this respect he seems to think, with an Englishman, that if the head and feet be well protected, other parts of dress are of minor importance.

Zyndul Abdin Shah, eldest son of Mir Ismael Shah, the Haiderabad Vuzir, was at this time governor of Shikarpur. As one instance of Sindi ignorance, out of many which could be enumerated, I may mention that the governor's brother asked us whether the Duryah or ocean had a periodical rise like the Indus, and if the water of the Ganges was salt or fresh.

On the 8th of April I left the party and returned to the river by a road that threatened us with many a fall before we got to the end of it. So rugged and rutty are the roads in Sind which lead from place to place, and more especially in the neighbourhood of towns, that exercise taken upon them, either mounted or on foot, approaches more to pain than pleasure. Communication between districts is kept up by roads on the edge of the desert, which, though somewhat similar, can be travelled over in wheeled carriages, and are less inconvenient than those in the alluvial valley. Carts are but sparingly used in Sind, though it is to he hoped they will ere long be more common; for although there will always be extensive tracts accessible only to the bullock and horse, still wheeled vehicles might be advantageously employed in all the drier and more elevated districts of the valley. The easiest way of journeying is upon the camel, though not at the snail's pace at which a caravan travels. The long-trot of a Sani, or running-camel, is quite another thing.

From B'hkur to Mittun-Kote the western bank of the Indus is in the possession of lawless tribes, which occasionally make stealthy visits to those of more settled habits on the opposite side of the river. Their object is plunder only; but, though expert thieves, blood is sometimes shed. This insecurity of property was indicated at Larkhanah by the new arrangement which is there first perceptible in the villages, the houses being either surrounded by a common wall, or a strong mud fort stands in the middle of the town, into which the inhabitants retire when danger threatens them. In Lower Sind, which is comparatively a quiet and well-ordered country, no such arrangement is observable in its villages. The predatory tribes are the Burdi and Muzari, both nominally subject to Khyrpur, though Mir Bustum Khan, ruler of that country, takes no effective measures to put down so disgraceful a system of pillage. While the blood of his subjects is made to flow, and their property despoiled, Bhyram Khan, the Muzari leader, is

[44]

rewarded with lands, and at the time we passed up the river was an honoured guest at the court of Khyrpur. The truth is, the territories of this state are split into so many independent principalities that no member of the family, even though possessing the power, feels himself authorized in employing it against these banditti. Were he to do so, he would be sure of making enemies, while, even though successful in putting down the robbers, he would gain no friends. The Amirs and their Sirdars are of the same Beluche origin as the guilty tribes, and this is another reason why the Khyrpur chief regards the misdeeds of these men with so lenient an eye, and is so little disposed to test the fidelity of his own followers in a struggle where the ties of kindred and similarity of disposition unite, it not to sap allegiance, at least to render all offensive operations lukewarm and ineffectual.

These observations on the weakness of the Khyrpur state are equally applicable to Haiderabad. Nothing but a strict adherence to the Chinese system of avoiding political relations with foreigners could have preserved peace in a country like Sind, so pregnant with the elements of discord. In pursuing this line of policy she has been favoured by her situation; for, with a dreary desert to the east, a high mountain-chain to the west, non-intercourse with the Panjab states, and the River Indus closed, her position was virtually insular. It was her object to maintain it so. Neighbouring nations were ill informed of the real resources of Sind, and, as usual where uncertainty prevails ignorance is prone to magnify everything, while the Amirs took special care that the received opinion of their military prowess should not lack the support of a haughty, and in some instances an insolent, bearing. But this unsatisfactory state of affairs could not last long. It was unjust to India that a river designed for the good of many should be engrossed by a few, who turned its advantages to no good account. The British government therefore wisely determined on throwing open the navigation of the

Indus. Once in treaty with an European power, it required no prophet to foretell that the crafty policy which had hitherto been the security of Sind could no longer avail it; for where power is portioned out, as in this country, among a number of independent chiefs, it is impossible but that difference of opinion will occur. Mir Mohamed Khan, who is now ostensibly the ruling Amir, is as a monarch virtually powerless; and should he be held responsible for the acts of his co-regal partners, misunderstandings will happen, distrust be engendered, and quarrels must ensue. Were our relations with Sind similar to those we have established with the protected Sikh states, there would be less distrust on the part of its Amirs, and more confidence on ours.

Wherever we landed between B'hkur and Mittun-Kote the print of tigers' feet was met with, and, what is singular, they were not once remarked below the former place. This was perhaps, partly owing to the nature of the country, which here is poorly cultivated, while the banks of the river are fringed to a varying depth with a thick cover of reedy grass and tamarisk jungle.

Buffaloes in this portion of the river were likewise more numerous than lower down: they had completely seamed the jungle with their tracks. When green food fails them they crop the upper end of the reed or feathered grass, and large districts were observed which had thus suffered. Numbers of these huge tame brutes lay at the entrance to almost every creek, enjoying the luxury of mud and water, with only, perhaps, the tip of the nose or the curved end of a horn visible above the surface. In wild solitary tracks, where the tiger may be supposed occasionally to prowl, the tingle of a buffalo's bell is a sound at all times grateful to the traveller's ear.

The wealth of many families in Sind consists in their herds of horned cattle; and of their produce, hides and ghi, Karachi exports a considerable quantity. The former are collected by a class of people called Memans, of the Mohamedan cast, who traverse the country solely for this purpose. The latter is brought up by Hindu merchants, and is, under the name of Karachi ghi, much esteemed in India. The buffalo, the animal which furnishes the principal supply, is milked in the evening, and only once in the twenty-four hours. Although a large portion of the Sindian population leads a pastoral life, the country is essentially agricultural. Nowhere have I seen a greater scarcity of the natural grasses than in Sind, considering how the Indus bisects and fertilizes the soil. It is a diverting sight to witness a herd of buffaloes swim the river; all is noise and confusion, and considerable tact is necessary on the part of those who command the movement. A herdsman bestrides a bundle of dry grass, seizes a sturdy animal by the tail, and on this singular carriage takes the lead. The other buffaloes follow, while laggards, and any that may be vagrantly inclined, are driven up to the main body by the cudgelling of men in the rear. The herdsmen are armed with long light lances, for the defence of themselves and their charge.

On the 19th we passed the village of Allah Chatchur-ke-gote, the property of Nihal Khan, a Beluche of the tribe of Murry. It had been attacked and plundered by Muzaris, from the opposite or western bank, three days before our arrival. A villager lost his life, and two were wounded.

On reaching Mittun-Kote on the 29th I found a letter from Captain Burnes, directing me to join him at Ahmedpur m the country of Bhawul Khan. I started the same day, and slept that night at Khan-baila a considerable town on the south bank of the Sutledj, eighteen miles from Mittun-Kote. The intermediate country had a rich soil, and its surface was often, as far as the eye could range, one continuous corn-field. It was harvest time; and crops of wheat and barley stood ready for the sickle, dressed in the rich livery of the season. Numerous labourers were in the field, all of whom spoke favourably of Bhawul Khan, or rather the Khan, as his subjects familiarly style him. The taxes are paid chiefly in kind, which is as agreeable to the ryot as it is favourable to their chief. Circumstanced as the countries bordering the Indus were until lately, money payments could only be made at a grievous loss to the grower, bu now that he has an open market for his surplus produce, in addition to his own government, the case is altered, though it will take some years before the change will be appreciated, as in the end it assuredly will be. Were the rulers of this and the other countries bordering the river but capable of looking a little forward, they would be truly thankful to the British government for re-opening the Indus; since, by this just proceeding, their countries, and consequently themselves, must necessarily be benefited. If this enlightened act has not hitherto been attended with that measure of success which there was reason to anticipate, the fault is our own. A more clumsy treaty, even after it was patched up by I do not know how many amendments, than that which professed to open the river Indus, has seldom been framed. One would have thought that even in the hey-day of monopolies and municipal privileges, before Adam Smith had enlightened the world with more sound opinions on commerce, enactments to the following effect could hardly have been penned:—

That every laden boat, without reference to her size or description of cargo, (be it Kashmir shawls or grain,) shall, for permission to navigate between the sea and Lahore, pay a duty of 50l. Again, it was enacted that no description of military stores should be sent by the Indus. By the first of these sage regulations the river was shut against the merchant, and by the second prohibitory clause the British government was deprived

Of a tangible and immediate good—that of supplying the arsenals of the north-west provinces by the direct route of the Indus, instead of by the more circuitous line of the Ganges.

During the late military operations on this frontier, the above treaty was necessarily infringed; and we may now hope to see regulations for the trade and navigation of the river more politic and sound. The country is here inundated by the periodical swelling of the Indus. When the waters retire, the seed is thrown down, and the farmer has no further trouble till harvest calls him forth to husband his crops. The rice grown here is of superior quality; but the straw of the other grain is short, and the ear light.

For a short distance beyond Khan-baila, the country bore the same appearance of plenty as that which we passed through the day before. It soon, however, changed, assuming a dreary unproductive aspect— sometimes that of a woody hunting preserve, at others of a moist marshy land. This character continued up to Ahmedpur, where I arrived about four o'clock in the afternoon of Sunday the 30th of April.

On the 2nd of May Captain Burnes had an audience of Bhawul Khan. Carriages for our conveyance to the palace were sent to the residence of Lieutenant Mackeson, agent for the Indus navigation, at whose house we were staying; but of these vehicles I cannot speak in terms of praise. They do not differ from the Rut or Hackery of Hindustan, save that they are drawn by mules, and not bullocks. When we reached the Khan's palace, five miles distant from Lieutenant Mackeson's house, what with bad roads, and want of springs to the carriages, all of us were severely punished. At first the jolting furnished matter for merriment, but before long the groans which, at every lurch, escaped my well-fleshed companion, told that with him at least it was no joking matter. In front of the palace were ranged the Nawab's disciplined troops—numbering about thirteen hundred men, clad in uniform, tolerably equipped, with banners waving, and music playing. They were drawn up in double lines, each two deep and facing inwards, forming an open column, down which the road led. The palace itself is a diminutive building of two stories, in a light agreeable style of architecture, more resembling an Italian villa than the residence of a warlike chief. At our visit the upper room was occupied by the select men of the tribe, while that below was crowded by others of inferior rank. Their appearance was most martial; nor have I ever seen any tribe which, in soldierly bearing, equalled these Daoudputras, as the Khan's own tribe is called. They are tall and bony men, with well formed, strongly marked features, and clear olive complexion, tanned somewhat by exposure to a desert sun. Their dark hair in flowing ringlets clustered behind the neck, or streamed over the face and dangled in front of the person. All wore large turbans, and were dressed in white, except about the waist, around which a lungi was gracefully folded. Every man had a large black shield, with no other ornament on its jetty surface than a few brass bosses. Ranged in single rows, each warrior chief, as he sat cross-legged upon the carpet with sword and matchlock at his knee, leant forward on his shield, and watched, with eyes fixed and mouth open, all that passed at the interview.

The room of audience was on the upper floor; and the skill of some native artist had been sorely tasked to ornament its walls and ceiling with paintings in various departments of his art;—flowers and landscapes, town and mountain scenery, the holy Mecca, and hunting feats of the Khan contributed to the collection.

On gaining the head of the staircase leading to this room, Bhawul Khan met us in person. The Nawab is about forty years of age, stout, and of a large frame, inclining to corpulency. He was plainly attired, but his manly look was improved by this simplicity of dress. After taking our seats, much conversation passed between the Khan and Captain Burnes. The commercial objects of the mission were fully explained by Captain Burnes, and perfectly understood by his Highness, who on his part promised every assistance.

From Ahmedpur we proceeded to Bhawulpur, a town with which I felt more pleased than with any the mission had hitherto visited. The situation of Bhawulpur is well known. Its streets are cleaner and wider than those of Haiderabad, the metropolis of Lower Sind, while its bazar, though not so large as that of Shikarpur, offers a greater variety, and has a more prosperous look. Within the place are some fine gardens laid out in the Persian fashion. Though the largest town belonging to the Daoudputras, it is seldom honoured by the presence of the Khan.

Bhawulpur enjoys a well merited reputation for the various silk articles which are here fabricated. The texture is generally formed of silk and cotton, and the cloth is justly admired for the beauty of its patterns, the lustre of its colours, and its enduring qualities. The trade in this staple article of their commerce was, at the time of our visit, remarkably brisk. We examined three establishments, having in all thirty looms, not one of which was without its web. Each weaver is restricted to a single pattern, to which from early youth he has been habituated. These men are comfortably housed in clean, well-aired apartments, and to judge of their condition by the appearance of their workshops, I should say that the Bhawulpur weaver is, comparatively, in possession of superior comforts to this class of hand operatives in Great Britain. They work in large sheds open in front, with chunamed sides and flooring. The rooms are ranged in line, close to the back wall, in which is a large square aperture to give a free circulation. The open area in front is usually ornamented with one or more shade-yielding trees.

While here, we had an amusing visitor in the person of a Monsieur Argoo. He had quarrelled with Runjit Sing and his countryman in the Panjab, and was proceeding to join Dost Mohamed Khan of Kabul. We were at dinner when the Frenchman arrived, but no sooner was an European announced, than Captain Burnes ran out to bring him in, and before many minutes had elapsed, Monsieur Argoo had taken wine with every one at table. The poor man's failing was soon apparent, for he proceeded to beat the tattoo with his elbows on the table, and as a tenor accompaniment, he made a knife vibrate between its under surface and his thumb. It was really done very cleverly, and the performance being highly applauded, the complaisant Frenchman knew not when to desist. Fatigue, sleep, and wine at length got the master, and we saw him safely to bed. Next morning at an early hour our guest was astir, roaming up and down the courtyard till he chanced to stumble on Dr. Lord, engaged in dissecting and stuffing birds. Watching him for some time, he exclaimed "Quelle patience!" and with a shrug of the shoulders passed into Captain Burnes's room. That officer was not yet dressed, on which Monsieur Argoo called out, "Why, Sare, the battle of Wagram was fought before this hour; and you still in dishabille! Vill you take vine vith me?" "No," replied Captain Burnes, "I never take wine before breakfast; but I shall order you some claret, as your countrymen, I am aware, like light wine in the morning." "Then, Sare," replied Argoo, "you insult me, you refuse to take vine vith me, and I demand de satisfaction." He ran out, and soon re-appeared, armed with a rapier, and asked Captain Burnes to send for his small sword, but the latter thought that, considering the shortness of their acquaintance, he had already sufficiently humoured this fiery little Frenchman, and Monsieur Argoo was politely requested to continue his journey, which he accordingly did that same evening.

This unfortunate gentleman had many good points in his character, but they were unknown to us at the time of his first visit. As a soldier and drill-officer, he was the first in the Panjab; but his drunken habits, and violent temper, made him disliked by his brother officers. At Kabul, in October following, we fell in with him a second time, so that his journey from the Indus had occupied him fully five months. Whilst on the road, his dislike to Mussulmans had nearly cost him his life. It was only spared on his repeating the Kulmah or Mohamedan creed. Immediately on his arrival being known to us, Captain Burnes sent him a kind note, inquiring if he could be of any service to him; but the good-hearted

Frenchman was so ashamed of his conduct at Bhawulpur, and so oppressed by this unexpected return, that he could not be persuaded to visit us; and on his failing to obtain employment from Dost Mohamed Khan he set out for Peshawar, without our having met him. We, however, learned that the day previous to his departure he had been employed in moulding leaden bullets, and that he had sworn to be revenged on the Mussulmans, for the ill-treatment on his former journey. The cause of Monsieur Argoo's failure in obtaining service, was his ignorance of the Persian language. Dost Mohamed Khan was partial to him, and though regretting his attachment to the bottle, offered him a regiment. Unfortunately for the Frenchman, the interpreter took advantage of his ignorance of the language, and in reply to a question on Argoo's qualifications for command, reported, as his answer, that if the Amir wanted a drummer, he could not suit himself better. The Frenchman required but little pressing to beat a tattoo, and the result was that he got his discharge that evening, and next day the interpreter (a brother adventurer) obtained the regiment.

Embarking in boats at Bhawulpur, on the 12th of May, we dropped down the Sutledj to Uch, and as the boats here brought to on the night of the 14th. I embraced the opportunity to visit the town. Darkness, however, had cast her sable mantle around ere we reached its suburbs, but this slight circumstance we had not in our wisdom adverted to. Now, as the streets of an eastern town are neither illuminated by the magic gas jet, nor even the dull oil flame, we had no alternative but Sawney's, to gang back again. We had gone about half way to the boats, when a loud barking of dogs, and the voice of some one in trouble, made us quicken our steps towards the hamlet from which the noise proceeded. Here we found a drunken Afghan, who had lost his way, battling manfully, dirk in hand, with a pack of curs that had beset him. He had lost his sword, for as he swept the ground with it in front, dealing forth, as the bewildered man no doubt thought, destruction to his enemies, it had slipped from his grasp, and he now stood making, occasionally, a desperate thrust with his dirk, measuring at each pass his length along the ground. An Afghan chief had arrived from Dhera Ghazi Khan, and this worthy was of his suite. He had been to Uch, and there made too free with the wine cup, an excess which the company of a countryman and friend whom he accidentally met with, may palliate, if not excuse. The drunken man was proceeding to the river's bank to rejoin his master, who was there encamped; so extricating him from the canine foe, and gathering up his scattered weapons, we took him under our charge and saw him safe home.

Burnes, speaking of Uch, says, "The place is ancient, and highly celebrated in the surrounding countries, from the tombs of two saints of Bokhara and Bagdad. The Ghorian emperors expelled the Hindu Rajas of Uch, and consigned the surrounding lands to pious Mohamedans.

An inundation of the Acesines, some years back, swept away one half of the principal tomb, with a part of the town; and though the return of the river to its original bed is attributed to the miraculous interference of the deceased saint, the people have, as yet, failed to testify their gratitude by repairing his tomb."

On the 18th we descended the Chenab to Mittun-Kote, at the confluence of the Panjab streams with the Indus, and here, before quitting that portion of the latter river voyaged by the Greeks, I may be permitted to offer a few remarks on the descriptions of the Indus given by Arrian and by authors of recent date. When the latter differ so widely from each other, the statements of the former should not be too keenly criticised. Burnes has been accused of under-estimating the size of the Indus; but with what degree of justice, the result of experimental steam-voyages will by this time have shown. It would, indeed, have been the safer side to err on, but he has done just the contrary, and drawn a too favourable picture of the capabilities of this river, both in his published work and practical notes. But if this may be said of the author whom we have named, what shall we say of those who declared the mouth of the Indus to be navigable to a line-of-battle ship, and to have a width of twelve miles? It is true that Colouel Pottinger spoke only from information obtained from the natives; but the results that sometimes ensue from the dissemination of loose statements, cannot be better instanced than by adducing the prospectus of a Steam Company for the navigation of the Indus, which was given to the public in 1834. This joint-stock scheme actually proposed stationing an old East Indiaman, as a depot or receiving ship within the mouth of the river. Why, this class of vessels could not, if laden, even sight the coast of Sind, far less cross the bar of its shoal-streams. Thus much for modern authorities; let us now hear what the ancients say. Arrian states the Indus to have a medium width of forty stadia, and to measure fifteen where narrowest: that in its course, from the confluence of the Panjab rivers to Pattala, it was one hundred, and lower towards the sea two hundred. These seemingly exaggerated statements have much perplexed the worthy Dean of Westminster, who, ignorant of localities, could not possibly be aware of the peculiarities of this stream. To me the measurements of the historian, though absurdly high, even taking the stadium at D'Anville's low estimate of fifty-one toises, contain all the evidence of a truthful narration. Let it be remembered, Nearchus commenced the voyage down the river in October, when the Indus is very low, and reached Pattala in July, when the periodical rise of the river is nearly at its height. The seasons would thus occasion great disparity in the accounts which have been transmitted to us of the river's estimated width. Indeed, Arrian expressly adds, "this is the breadth when it spreads its waters most." His measurements, therefore, embrace rather the belt of country inundated, than the thread or proper channel of the stream.

We now, at least, know what the Indus is not, and even this negative information may prevent much disappointment. The difficulties that arise, and the angry feelings engendered, through ignorance of matters which it is the province of physical geography to explain, need not, after the instances just quoted, be more than alluded to in this place. Proper vessels are now upon the Indus, and its capabilities for steam-navigation will be made the most of; but we cannot help reminding such of our Indian friends as are interested in the subject, that not only are the native craft of the river well suited to its peculiarities, but are also equally adapted to the commerce for which the Indus now is, or will shortly become, the highway. In conclusion, we may remark, that there is no known river in either hemisphere, discharging even half the quantity of water that the Indus does, which is not superior for navigable purposes to this far-famed stream. In this practical age the beauty of a river is measured by its utility; and although few people could sail without emotion upon the waters that once bore the bark of Alexander, there are numbers who would willingly give up all its classic associations, could they, by so doing, obtain for it the clear channel of an American stream.

Chapter IV

When the Dheraját was a province of Kabul, Mittun-Kote belonged to the district of Dhera Ghazi Khan; but on the dismemberment of that kingdom it was seized by the Daoudputras, and Saduk Mohamed, father of the reigning Khan, gave it in fief on easy terms to Hafiz Mohamed Khoreishi, a holy man of the town. The son of this saint, Miha Khoda Buksh was ejected on Mittun-Kote's being taken possession of by Runjit Sing, above eighteen years ago. The dispossessed Pir has fixed himself at Chatcher, a village on the opposite bank of the river, fronting Mittun-Kote, that his eyes may be daily gladdened with the sight of the dome of a ziarat, which twenty-five years before he had built over the home of his childhood and the ashes of his father. The Seiks have been urgent in their request to Miha Khoda Buksh to resume his jaggir, but in vain, the old man will not consort with kaffirs. He has, however, strong hopes that Mittun-Kote may yet revert to Bhawul Khan, hopes strengthened, if not engendered, by the dome ever present before his eyes.

Whilst at Mittun-Kote, seeing a crowd one day congregated round a well, I walked to the spot and was witness to the following trial by an ordeal, which we may term that of "water and the bow and arrow." The water in the well was eighteen feet deep, and in its centre stood an upright pole. Two criminals were to be tried for theft, one of whom was already in the well, clinging to the pole, with only his head above water. A little on one side, with his back to the criminal, stood an archer with bent bow and an arrow on the string. On a given signal the arrow was shot away, and the culprit descended below the surface of the water. No sooner had the arrow reached the ground, than a young man swift of foot left the bowman's side, and made towards it; on his reaching the spot where it fell, another runner, equally fleet, snatched up the arrow and set off for the well. As he neared us at a winning pace, all eyes looked over the parapet into the well, for the criminal's re-appearance. His friends breathed short, while hope and fear were depicted on every countenance. At last, the runner reached the goal, and the next moment the head of the suspected person emerged from the water. A loud shout proclaimed his innocence and the crowd's satisfaction.

The other criminal, an old man, now prepared to descend into the well, but before doing so a lock was shorn from his thin gray hairs, and fastened to the arrow as a charm to impede its flight. He was the reverse of confident, and his looks were certainly not in his favour. Prayers were offered, and many fingers pointed to the heavens, while voices exclaimed "Allah will clear the innocent." The trial was gone through, and with the same happy result as before. These injured men were now placed upon the backs of two bystanders, and so mounted, were led through the crowd to receive its noisy congratulations. This over, their female relations came forward and contented themselves with imprinting a silent kiss upon the cheeks of the once-suspected men, who had thus established their innocence in the opinion of their countrymen, and the sound state of their lungs in ours.

By the 22nd of May, permission from Runjit Sing having arrived for the Mission to proceed to Attock by the Indus, the fleet on that day was again in motion, pursuing, with a favourable breeze, the voyage to Dhera Ghazi Khan, the next commercial mart where a halt was to be made.

Between Mittun-Kote and Dhera Ghazi Khan a low alluvial tract extends far inland on both sides of the river, which, though studded with farming hamlets, had no large villages; some were visible, situated above this alluvial bottom, but they were too distant for me to visit them. To the east the eye ranges over an uninviting level, but on the opposite bank are seen the Suliman mountains, which rising about Mittun-Kote, continue parallel to the Indus, till they disappear midway between the Upper Dhera Kalabagh, in the table-land south of Sufeid Koh. This country is well watered, both from canals and the inundation, and as might be expected, the soil is rich and productive. The eastern bank is inhabited by Mussulmans, Hindus, and Seiks. The west solely by the first of these sects, who are mostly Beluche of the Gurchani, Dizuk, Sagri, Dushti, Gopang, Koza, and Kalora tribes. The Kaloras were the tribe which ruled in Sind prior to the Talpurs, and Abdul Nubbe was the last of the race who possessed authority in that country. His vindictive spirit and ferocious disposition forced, for self-preservation, the friendly and powerful tribe of Talpur into rebellion; and the result was the dethronement of the tyrant, his tribe's expulsion from Sind, and Futi Ali Khan's succession to the vacant musnud.

The Kaloras, now harmless wanderers, were indebted to the charity of a Kabul monarch for the means of subsistence. He gave them lands in the Dherajat, and this estate their descendants still retain, though somewhat curtailed of its fair proportions by their present masters. But the Kaloras have no cause to revile the Seiks, when they contrast their own favoured condition with the other Mohamedans under Runjit's rule. The Maharajah has shown unusual forbearance towards this unfortunate community. No troops are quartered among them, and here the Mohamedan is even permitted to raise his voice in prayer. The Kaloras are held in much consideration, not only as having once been rulers, but also for the strictness of their religious observances; and Runjit, with his usual discrimination, does not despise even the prejudices of an opposite creed, when, by a little hypocrisy, he can add to the stability of his own power.

On Tuesday, the 10th of May, we moored abreast of Dhera Ghazi Khan. This town stands on the alluvial bottom of the Indus, four miles inland, and upon the west bank of the stream. The country here for many miles round is inundated, and the town itself suffers when the river's periodical rise is unusually high. It is surrounded by date groves, from the produce of which the Seik government draw a considerable revenue. This town is admirably situated for traffic with the tribes among and beyond the mountains. At the foot of a pass, and on the bank of such a river, a trade, alike beneficial to the immense regions lying to the west, to India, and to Britain, might here be established. The day, we trust, is not distant, when an annual fair will be held at this place. What may be the ultimate result of this, it might be rash to predict, but that the measure would in no ordinary degree prove successful, the map itself seems to testify. It shows not only the immense regions to be drained of their raw produce, but also the millions of inhabitants who, unless we ourselves are to blame, will one day be supplied with British manufactures.

What is further favourable to Dhera Ghazi Khan becoming an emporium of trade is the festival of Sukki Surwar, which is yearly held in the gorge of its mountain-pass. The rejoicings continue for five days, and bring together from districts far apart the saint's numerous followers. Many thousands of persons are thus congregated, and, while the fair lasts, the streets of Dhera Ghazi are thronged with merchants and devotees.

While here, we had an opportunity of observing how Mussulmans on the Indus spend their Sunday (our Friday) when dwelling in a town. In the suburbs a large concourse of people had assembled. They formed a hollow square, within which were the palwans, or combatants, the musicians, and a few Seik Sirdars. Seik soldiers paraded to keep order in the crowd, while their officers presided as umpires and distributed the rewards. The spectators were of both persuasions, Mussulmans and Hindu. The palwans were Mohamedans. I inquired of a decrepit and aged man the nature of these holiday recreations, when he replied with a sigh, "Ah Agha Jan, in bygone times we had games and other sports. Under the Duranis the victor had a horse given to him, or he was crowned in the ring, amidst the shouts of his townsmen, with a Kashmir shawl, or had a golden-hilted sword presented to him; but these people" (added the sarcastic old man, as he cast a glance of contempt upon the Seiks within the ring) "give you a doputtah."

The musicians struck up, and two young men came forward to wrestle. Striking the palm of the right hand against the folded left arm, they advanced to the centre of the ring, where, after smearing their hands and arms with sand, they stood on their defence. Eyeing each other with an eager and steady look, they paused for some time, measuring their adversary, each endeavouring to close with some advantage. At length they met, when, grasping each other's arms, their heads touching, the encounter for some time continued much after the manner of a ram-fight. Violent struggling followed, each trying to get his head under the breast of his opponent, which, when accomplished, the fall was sure. In this way one of the men was thrown, and while another match was arranging two children were led into the ring, and wonderful indeed were the gymnastic feats of these minor performers. They threw numerous somersaults, and hopped on one foot round the ring. Next, they swung their arms to and fro, jerking at the same time the body from an inclined to an upright position. Then, stretching themselves along the ground, face downwards, they rose to the full length of their arms, and kept repeating the movement, rising and lowering the chest, whilst only the hands and toes were permitted to touch the ground; thus the muscles of the body were brought into play, but more especially those of the chest and arms. The children were not more than five years old. This exercise however, though violent, was play to these little fellows, for they were not stimulated by rewards, but did it apparently to amuse themselves, none of the bystanders, except the Seiks within the circle, taking any notice of their play; and when called out of the ring to make room for another wrestling-match, they were as sprightly and fresh as when they entered it. Should they continue such feats, and reach manhood, they will be muscular men. The concourse which formed the ring itself was an interesting spectacle. Here was to be seen the half-civilised and gaily dressed Seik, who, en déshabille, draws a lilac scarf across his shoulders, over his anqarkha or white muslin shirt, and, instead of a turban, wraps round his head a small yellow band, the nation's favourite colour. With these effeminately attired but soldierly figures mingles the rude Beluche, whose shaggy locks, flowing robes, long matchlock, and huge shield, lend to his person a more independent, if not martial air. These rough-looking figures form a strong contrast to the handsome appearance of the Seiks, lounging about in their white flowing draperies, with their gay-looking gold-hilted swords, whilst here and there a naked savage in the character of a fakir, renders the tout ensemble truly Eastern, and the scratching inharmonious music contributes not a little to complete the effect.

Whilst at Dhera Ghazi Khan, a singular alteration took place in the appearance of the Indus, which may, perhaps, be worth recording. From the day of our arrival, the 30th of May, to the 6th of June, the river rose slowly at the average daily rate of an inch and a half. On the last of these days its width was 2,274 yards, its whole volume flowing on in one stream, and its surface unbroken by a shoal. On the following night the river fell eighteen inches, and next morning its bed was one confused mass of sand-banks, more resembling the wreck of some noble stream than the Indus in the month of June. On threading my way amongst the shoals, the principal channel was discovered on the eastern side of the bed, deep and rapid, but in width shrunken to 259 yards. Admitting the river to have been at its usual height on the 6th of the month, I am inclined to attribute its rapid subsidence, not to any deficiency in the river's ordinary sources of supply, but to the escape of a large body of water under the following circumstances. On our passage up the river we occasionally came to districts where the level of the stream was above that of the inland country, which was only preserved from inundation by somewhat higher land banking the river. When the Indus rises sufficient to overflow this natural embankment, the rush of water that follows soon reduces the barrier's height. The low-lying district is flooded, and the quantity of water thus abstracted from the river alters, for a time, its appearance for the worse. Its equilibrium is, however, soon restored, and it resumes its beauty.

From Dhera Ghazi Khan, Lieutenant Leech and Dr. Lord crossed the desert to Multan, and rejoined the Mission at the Upper Dhera.

On the 7th of June we continued our progress to the northward, and at night experienced a violent thunderstorm. The wind throughout the day had been blowing from the north, but towards sunset dark clouds were seen to gather upon the summits of the Suliman mountains, and about nine o'clock at night the storm burst in severe gusts of wind, with heavy rain and lightning from the south-west. So vivid and fiery was the electric fluid, that it almost seemed to scorch us as it played above our heads, while its startling proximity involuntarily made us crouch to avoid the anticipated stroke.

We had not left Dhera Ghazi Khan many days when we remarked a visible change in the aspect of the country, and especially in the bed of the Indus. In fact, the valley and the bed of the river are here one and the same, since on both sides the stream is walled by banks thirty feet high, over which there is no evidence of its waters ever having risen. No canals pierce these barriers, and from this point the agriculture dependent on the Indus for irrigation is restricted to this sunken valley, which may be estimated at from five to ten miles wide. In this depressed bed the stream shifts its path, though it would seem but slowly, since, by Macartney's description of the Indus in 1809, it would appear that a lapse of nearly thirty years has produced no great alteration in this portion of its course. The river continues to run down the west side of the valley, and, according to the natives, is still, by the abrasion of its west bank, working its way in that direction. A broad fertile belt of rich alluvium is thus left to the right of the stream, and at some places under the west bank also. These grounds, unvisited by the river for so many years, have, by the annual decay of their rank vegetation, attained an elevation that exempts them (but that is all) from the general inundation of this low-lying district. They are, however, intersected by innumerable mazy off-shoots from the main stream, and in fact the whole of this low valley is liable to inundation. Here, therefore, are no towns or villages, but numerous hamlets and farm-steadings are spread over its moist surface, while the domed mosques of such towns as Dhera Din Punah, Leia, and Eajun, stand upon its high bank overlooking the valley.

The foregoing description of the bed of the Indus requires to be modified with regard to some circumstances affecting its western shore. The Suliman chain on this bank is, between Dhera Ghazi and Dhera Ismael Khan, from thirty to sixty miles distant from the river, and by the drainage of these mountains has the west bank of the Indus in many places been destroyed, so that when the river is full a considerable tract of country is flooded through the openings thus formed. The streamlets from the range of mountains do not, as represented in the maps, join the Indus, their entire volume being ordinarily consumed in agriculture. Single-embanked dams, thirty miles in length, skirt the base of this chain, and receive their drainage, which is here the only means of irrigation,—water, except near the river, being too far from the surface to be obtained by wells. After long-continued rain these embankments sometimes give way, and then the pent-up water rushes down the plain and moves onward to the river with a wasting velocity and a wantonness of strength which at first nothing can oppose. The towns exposed to calamities from this cause are protected by a strong mud wall drawn around them.

The earthquake of June 1819, which devastated the British province of Kach'h, was felt far up the valley of the Indus, though the Sindis point to Maghribi, and the countries eastward, as the centre of its vibrations. The town of Dhera Din Punah on the west bank of the river, which we passed on the 18th of June, suffered by that convulsion. The ground upon which the town stood sank from four to six feet, and, to increase the horrors of its already affrighted inhabitants, the streets were flooded for fourteen days, from newly-opened chasms in the Suliman chain.

Visiting one evening in this neighbourhood a village of Jat Mohamedans, I was pleased at witnessing an agreeable usage of the tribe. They were distributing among the poor the milk of a large herd of buffaloes. It is their custom to do so once a month in remembrance of Abdul Khadir, a Mohamedan saint. The pastoral tribe in Lower Sind do the same thing, and there Hindu and Mussulman alike share in this charity. How seldom does superstition wear so attractive a garb as it does in this instance, where, in doing honour to the memory of a good man, rival sects for a time forget their difference, and unite in befriending the poor!

As the river was now high, to avoid its strong current we sometimes for a distance threaded one of its many parallel branches. In one of these, eighty yards wide, its banks either level with the surface of the stream or just submerged, while the tall grass with which they were thickly clad was above the water, we were startled to hear our words repeated in a clear soft tone from among these rushes. This beautiful water-echo accompanied us to the end of the narrow channel.

As we advanced to the north, the Takht-i-Suliman, or the highest mountain in the chain became daily more conspicuous, and on the 21st of June, the day preceding that of our arrival at Dhera Ismael Khan, I ascertained its height by trigonometrical measurements to be 10,086 feet above the river, or in round numbers 11,000 feet above the sea.

Chapter V

The old town of Dhera Ismael Khan, with its wood of date-trees, was swept away by the Indus in 1829. It had been long threatened, for in 1809 it stood within a hundred yards of the stream, but its fate was not consummated until twenty years after its perilous site had been remarked by the Honourable Mr. Elphinstone.

The new town is well laid out. Its streets are straight and wide, though as yet houses in some of them are but thinly scattered. They are built of sun-dried brick, consist of a single story, and rise from a basement or platform about a foot in height. The bazar is roomy and well supplied. There was an airy clean appearance about this new town, that augured comfort and health to its inhabitants. I regret, however, to observe that the result of further observations in the Dherajat did not confirm the first of these suppositions. The country is abundant in both the necessaries and luxuries of life; and yet its peasantry are poorly clad, indifferently lodged, and, by their own account, worse fed. This remark is applicable to the west bank of the river, where the spirit of the people is embittered by Seik bondage; but it may be truly said that, from one cause or another, this is more or less the condition of the lower classes throughout the entire valley of the Indus: "The invasion of another conqueror, who would reduce the whole under any form of regular government, and open the communications again, would be a benefit to the country, instead of an injury or oppression; and if the Abdallis should in this instance tread in the steps of the Macedonians, one general despot who should govern the whole, and for his own interest protect it, would be better than a variety of petty tyrants, who desolate each other's territory without obtaining security for their own; or the predatory incursions of the barbarous tribes, who not only rob but annihilate the industry of the merchant and the cultivator." Let us substitute the word Britain for the Abdallis, and a mild government for Eastern despotism, and then we hope that the day anticipated by the worthy Dean has at length dawned.

Leaving Captain Burnes' party at Dhera Ismael Khan, I started for Kalabagh on the 2nd of July, with instructions to continue along the west bank of the Indus for the entire distance, should it be found practicable. Four days afterwards we came abreast of a mountain-chain, which in a northerly direction edged the stream for five-and-twenty miles. For the first two days we tracked along its base. A belt of good land lay between it and the river, of a varying width, but nowhere exceeding two thousand yards. It gradually lessened as we ascended the stream, until, on the afternoon of the 8th, we came upon the rock itself. This narrow fringe of cultivable land is shared by various Afghan families, whose means of existence are necessarily precarious, as the Indus is yearly reducing the size of their already contracted domains. This tract, where uncultivated, is covered with date-trees, not, however, that kind from which,

"With fruit and ever-verdant branches crown'd,
Judea chose her emblem; on whose leaves
She first inscribed her oracles, and all
The fortunes of her state,"—

but a species of dwarf wild palm that produces no fruit.

The difficulty of tracking now hourly augmented, until, on the afternoon of the 10th, a jutting portion of the mountain forced us to halt. Three hundred yards in advance there was firm footing, but in the intermediate space the mountain was scarped down to the river, which here, ten fathoms deep, rolled onward at the rate of seven miles an hour. The pelu-tree (Salvadora Persica) had taken root in crevices, at present hidden by the swollen river, and, though an impediment to trackers when the water is low, they were now extremely serviceable to our advance. From the sloping surface of the mountain the trees shot their strong boughs above water, about four yards outside the rock; and up this hack channel a couple of boatmen, after several failures, made good their way, and then returned to us, floating down the river upon mussuks. We thus succeeded in getting several warps (track-ropes) fastened above that portion of the mountain which retarded our ascent. The boat was now swung out into the stream, and we were proceeding to haul her ahead, when a change of current carried us forcibly away from the bank. To keep her from capsizing we were compelled to let go the different warps; and when we got beyond the shelter of the mountains it was found to be blowing a perfect gale, so that our only alternative was to scud before it, under a close-reefed sail, for the opposite bank. During the night the gale abated, and the wind changing to south, we recrossed the river, and landed on the west bank, about 100 yards above the scarped rock which had given us so much trouble.

At this place are the ruins of the castle of Kaffir-Kote, equally remarkable for its strange site and massive architecture. On the very summit of the mountain-chain several time-worn turrets of imposing appearance are seen, from which a dilapidated wall runs right down the face of the rock into the river. The natives of these parts assign to this castle an era long antecedent to the Hejira; and in this they are supported by its traditionary name. On comparing the numerous pigmy mud forts of modern times with the remains of this giant of antiquity, the result is not favourable to the exertions of the present day; or perhaps it would be more correct to infer that these countries, under the Hindu Rajahs, possessed greater power than they have done since the Mohamedan conquest. Slavery, too, would seem to have been prevalent in those days, for without such a supposition it is impossible to account for the remains of many similar structures in Afghanistan and the adjoining countries. Freemen would never have consented to the erection of such stupendous edifices, on sites so arbitrarily chosen, and so little calculated for the general good; and we may therefore conclude these to have been built by forced labour, and to have been so many mountain-eyries, of tyrant chiefs: or, if we view them in a more favourable light, the traces of wealth and knowledge that these relics of a younger world present, fill us with wonder at the mechanical skill required to raise such piles, or at the density of population, if physical strength alone were employed. But where now are those giants of the earth, those sons of Anakim's generation? Gone for ever: and whether we look to India's excavated caves, or to the banks of the Nile, in Egypt's mystic land, no clue has yet been discovered to guide inquiry through the dark ages that have followed the bright era of their origin. A moral catastrophe, antecedent to Alexander's invasion, seems to have blighted science and thrown backward the intellect of man. The round towers of Ireland, the pyramids of Egypt, the caves and other undeciphered Indian antiquities may be referred to this mysterious era; and an unrecorded irruption of savage hordes may perhaps have been the Lethean wave which swept over them.

Immediately after passing this ruin, we found ourselves in the country of the Esaw Kyl; and on clearing the mountains next day we reached Kundul, the frontier village of the tribe.

From Kundul we could discern the Salt range, which seemed to bound the valley of the Indus on the north. From this range, another swept in a semicircular curve to the south-west, till it almost joined those we had just left behind. The land thus shut in forms the country of the Esaw Kyl, and is a comparatively high-lying plain, resting one side upon the river, and enclosed on its three others by mountains.

We had not been long in the village when Khan Beg Khan, a person of consequence deputed by the chief of the tribe, paid us a visit. He came, he said, from his master Ahmed Khan, to welcome the English to his Kyl, and to furnish us with sursat, or daily rations. After due acknowledgments on our part, Khan Beg Khan took leave with an assurance that to-morrow he would send a strong party to drag the boat; a service which, having declined his other kind offers, I thought it politic to accept.

The morning brought us the promised trackers: but to drag the boat against a strong current under a constantly falling bank, thirty-three feet high, was more than we dared to try; so, spreading our canvas, we sought the eastern shore, along the low flats of which we tracked throughout the day, and at nightfall again crossed to the west side of the river. We made an excellent day's work, and, although it was dark, hit the bank at Shaikh-ke-Shair, a village at the confluence of the Kurum, a stream that here joins the Indus.

Late as was the hour of our arrival, the nephew of Ahmed Khan was at the river-side to receive us. What conversation we had was carried on, through an interpreter, in the Persian language, as Alum Khan knew only Pushtu, the vernacular of his country. The chief, he said, would visit us next day; a compliment I vainly endeavoured to shun, on the score of my poor accommodations being unfit for the reception of so great a personage. On taking leave, the young man pressed us to accept of a guard for the night, affirming with much sang froid, that, although such a precaution was unnecessary in the midst, of his own peaceful tribe, still there were hill-men, against whom we should be on our guard.

[71]

Next day before the sun had well risen, I was surprised by the chief's approach. An old bechoba was hastily pitched, and into it with due formality, Ahmed Khan was inducted. He opened the conversation by expressing deep regret that the difficulties of the navigation had prevented Captain Burnes from visiting the Esaw Kyl. He hoped, however, the day would yet come when he might prove to the Indian government the sincerity of his respect and esteem for our nation. "True," said the chief, "my country is but 'ticka zumen,' a spot of earth, and the tribe, in strength, not what it once was; yet, such as we are, I and mine are at the service of your government." In vain did I assure him he was mistaken, and that the English nation sought not for territorial aggrandisement, but that in interesting itself in the tranquillity of nations bordering the Indus, its views were far more liberal and philanthropic. I then carefully explained to the chief the purely commercial character of Captain Burnes' mission. That its object was to determine the navigable capabilities of the Indus, that the boats of the merchant might be suited to its streams; to note what descriptions of raw produce, and to what amount the adjacent countries could exchange for articles of British manufacture, and to mark the taste and predilections of their inhabitants, that our merchants might adapt their investments to the wants of their customers. Ahmed Khan listened attentively, and asked many questions, where he did not clearly comprehend my meaning. When I had finished, he remarked with a quaint incredulous smile, "it might be so: but the Seik rule was a harsh one."

Conversation now took a more discursive range, and for an hour the chief sat asking innumerable questions about Europeans, their customs and inventions; but on no subject was he more inquisitive, than that of steam, and the various uses to which it is applied. He had heard that quicksilver was employed to generate it, and was surprised to learn that, for common purposes, water only was used.

[72]

The chieftain of the Esaw Kyl is about forty-five years of age, of a mild, placid countenance, and, though his figure is not handsome, there is something elevated and prepossessing in his demeanour. His escort consisted of twenty matchlock men. At parting, he again expressed great anxiety to meet Captain Burnes.

No people west of the Indus are more impatient under the yoke of Runjit Sing than the Esau Kyl. A small Seik detachment, quartered in their country, was lately cut off to a man, and, to avenge this insult, an army was now on its march from Lahore. But Runjit, ever prudent, had secretly proposed an amicable arrangement to Ahmed Khan, who, sensible of his own weakness and the Maharajah's power, was prepared to accede to the terms offered, provided Runjit would not insist on stationing another Seik detachment among his tribe. Rather than submit to this, Ahmed Khan expressed his determination to take to the hills and try what modification in the Maharajah's sentiments a guerilla system of warfare would effect.

The water of the Kurum river is of a bright red colour. By this and other mountain streams the lands of the Esaw Kyl are irrigated. The Indus rolls past unheeded, as it here flows in too deep a bed to be turned to agricultural purposes.

Taking leave of the Esaw Kyl, whose hard fate I sincerely pitied, we kept tracking up the west bank, and at the village of Muddut Kyl, detected the first pebble in the river's channel. Three miles higher, at Chandina Ka-gote they were visible in its banks. Seven miles more brought us, on the 16th, to the town of Kalabagh, where Captain Burnes and his party had already arrived.

Having reached the mountains, I shall close this chapter with a few general remarks on that division of the Indus which lies between Mittun-Kote and Kalabagh, a portion of its course yet little known. The season it should be remembered, in which we voyaged, was that of the river's periodical rise, and the temperature of February does not differ more from that of July, than the

[73]

shrunken stream of the one month from the full channel of the other. At some places, so diffused was the stream, that from a boat in its centre no land could be discovered, save the islands upon its surface, and the mountains on its western shore. From Dhera Ismael Khan to Kalabagh, the east bank was not once seen from the opposite side of the river, being either obscured by distance, or hidden by intervening islands, which, at this season, thickly speckle over its channel. Some are level with the water's edge, while others below it are only known by their sedgy covering. In other months, they are the resort of the inhabitants from both shores, many of whom, delighted with their fine pasturage, prolong their stay till dislodged by the rising river. Such laggards I have seen caught, and have enjoyed a hearty laugh at their unceremonious removal. When this is about to happen, the inmates are soon astir. The young men go in search of the cattle, whilst others speedily unroof the reed-built cot, and transport such part of its materials as may be useful in the erection of their new habitation, to a boat which they take care to have at hand. Between this vessel and the hamlet, parties may be seen hurrying to and fro, with bundles on their heads, their arms filled with children and earthen jars, and dragging rafters and other fragments of their houses after them. But in this month (July) the islands are abandoned, and as the boat swiftly glides amidst the mazy channels that intersect them, no village cheers the sight; no human voice is heard; the only sound is the plover's moaning call as it hovers above the falling bank, and dexterously seizes its prey while yet in the air, or skims it off the water. Here and there a boiling eddy rises to the surface, and even the wild swirl of its gushing, turbid current, is grateful to the ear amidst the profound stillness. A small grey speckled bird, that loves the water, nestles on these half-drowned islands, hanging its neatly constructed little nest to the top of a flexile grass stalk, and rears its young in security, when all is flooded beneath and around it. Lower down the river, about the vicinity of Mittun-Kote, the low sandy islands that disappear before the first wave of inundation, are, in the spring months, studded with the eggs of the plover. The bird's unfailing instinct thus beautifully exemplifies the truth of Solomon's words, that "for every thing there is a season, and a time for every purpose under the heavens."

As the eye wanders round, clumps of seeming trees edge the horizon. These may be plantations around villages on the high bank, or Talli trees in the river's bed, which the stream has respected for the last dozen years, —a long duration for all that blossoms here; or perhaps they are only bushes magnified by the atmosphere. The sun rises, the mirage is broken, and the last suspicion proves correct.

Out of sight of land, the voyager may for hours be floating amid a wilderness of green island fields, and when he supposes himself far from man, is sometimes startled at hearing a human voice from amid the expanse of rushes which surround him. It is the solitary bulrush-gatherer, who, with only his mussuk for support, braves all the dangers of the stream to procure the root of the bulrush for food for himself and his little ones. These people resort to such islands as are within a foot of being submerged, and, stationing themselves on the windward edge, seize hold of the rushes when detached by the action of the stream; nor does a plough turn up a furrow with greater precision than the current's surging waves slices down these ever-changing islands.

Chapter VI

The romantic site of Kalabagh in a gorge of the great salt range, through which the Indus rushes forth into the plain, was remarked and admired by Mr. Elphinstone's party in 1809. Its situation is certainly more picturesque than judicious. It is the hottest place between Attock and the sea, and it would require little trouble to prove it the most unhealthy. The water of the Indus is here reputed unwholesome, while an alum manufactory in the centre of the town keeps its inhabitants in an atmosphere as noxious as it is disagreeable. Many of the natives of the place suffer from a swelling resembling goître, which they attribute, and I should conceive justly, to the tainted air they are constantly inhaling. To a stranger the effluvia given out by the burning beds of alum is highly offensive.

The heat of this place must be excessive. Its inhabitants never think of passing a summer's day in-doors, but, quitting their houses, seat themselves under the umbrageous banian trees (Ficus religiosa), which here at intervals shade the river's banks. In these cool retreats, with the water actually surrounding their couches, the idle and the aged of the male population sleep or languish out the day; while their more thrifty partners divide their time about equally between the river and their spinning-wheels.

Bathing is here a great luxury, and much in fashion, especially with the women, who when so engaged expose their persons with an indifference which proves they can have but little delicacy, and still less sense of shame. But let us be just to the fair ones of Kalabagh. Scenes that to a stranger appear indelicate, are not so viewed by the husbands of these ladies, who themselves accustomed to frequent the river from infancy can see no impropriety in their better halves thus unceremoniously enjoying the luxury of its cool waters.

In truth the population of the banks of the Indus are almost amphibious. The boatmen of Lower Sind, for example, live, like the Chinese, in their boats. If a native of the Lower Indus has occasion to cross the stream, a pulla-jar wafts him to the opposite shore. At B'hkur the mussuk supersedes the pulla-jar, and from Mittun-Kote upwards every man living near the river has one. Kassids so mounted make surprising journeys, and the soldier with sword and matchlock secured across his shoulders thus avoids the fatigue of a long march. But the Hindu most enjoys the Indus, and delights to sport in its stream. The higher we advance up the river, the more manifest does his predilection for its waters become. At Attock the very boatmen are many of them Hindus,—an employment quite foreign to Brahma's followers in the lower course of the Indus. The Sunday amusement of this class is to wanton in its waters. Confined to their shops throughout the week, with them the seventh day is one of relaxation and enjoyment. Early in the forenoon they repair to the river or canal, and there upon their mussuks float and talk till sunset. I have seen in one group a father and two children, the latter on dried elongated gourds, clinging to their parent, who bestrode a good-sized mussuk. Close to them came twro grey-haired men apparently hugging each other, for they rode upon the same inflated skin, which, but for the closeness with which they embraced, it would have soon parted company. Next came sailing down an individual lying much at his ease, between the four legs of a huge buffalo's hide, while boys moved in all directions, mounted as they best could, some on gourds and some on skins.

[77]

The Hindus of these regions differ considerably from those of Hindustan. They are less fettered by religious observances, unawed by Brahmins, less rigid in their diet, and altogether assimilate more to their Mohamedan neighbours. Conversion among them to the latter creed is not a rare occurrence though in all cases which have come under my observation, the motives were unworthy—love of money and ambition in the men, and affairs of the heart with the women. But the Hindus of the Indus have also their customs and superstitious rites. The bodies of the dead are burned, as with the rest of Brahma's followers; but children dying before they have teethed are thrown into the river. Many are the propitiatory offerings which are hourly committed to the Indus. A few reeds smeared with mud forms a little raft, on which the devotee places as many lights as it will carry, strews it with rice or other grain, and having muttered some words of mystic import over this richly freighted fire-ship, the little bark is launched upon the stream. Often of a still evening have I watched the flickering lights of these votive offerings, as they were borne away by the current, and have been tempted to liken the river to Time, the Ocean to Eternity, man the frail, faintly illumined bark, and life its perilous and chequered voyage.

The alum manufactory employs three hundred labourers of different descriptions. The quantity of this article daily prepared is one hundred and twenty-two maunds, at an expense of one hundred and ten rupees. At the works its price is two rupees per maund, and on its removal the government levy a tax on every camel load, or eight maunds, of two rupees and a half.

A few days after our arrival at Kalabagh, the Seik army alluded to in the last chapter appeared on the east bank of the river, and there encamped. A party of Ghazi, or champions of Mohamedanism, had collected on the west bank to oppose their passage across the Indus, and as our little camp occupied the ground where the Seiks would probably land, a civil message was sent,

[78]

requesting we would move elsewhere. This, however, proved mere gasconade, for the army crossed without encountering the slightest opposition, and not many days afterwards Ahmed Khan, by concession, made his peace with the Maharajah.

The boatmen of Kalabagh having reported the upward navigation to Attock impracticable at this season of the year, Captain Burnes was detained here some time by the difficulty of procuring bullocks to convey his party by land. As soon as he had obtained them he crossed to the Indian side of the river, and, under a Seik escort, left Kalabagh about the 22nd of July.

My instructions were to make the best of my way to Attock, by the river; or, failing in that, to hasten there by land, and thence descend the stream. I accordingly made choice of the strongest and fittest boat the place afforded, and commenced beating up for a crew to man her; but at first, neither the Malik's threats nor high wages would induce the boatmen to volunteer. At length, thirty-seven men were obtained under an express stipulation that they were not to go higher than Mukkud, a town only twenty miles above Kalabagh, and on the 20th of July we commenced the ascent.

The boat employed on this part of the Indus differs, though not materially, from the Sind Dundi. It is strongly built, and the extremities project more than with the Sind boat. The utility of the elongated bow and stern is very apparent in navigating the Indus where its banks are high and rocky; for when, for example, a strong current sweeps round a projecting point, the bow of the boat acts as a lever, and enables the trackers to swing her clear.

Masts and sails are not used here. In a channel so contracted, and with banks so high, the breeze is necessarily variable, whilst the wild swirl with which the wind comes over the stream, as it gushes down the lateral ravines, would endanger better boats than any which the Indus can boast.

On starting, the crew, in tracking the boat clear of the town, had an opportunity of trying their skill, and I was glad to find that there was a fair proportion of good hands among them. Towards sunset we reached the point where the Swan river flows into the Indus, and there we halted for the night. Just above the town of Kalabagh, the width of the Indus was 481 yards; nor during this day did the stream anywhere seem of a much less breadth. The trackers had no great difficulties to contend against, and I already began to augur favourably of the termination of the voyage.

Seven miles above Kalabagh we passed a rocky precipice, rising immediately from the river, the table summit of which is the site of Ding-Kot a place of some celebrity in the early annals of Hindustan.

Next day we arrived at Mukkud; having thus made, without any extraordinary exertion, twenty miles from Kalabagh. Here the boatmen left us, although I made the most liberal offers to induce them to remain. From this to the 27th I was detained endeavouring to obtain a new crew. The Seik authorities of the place gave me every assistance; but they had even less influence with the boatmen than the Malik of Kalabagh.

The day of our arrival at Mukkud, believing that Captain Burnes might still be in the neighbourhood of Kalabagh, I felt anxious to communicate with him, that an order might be obtained from the commander of the Seik army, to their functionaries here, stimulating them to use every endeavour to complete my boat's crew. I accordingly wrote a letter; but as time was now doubly precious, I resolved to be the bearer of my own despatch, and to drop down with the current upon a mussuk, and come back by land the next morning. So after stripping, and tying a suit of clothes upon my head, I audaciously pushed off from the steep bank and launched into the stream; but scarcely had I advanced two yards, when, losing my balance, the buoyant skin jumped from under me, and I had to regain the bank as I best could.

A thousand times had I seen the mussuk used; and although I had never before tried it myself, I thought there could not be any great mystery in managing a contrivance so simple that children were permitted its use. I was, however, mistaken; knowledge is not intuitive, and, like all other polite arts, the skill to ride or swim steadily upon a mussuk is not to be acquired without some application. Inattention to the axiom on the present occasion, not only procured me a good ducking, but had nearly cost me my life. After my mishap, the man who was to have been my companion on the river proceeded with the despatch alone.

Mukkud is the principal town in the country of the Sagri Patans; but though the tribe itself be yet free, their capital is in possession of the Seiks. The town is built at the apex of the angle formed by the junction of the Bundewan rivulet with the Indus, and so close to the steep banks of both, that the latter, whose periodical rise is here about fifty feet, now washes the lower story of some of the houses.

The bed of the Indus in the plain is so wide, that local rains produce no great change in the general appearance of the stream. The effect of heavy rain among the mountains is different; for, during the four days of my stay here, the river apparently from this cause alone rose nine feet.

Whilst at Mukkud, the Bundewan, a rivulet usually so small that it may be said to trickle rather than flow, was at times much swollen. One day in particular, it afforded me a good opportunity of observing the changeable character of mountain torrents. The rivulet had dwindled to its usual insignificancy, when a rain-cloud burst over the valley, and poured out a constant stream for ten minutes. The boys, aware of what was coming, repaired with their mussuks to a spot on the bank of the rivulet, a mile above its emboucher. About half an hour had elapsed when the roar of the coming torrent was heard, and presently the front wave of what was now a wild foaming river rolled past, which it no sooner had done than the assembled merry group plunged into its frothy stream, and as they sported like ducks upon its red surface, seemed equally delighted with the velocity and the foam.

The force of these torrents is indeed remarkable, and the cutting power of water can nowhere be better understood than by an examination of their dry beds. One in this neighbourhood, which I inspected, had a channel thirty-six feet wide, and perpendicular walls for its banks three and a half feet high. These banks were composed of pebbles and rounded stones, many of which were upwards of a hundred pounds in weight. The debris had closed their interstices, so that the whole had the look and almost the strength of a conglomerate formation. Had this channel been artificially hollowed the walls could not have been formed with more regularity.

Every day during our detention at Mukkud a corpse floated past the town; but those sickening scenes which often startle humanity on the banks of the Ganges are unknown here: life, I am inclined to think, is oftener lost in mountain torrents than in the main stream.

Our crew being at last completed, we left Mukkud on the 27th, and toiled against the stream till sunset. At day-break next morning we were again at the track-ropes; but the most unwearied exertions brought us in the evening no further than Tora Mala, a village distant but five miles from Mukkud. The ascent had now become extremely laborious; though not hazardous, as the obstructions we had to surmount were not in the river's channel, but arose from the wall-like nature of its banks. Quitting the boat here I landed and examined its channel as high as Sharki, a village on its western shore. To this place I concluded the boat might possibly be dragged; but all hope of being able to advance higher was completely cut off by perpendicular banks several hundred feet high, which a little above Sharki buttressed the river.

The method of tracking in this rocky section differs from that pursued further south only in the greater number of men employed, and the additional precautions used. A boat that ascends from Kalabagh to Attock in winter, when the river is low, must have a double crew; but during the summer, when the Indus is swollen, the voyage is altogether impracticable. Independent of other obstacles to the boat's upward progress, the great rapidity of the current is at this season an insurmountable impediment. From the wavy outlines of the precipitous banks, it is often necessary to cross from one side of the river to the other. In these cases it is more galling than I can well describe to find your boat, whilst you are crossing a stream two hundred yards wide, borne away by a sweeping current, and, despite the best efforts of her crew, landed below an impending cliff which can only be doubled by re-crossing and working up the bank you have just quitted. These unprofitable traverses kept me, as I have already stated, two days between Mukkud and Tora Mala.

In May of this year (1837), two months earlier in the season, the Seiks succeeded in getting five boats up the river: with fifty men to each boat they vanquished not only the physical obstructions, but, by the active friendship of Sultan Mohamed Khan, ruler of Kohat, were enabled also to overcome the difficulties resulting from the hostile disposition of the tribes along the banks. These boats were sent back about the 5th of this month; three reached Kalabagh, but the other two were wrecked on the way down.

These boats were requisite for the completion of the Attock boat-bridge, and as the Seiks of Peshawur had been worsted in a conflict with the Afghans, Runjit Sing was extremely anxious to throw troops across the Indus for the protection of that rich, but to him, unproductive plain. Under these pressing circumstances, the boats in fifteen days were brought from Kalabagh to Attock. But what the Seiks had considered a hard task in May, with unlimited means at their command, would, I imagine, have been impossible even for them in the month of July.

There is no intercourse by the river between Attock and Kalabagh. The boats of the former place are restricted to the use of the ferry, and to the formation of bridges across the Indus when necessary; while those of the latter, besides the usual duties of the ferry, have to keep the alum works in fuel. In these wooding parties, two or more boats sail in company. When tracking is difficult, their crews banding together, first drag up one boat, and then return for another.

Convinced of the utter hopelessness of any further attempt to reach Attock by the river, I now proposed to fulfil the latter part of my instructions, and proceed there by land. The boat was accordingly dropped down the stream to Mukkud, and discharged. After some detention at this place, two ponies and a guide were procured, when, thanking the Seik authorities for the aid they had afforded me, Gholam Hussein and myself commenced our journey. As the Sagri Patans are unfriendly to the Seiks, whose guests we were, it was necessary to make an easterly détour to avoid the lands of that tribe. Our road at starting led up the Bundewan's bed, where we were caught by a pelting shower of rain, and fated to stand longer than was pleasant, bridle in hand, soaked to the skin and crouching under cliffs in its time-worn sides. Around us was a picture of desolation. Hemmed in by hills, nothing could be seen but the rugged summit of walls of concentrating ravines, the aspect ot which was arid and ferruginous. When the rain fell, a thousand cascades came streaming down their furrowed sides and drove us from one nook to another, as the waters found an entrance. At length the weather cleared; we wrung our clothes dry, mounted, and arrived on the second day upon the banks of the Swan river.

Our guide was a Mohamedan, and heartily hated his Seik employers. He seldom spoke, but to anathematise the Kaffirs, and throughout the journey continued to call down curses on their race. I asked this man what he would do, were he to meet an unarmed Seik? "Murder him," was the laconic and savage reply.

East of the Indus, the Sagri Patans are the only people who have not yet submitted to Runjit Sing's authority. The lands of this tribe stretch along both sides of the river, north and south of Mukkud. On the west bank, their country lies between the Kuttock and Bungi Kyl territories, while on the opposite bank, the Awans are found to the north and south of them. The tribe is both pastoral and agricultural, feeding large flocks of sheep and goats by the river's side, and cultivating the ground inland. The fleece of the Dumbi or large-tailed sheep, is beautifully white, and the wool was now selling at ten seers for a rupee. The Sagri have no chieftain, but their place of resort and council is the valley of the Nirrah, on the east bank of the Indus, and close to Torra Mala. It is described as well stocked with fruit trees, with a fertile soil, and of sufficient extent to support 150 horsemen. Here some of their principal families reside. The Sagri have a high reputation among their neighbours for bravery, and are accounted good swordsmen. They are of Afghan origin, and speak Pushtu. Many of them are in the habit of serving as mercenaries, both in Afghanistan and in India. This tribe could muster from 800 to 1,000 foot soldiers, and about 200 horse.

When the Seiks in force overran their country, the Sagri Patans made no resistance, and the former having built a fort in the Nirrah valley, quietly took possession of the land: a tribute was then fixed, and the Seiks withdrew. The tribe, however, accuse Runjit Sing of acting towards them with duplicity and bad faith; and from the various circumstances which have come to my knowledge, I believe there is truth in the charge. Some time ago the governor of Mukkud sent to acquaint the Sagri that he had received Runjit Sing's commands to levy a heavier tax than the one which had been fixed, and that in compliance with his master's instructions, he had now sent properly qualified persons to measure and re-assess their land. The Sagri sent one of their body to remonstrate; but this deputy on the plea of sedition, was imprisoned in Mukkud, and for his ransom a fine of 700 rupees was demanded. The tribe retaliated by seizing a number of Seik ryots, and threatening to detain them until their clansman was released. The Seik governor replied, they were welcome to do so, on which, the Sagri paid the money, and on their deputy's being released, the tribe with one consent rose in arms. The governor of Mukkud thinking, I presume, that he had not rightly interpreted his instructions, was now solicitous for an amicable accommodation. Trusting to the oath of this unprincipled functionary, the Patans sent seven of their number to arrange its preliminaries, and these men, strange to say, the infatuated governor likewise confined. No sooner was the fate of this deputation known in Nirrah, than the heads of families assembled, and after a short deliberation, the following message was sent into Mukkud: "Three times have the Seiks broken faith with us, and friendship henceforward between us can be no more. Our imprisoned brethren you may destroy, but to the Sagri revenge is sweet." Between Mukkud and Nirrah the Seiks had built a little fort called Nukka, to assist in keeping up the communication with their troops in the Sagri country. The commander of this garrison seeing the tribe's preparations for war, applied for reinforcements, and accordingly, between fifty and sixty men were sent from Mukkud. The party never reached Nukka. The Patans had early intimation of what was contemplated, and assembling their strength, patiently waited in ambush for the approach of the detachment. The place selected was a narrow path-way, commanded by rocks overhead and at both ends. Every Seik soldier was massacred, and a few mercenary Afghans met a similar and more merited fate. After thus committing themselves, the tribe, until May, 1837, kept up an exterminating system of warfare, robbing upon the roads, plundering villages, devastating corn fields, filling up wells, and cutting off every small party they succeeded in way-laying. When pursued in force, they crossed to the west bank of the Indus, and harboured among the Kuttock and other friendly clans. The country east of the river, from the Swan on the south, to the Hurru on the north, felt the effects of their depradations, and it was the diminution of the revenue from this region which brought the transactions we have briefly sketched to the knowledge of Runjit Sing. Orders forthwith arrived from Lahore to cease persecuting the Sagri, to restore the prisoners to freedom, and to tax the tribe only to the amount they had formerly paid. These lenient measures on the part of the Maharajah are fast reclaiming this lawless, but justly incensed tribe; their lands are again becoming settled, and the deserted fields of Nirrah have resumed their beauty: men who have been deeply wronged are easily re-excited, and I feel certain that the sight of a Seik detachment in their country, unless its strength made it formidable, would again rouse the Sagri to acts of violence.

On quitting the banks of the Swan river, we proceeded in a more northerly direction over a country where ruined hamlets and uncultivated fields bore ample evidence to late unsettled times. This was succeeded by a quiet district, where numerous smiling villages contrasted favourably with the desolate condition of those we had left behind. Its cultivators were Jats and Awans. The former are to be met with along the banks of the Indus, from its mouth to Attock, and also in the Panjab. The latter are chiefly confined to the east bank of the river, and to that portion of it lying between Attock and Kalabagh. The Malik of the last-named town is chief of this tribe. The Awans are willing to take a daughter from the Jats, but will not give a female of their own to any of that tribe. The Afghans look upon both as one people, though the Awans profess to be descended from no less a personage than Hazrat Ali. Both tribes are followers of the Prophet, and their vocation is the cultivation of the soil.

[87]

Pressing on by forced marches, we forded the Hurru river on the 3rd of August, and next day entered Attock.

Chapter VII

By noon of the following day, I was prepared to descend the river from Attock to Kalabagh. Here there was no difficulty in procuring both boats and men; a large establishment of each being kept up by Runjit Sing for the construction of a boat-bridge, which he yearly throws across the Indus, which river between these two towns is called by the inhabitants on its banks the Attock. After breakfasting with Captain Burnes's party, which had arrived here early in the forenoon, I went down to the lower gate of the fortress where the boat lay. Before embarking, I measured the width of the stream here, and found it to be two hundred and eighty-six yards, but a little lower down where its channel is usually spanned by the bridge of boats, it is much more contracted.

At llh. 55m. in the forenoon we cast off the painter, pulled out into the stream, and as we passed the ferry, sounded and found the depth of water ten fathoms. Having gained the centre of the river, the boat was permitted to drop down with the current, and her crew instructed to keep her at all times as much as possible in its strength.

In a quarter of an hour from the time of departure we approached a spot where a bulging rock on the left hand split the stream into two channels. The boat was steered to the right down the larger, which had a depth of twenty fathoms. The island thus formed is named Berri by the boatmen. A short distance below this island the ruins of a place called Petore were descried among the mountains on the left bank; on breasting which we emerged from the Attock slate, by a range of which, thus far, the river had been margined.

The plain we now entered was very circumscribed, being only three miles in length, and bounded on both sides by hills at no great distance. The space between these had permitted the river to expand, and reduced its depth to four and a half fathoms. The banks were shelving and pebbly, and the course of the stream nearly due south. Several good-sized villages are situated hereabouts, whose inhabitants were now employed washing the sand of the river in search of gold. The Macedonians found no gold in India, and it is a singular fact that none of the eastern tributaries of the Indus yield it, though the parent stream does, and likewise every rivulet from the westward.

Before reaching the end of the plain a range of black-looking mountains a-head was seen, apparently crossing the river's bed, and even when we were close upon them, no gorge or exit could be detected. The confluence of the Hurru river, which here joins from the eastward, had just been passed, when our boat was forcibly carried by a violent current under the high impending cliffs of the left bank, and on sweeping round a corner we discovered, when we had time to look about us, that we were surrounded by mountains.

From Attock to the Hurru, the Indus, though rapid among the slaty ridges, yet flows calmly on; but below this it assumes a very different character, which it retains to within a league of Sharki, a village, it may be remembered, where I was discomfited in an attempt to reach Attock by water from Kalabagh. For the whole of this distance, huge boulders and long ridgy ledges occur in the channel of the river; over and among which the mighty torrent tumbles and roars: its power is immense, and one is almost led to suppose that it would be sufficient to remove from the bed of the river many of the greatest obstructions. The course of the river is very crooked, and its bed being narrow, the immense volume of water pent within it rushing on with great velocity, has not space to sweep quietly round the corners, but is precipitated against the bank that faces the line of its direction, and is there heaped up several feet, above the general level. At all such places we find a fall in the river, and immediately below it a dangerous eddy. The fall may have a height of four feet, measured on the bank which causes it, but it speedily lessens as it runs off towards the opposite side, where it sinks into the eddy.

Two miles below the Hurra is Nilab, where the ruthless Tamerlane, when he marched on India, crossed the Indus. The town formerly stood on both sides of the river, though it has now dwindled into a miserable village on the eastern bank. The stream is here contracted, and twenty fathoms deep. The blue colour of its waters has given the name to this place. It possesses a ferry-boat, and from hence there is a road to Peshawur.

The river from Nilab continues for eight miles to flow nearly due west, between blue limestone hills, that rise slantingly from its bed to a height of seven hundred feet. These hills are thickly studded with Fulah bushes, whose evergreen foliage upon the bare glassy sides of the blue rocks, looked exceedingly beautiful as we swiftly glided in silence along their base. This scene soon changed to one more stern, and more exciting. On nearing the end of the reach, a noise of angry water was heard, when the boatman informed me that we were approaching the whirlpool of Ghora-Tarap the first danger that occurs on the river below Attock. The crew now went to prayers, then seizing the oars, they fixed their eyes upon the steersman, watching for his signal when they were to exert themselves. The danger here is caused by a series of those eddies which I have described as formed by the sharp angular turnings of the river, when compressed and cased in by high rocky banks, that admit of no lateral expansion. The steersman passed his boat down where the fall had a height of perhaps eighteen inches, caring little for this risk, but fearful of the attendant eddy. Though the fall was shot with startling rapidity, the boat when over seemed spell-bound to the spot, and hung for some time under the watery wall in spite of the most strenuous efforts of her crew. At last she moved, the men cheered, and out she darted into the fair channel. At Ghora-Tarap the depth was thirty-one fathoms, and the width of the stream, though I had not the means of measuring it, could not have exceeded two hundred and fifty feet.

At 3h. 20m. p.m. we reached a watch-tower of the Kuttocks overlooking the river. Here the high limestone hills, among which for the last seventeen miles, the river had held its course, gave place to others of less altitude, which continued to bank the stream through the remainder of this day's voyage, which closed ten minutes before seven p.m. at Muncu, a village forty-two miles from Attock. From 5h. 20m. to 6h. 10m. the boat was delayed by a sand squall, so that we had averaged during the passage seven miles an hour.

Not far below the watch-tower a Kuttock hailed us from the right bank, and ordered us to land; taking aim at the same time by way of enforcing his command. We proceeded to obey, but intentionally plied the oars so sluggishly, that the current had borne us beyond the range of his matchlock, ere the Kuttock had discovered he had been outwitted. It was evident that he was terribly enraged, for we could see him leap from rock to rock with the agility of his own mountain goats; but if he had also possessed the antelope's speed, it would have availed him nothing among the craggy rocks that here buttress the river.

Next morning at 4h. 35m. the fastenings were let go, and out we swept upon the dark glassy surface of the river, still banked by the same hills as on the preceding day. It was necessary to be wary, for the deep channel was yet but faintly lit up by the grey dawn of morning, and scarcely had we cleared Muncu when the usual noise gave warning of rocks being near. These and a few

others which succeeded to them were soon left behind,
when we moved forward upon a comparative clear
stream, till at 6 a.m. we were abreast of the Toe river, and
the Soheili rocks lying off it. Having cleared this danger,
we steered down along the right bank much
incommoded by the turbulent water which, throughout
the whole of this reach, is boisterous even where there is
no apparent cause for such commotion.

At 10m. to 7.a.m. we passed through the Dubber
mountains, a range that here extends on both sides of
the river. The acute turnings among the steep bluffs
caused by these mountains gave rise to numerous
violent eddies, over which, had the boat's beam been
less, she could not have safely ridden. In these we were
often completely drenched by the surging waves, which
flew up in jets when the boat came in contact with the
whirling and angry current. We had passed but a few
miles below these eddies, when Sharki came in sight.
The Dubber range may thus be styled the barrier gate of
the Indus, for its southern bluffs are in sight from that
village, and are the same which, as already related,
deterred me from advancing higher up the stream.
Hence to Kalabagh the river flows smoothly, or in a
comparatively diffused stream free from rocks and
other impediments. We reached that town a little after
noon, having averaged from Muncu six and three
quarter miles an hour.

What a contrast does the Indus in this part of its
course present to the shoal and wide-spread river of the
plain! Here it gushes down a valley varying from one
hundred to four hundred yards wide, between
precipitous banks from seventy to seven hundred feet
high. Its character, however, is not that of a brawling
stream, or a swollen mountain torrent, but as if
conscious of its own magnitude and strength, the noble
river pursues its course in silence, except where chafed
by obstructions which itself has caused. The country,
down the centre valley of which this ceaseless tide is
rolled, may be described as a moderately elevated table-

land, extending from Attock to the Great Salt range. The banks of the river throughout the whole of this distance are formed of hills that rise immediately from its waters, in bold bluffs or steep weather-worn slopes. At some places rising in mural precipices, at others rugged and broken, the blackened sides of the impending cliffs cast their dark shadows across the leaden surface of the narrow river, and tinge its waters still deeper with their gloom. Compressed by rocky banks several hundred feet high, the sullen stream, where not opposed, glides smoothly onwards, and but for the ever-changing form of the overhanging crags, and the varying outline of the banks, the boat would seem motionless, though borne on by a current of nine miles an hour, so stealthily does the river flow where its depth and velocity are the greatest. It is where the surface of the stream is ruffled and broken by opposing rocks, that the angry spirit of the river is roused and the turmoil is dreadful. The enormous body of water is crushed against the obstruction, and becomes white with spray and foam. If it be a rocky ledge in mid river, the water, after rising up its face, rolls off in huge waves that extend across both channels, forming dangerous eddies; and to keep clear from their whirling and tumultuous vortex requires both nerve and skill; whilst at the lower side of the ledge the river keeps dashing on, roaring among its jagged points and cresting them with foam.

From Nilab to within two miles of the Kuttock's watch-tower the river was quite a sluice. Black bluffs here encroached upon the stream, and produced fearful eddies. We must have passed down some of these narrows at the rate of nine miles an hour. In approaching them no noise is heard except a sort of gushing sound, till on turning a corner, the thunder of broken water falls upon the ear, its foam being just visible at the further end of a dark rocky vista. The boatmen kneel and commend themselves to their Maker; then seizing the oars with a firm grasp stand prepared to act. The noise becomes deafening, and the rocks are soon under the bows. To hesitate between the channels would be certain destruction: and here every one must admire the courage and firmness of Attock boatmen. Their nerve greatly lessens the hazard of this dangerous voyage, as does also the peculiar structure of their boats.

From the middle of May to September, the upward voyage may be pronounced impracticable. The downward voyage may be performed at all seasons of the year, although not without risk when the river is full.

The villages in this section of the Indus are perched on the verge of its banks, so that the inhabitants of many of them could at this season draw up water from their balconies. They stand on the bare rock, without a blade of vegetation near them. The heat of such houses may be imagined. They are generally forsaken in the middle of the day, at which time the inhabitants resort to the trees scattered up and down in the neighbourhood. A rough bed frame is placed under their shade, and on these the old folks dream away the day. The thrifty wife brings out her spinning-wheel, and parties so employed may be seen under every green tree.

Chapter VIII

That our old acquaintance the Malik of Kalabagh had more authority over his sepoys than over his boatmen, was evinced by the promptitude with which he furnished a party to escort us through the lands of the Bungi Kyl into the territories of Kohat, the route by which I was directed to join the mission at Peshawur.

When prepared to start, I dismissed the Attock boatmen with a small present, giving them the option of accompanying us back to their homes by the way of Peshawur and Kohat, or remaining with their boat until the navigation was open. They chose the latter alternative, and we parted. Kalabagh stands on the southern face of the salt range, just outside the gorge by which the Indus enters upon the plain. Behind the range is the Pass of Shukur Durah, up which our road lay. It was therefore necessary to boat the horses round the dividing mountain, in doing which, we had a good opportunity of observing its formation. The salt occurs here in compact glassy strata, dipping at an angle of $65°$, but its large protruding blocks have no determinate form.

Not far up the Pass is the residence of a fakir, who has devoted the best years of a long life to the charitable office of supplying water to travellers. In Shukur Durah the springs for twenty miles are either salt or fetid, and under a sultry summer sun this journey is always one of pain and fatigue; to the exhausted and thirsty traveller, no sight can therefore be more welcome than this good man's humble dwelling, nor any thought more cheering than the anticipation of the long array of earthen pots, brimful of the cool delicious element which he is sure to find within.

We met several parties coming down the ravine laden with dried grass for the Kalabagh market. These people called at the water-stored hut, and on leaving it, took the fakir's empty jars down to the brink of the river, where they left them to be brought back full by the first traveller returning from the town. For two miles we proceeded up the Pass in a northerly direction, over a tolerable road, having the salt range to our left hand, and sandstone hills to the right. We then quitted the salt range, but continued to zigzag on through the sandstone, the defile becoming narrower as we advanced, whilst the road was so obstructed by large stones and rocky ledges, as greatly to impede the traveller whether mounted or on foot. This path continued to ascend without any improvement till we reached a cleft in the hills called Mussun, ten miles from Kalabagh, where some water trickles down the rock, but so fetid that it would be considered undrinkable were it not that no better is to be had. Here we passed the night.

Next day, the 9th of August, a march of thirteen miles brought us to the village of Shukur Durah at the head of the Pass. On quitting Mussun, the defile opens, the mountains become rounded, and small patches of cultivation are seen to skirt their base.

The country we had just passed through is inhabited by the Bungi Kyl, a tribe of Afghan origin, whose thieving propensities and vagabond life are notorious among their more correct and wealthy neighbours. They occupy both banks of the Indus for some distance north of Kalabagh, and are almost equally numerous with the Sagri Patans, but are neither so industrious nor respectable. Their flocks are small, and there are but few of them; while their limited extent of cultivated land is scattered here and there in patches undeserving the name of fields. The country is wild in aspect, and its soil unkind; and to rear the coarsest grain requires patient labour and a continuance of favourable weather. Should abundant showers not fall, the barren sandy soil is scorched by the July sun and deadened to vegetation; then it is that famine drives the poor starving wretches forth to prey upon their more favourably located neighbours. This predatory tribe live chiefly upon the west side of the river; but its opposite bank is the principal scene of their depredations. If hotly pursued, they will at all times rather abandon their stolen booty than risk their lives in its defence. Murder with them is a rare crime.

The Bungi Kyl are nominally subject to the Malik of Kalabagh, whom they assist in all his contests with the neighbouring chiefs; but they are not bound to serve abroad. In their disputes among themselves, the malik's award is final; and when a fine is levied, the judge, after taking a moiety to himself, distributes the remainder among the principal men of the tribe.

Should an individual who has been plundered by the Bungi Kyl have the hardihood to follow the thieves into their lone haunts amid the wild recesses of this savage region, he will, if poor and a stranger, recover the greater part of his lost property; but should he chance to be a person of consequence, he will fare still better, for the whole will be restored, and he himself feasted.

To rob from one another is accounted dishonourable among them, and the same feeling keeps them from disturbing the peace of their friends the Sagri. Grain left in the field is generally as safe as when stored in the court-yard. Sometimes, however, their inherent vice breaks out, and the more honest tribesmen sufler. On such occasion, which they profess to look upon as lamentable instances of national degeneracy, the heads of families are assembled, and the thief is compelled to restore the property, and is mulct in a fine sufficient to feast his judges. To this entertainment all parties sit down, the thief amongst the rest, silent and moody at the unfortunate discovery, the others talkative and jovial, and luxuriating at his expense. But these honourable and justice-loving vagabonds have no such clear perception of the distinction between "meum et tuum" when the goods of a stranger come within their grasp.

Hospitality, the most prominent virtue of a rude people, is not better observed by the noble clan of Durani than by the thieving Bungi Kyl. A stranger when he has broken bread with one of the tribe may afterwards feel perfectly secure, and at his ease among them.

At the village of Shukur Durah we were met by Agha Maheide, a Persian gentleman, deputed by Sultan Mohamed Khan to escort Captain Burnes up the west bank of the river should he have preferred journeying on that side. Agha Maheide came well attended, which enabled us to part with our Kalabagh escort sooner than we otherwise could have done.

On the 10th we set out together for Kohat. The first halt we called, was at the fine large village of Kurrilsum, three miles before entering which we crossed the Lun rivulet. The name of this petty stream implies salt, an appellation it well deserves, for its waters were brackish; all the horses, however, and many of our party drank of it.

The country both to the east and west was rugged and mountainous, but that portion over which we journeyed gradually improved, until the soft features of its grassy valleys presented a pleasing contrast to the broken and pointed summit, the savage cliffs and the grim iron visage of the sandstone district between Kalabagh and Shukur Durah.

Next day a pleasant ride over a fine country with an agreeable chatty old man for a companion, for such we found Agha Maheide, made me regret that the march was not a longer one. Twelve miles from Kurrilsum brought us to the small river Toe, on the green banks of which, shaded by trees and cooled by its crystal stream, we lounged through the heat of a sultry day. This clear brook has its source from springs in the Tiri country, but its principal supply is from snow, which in that elevated region lingers at the bottom of the deep ravines till summer is nearly spent. To this river the lands of the Bungush owe their fertility, and well do the inhabitants deserve their good fortune. Nowhere had I seen land cultivated with such praiseworthy care. Nearly all the water of this little stream is made to flow in many meandering channels, scattering its blessings everywhere. From our encampment on the Toe, four villages were to be seen within a distance of two miles, all watered by this river.

Four miles south of the Toe the lands of the Kuttucks end, and those of the Bungush commence. The former are termed, in allusion to their sterility, khushk or dry, while the latter are called aube or wet. The Kuttuck depend on rain for their crops, but the Bungush irrigate their fields from the Toe and other perennial brooks.

The place of our encampment was a ziarat called Turkumul, round the burial-ground of which the whole country seemed to have piled their grain. On the march we had passed two other villages, where I remarked what appeared to be a similar provident care for the sustenance of the departed in the land of spirits. In one place of sepulture, the usual household utensils were stored, and I verily thought with the same pious and kindly feeling that makes the relatives of a North American Indian bury him astride his war horse, or in his canoe paddle in hand. But such was not the case. Here the dead sentinelled the chattels of the living. In troublesome times, when a man is fain to quit his native village until the return of order, he prefers trusting his valuables to the sacred guardianship of such a place, rather than to his weak and failing brother. I inquired of Agha Maheide if such was really the case, and whether thieves would not be induced to violate the repository from the certainty of being able to do so with impunity. The old man put the forefingers of his right hand to his lips, and looked at me, exclaiming, "God forbid! bad as men are, they are not yet so utterly profligate." Religious feeling thus accomplishes what the government is unable to do: it ensures the safety of property: nor can, perhaps, a stronger instance be shown of the firm hold which superstition has over the human mind. Here we find it overcoming the worst passions, and the most confirmed habits of depraved men, much in the same manner as in the dark, solemn oak groves of the Druid, the impious were deterred from touching aught beneath the consecrated shade.

In the evening we moved forward to the village of Doda, the country continuing beautiful. We had mountains to the east and west, while the intervening plain was ribbed by parallel ridges connecting them together. The long narrow valleys, rich and sheltered, lying between these lateral chains, looked the very abodes of peace and comfort. In one of these valleys which we crossed during this day's march, a village called Shadi Kyl was built on the slope of its northern ridge. Before the doors of the houses a small clear brook glided by in a shallow bed, bordered with grass and with a row of mulberry trees. From the bank of this rivulet the fields spread out, clothing the region with one sheet of green. This valley and some others like it, were, however, but the exceptions, for since the Seiks seized Kohat its ruler has been compelled to levy a tribute on his people, which they, though perhaps able, are not willing to bear. Many have, in consequence of this, abandoned their homes, while the lands of others are suffered to lie fallow. We saw several deserted villages, and in one fine large valley there was not a single spot that evidenced the presence of a husbandman.

On the following day we marched for Kohat. When within four miles of the town we were met by the Lieutenant-governor Kheirulah Khan, a grand-nephew of Sultan Mohamed Khan. He came gaily attended, and a rabble crowd accompanied him, among which, with banners flying, music playing, horses careering, and spearsmen exhibiting, we entered the fortress under a salute of thirteen guns.

The geological formation of the country between Kalabagh and Kohat is sandstone and limestone. The latter did not appear till we had passed the village of Shukur Durah, when it was visible in the first ridge we crossed, and continued on to Kohat. Its presence not only brought fertility to the soil, but good water to the surface: whilst all the streams among the sandstone are more or less brackish. The height of these ridges varied from five hundred to one thousand feet. At some places the sandstone rose out of the ridge in mural precipices, while the slopes were strewed with slabs and fragments of limestone, looking as if the sandstone had been protruded through the rock. On the summit of these walls a piece of iron slag was found, which would seem to refer their disruption to igneous agency. Through these ridges the Indus has cut its channel, and it is where this occurs that its stream is so boisterous. At Hassan Abdal and Fatteh Jungh, on the Indian side of the river, not only have we the blue limestone formation, but springs both of naptha and water similar to those of Kohat.

From my apartment in the fort, the eye embraced at a glance the whole plain of Kohat. It is a very fine extent of country, in diameter about seven miles, and susceptible of the highest cultivation. Its numerous enclosures irrigated by the Toe, have more the appearance of an assemblage of gardens than fields. Of gardens, however, there are but few, as the Seik soldiers, on capturing the place, felled its fruit trees for fire-wood!

The town of Kohat is a paltry-looking place, containing a population of about 2,000 souls. It has some copious springs, which supply the town with water, and are besides used to irrigate the land. Here is a Mohamedan ziarat, and a Hindu Dharmsala. The former named Hadji Bhader, has a pretty little mosque attached to it, in the court of which a fountain supplies water for the ablution of the faithful. The running streams in the neighbourhood of the town are margined by the willow-tree, and a few others of larger growth indigenous to India are scattered along their banks. Kohat, although deprived of its gardens, is still a delightful residence; and to the Afridi and other wild tribes, inhabiting the savage mountains to the north and west, its willow-banked streams and luxuriant plain must indeed make it appear an elysium.

On the top of a scarped rock commanding the town, the Seiks have erected a triangular fort, the apex of which faces east; and although not a very sublime military work, is sufficiently strong to resist such troops as are likely to attack it. Its length is two hundred yards, and its greatest width fifty. It mounts two brass three-pounders. Within the walls there is a well; but as its waters are brackish, the garrison is supplied from the town.

One morning, during my sojourn at Kohat, two Seik soldiers entered the durbar, and in a bullying strain enquired of Kheirulah Khan how long he intended putting them off with evasive answers, instead of paying them the tribute-money, to receive which they had been deputed. This was the revenue of a small mountainous district called Tiri, which is managed by Sultan Mohamed Khan for Runjit Sing. It yields about a thousand rupees per annum. More than twenty Mussulmans hung their heads in silence while the audacious soldiers all but insulted their governor. Kheirulah Khan had recourse to entreaty to soothe these violent men. It was evident that he felt their taunts keenly. How keenly, those only can judge who know the angry feelings that exist between the two creeds. For a Mohamedan governor to be thus rebuked in his own durbar, and that too before a guest, by a couple of unarmed Seik soldiers, was an insult which I could not have imagined one of the faithful would so tamely have endured. I could not, however, but admire the patient and cool tact of Kheirulah, who, while his blood must have been boiling in his veins as he listened to the cutting language of the fellows, was yet careful neither by word nor deed to commit his master.

While here, a handsome youth one day entered the Bechoba and threw his turban at my feet. He was in love, he said, but his passion was not requited. Hearing of a firingi passing through the country, he had come many miles to solicit a charm by which the heart of his lady-love might be softened He was greatly disappointed when I declared to him that I had no such treasures to dispose of, and although I took some pains to explain the absurdity and worthlessness of the tasseems or charms by which the fakir dupes the simple, he left the tent melancholy and incredulous.

Chapter IX

I was unwilling to quit Kohat without visiting its sulphur mines and naptha springs. On communicating my desire to Kheirulah Khan, a guide named Gholam Khader, was ordered to be in readiness, and at an early hour on the morning of Monday the 14th, we started for the Kuttock village of Sheikh, in the neighbourhood of which lay the objects of our visit. The road led in an easterly direction along the southern base of the Afridi or Khyber chain, a broad belt of high mountains which here separate the two plains of Peshawur Kohat. Towards evening we reached the Kuttock village, somewhat jaded by the heat and a march of thirty-six miles.

A servant was to have accompanied us with refreshments; but unfortunately, at starting, in the darkness of the morning, we got entangled among the cultivated land of Kohat; and when relieved from this provoking dilemma by the growing light of day, neither he nor the sumpter-mule were visible. The villagers, however, on our route, brought us fire, wood, and water, and as the tea-pot was always to be found in my own saddle bags, we managed matters pretty well.

Three miles north by east of Sheikh is the opening in the mountains in which both the sulphur mines and naptha springs are situated. On entering this ravine, the springs, five in number, were discovered at its bottom, small in size, and not very productive. They may yield, perhaps, five gallons a day. The colour of the naptha is dark green, its smell highly sulphurous, and its temperature that of the atmosphere. This ravine had evidently been rent assunder, as the projecting points of one side were faced by corresponding indentations on the other. Its whole length is not more than three hundred yards. The formation is limestone, large masses of which, scorched but not calcined, are strewed around. Salt water impregnated with sulphur oozes down the bottom of the ravine.

After reaching the upper end of the naptha ravine, you turn to the north, and ascending for four hundred yards, arrive at the sulphur mines. The limestone is here much calcined, and the sulphur is found either incorporated with or encrusting the stone. Where this deposit occurs, the hills seem to have been once coated over with slabs of a reddish-brown colour, which, burst by some pressure from within, now strew the surface with their fragments. When the strata are exposed to atmospheric influence, the stone is of a blueish colour, and so friable, that pieces may be picked out of them by the hand.

The sulphur is obtained by putting a quantity of the ore into an earthern vessel, upon the top of which three other vessels are luted one above another. The two central pots have apertures at top and bottom; the upper one is closed at the top. A fire is applied to the lower vessel and continued for twenty-four hours; at the expiration of which time, the earth will have parted with its sulphur, and the pure mineral be found adhering to the upper and intermediate vessels.

This sulphurous district extends twelve miles from Sheikh, in a south-east direction. It is but nine miles from Khushalghur, a village on the west bank of the Indus, from which the downward navigation is at all times open. When we recollect the inexhaustible supplies of salt that are found near that river, that veins of good coal have been discovered, and that the neighbouring district of Bunnu and Tak are rich in iron and other ores, we cannot but pause to admire the wisdom of a kind Providence in storing these natural treasures in a situation so favourable for the supply of a wide circle of population. From these magazines the valley of the Indus and the Panjab can by an easy water communication be supplied; and when progressing civilization shall have unlocked these elements of natural wealth, a great change, political and moral, may be expected.

On our return from the mountains, instead of proceeding direct to the Kuttock village, we spread our saddle-cloths under a fulah bush in the bottom of a shallow ravine, and there awaited the hour of noon, as I was anxious to get a mid-day observation. Whilst here, we were visited by Hussein Khan, the Kuttock chief, who expressed great surprise that on so sultry a day any man should prefer the oppressive heat of the jungle to the cool shade of the village. I got rid of the chief by promising to call at his house in the evening; but I soon found that he had good reason for his surprise.

This was one of the most trying days I ever remember to have spent. The bush was too small to screen us effectually, and the wind came down the ravine heated as from an oven. To remain in the ravine until the evening, as I had intended, was impossible. Our mouths became parched, and the skin peeled from our lips. We could bear it no longer; and at 3 o'clock in the afternoon we saddled our horses, and made our escape into the village.

After passing an hour with Hussein Khan, who, I could see, smiled at the promptitude of our visit, we again mounted, and putting our horses into a brisk trot, we reached Gumut, twenty miles west of Sheikh at 8 o'clock in the evening. The moon was shining brightly as we entered this village, which I perceived was large, and composed of three detached clusters of buildings, each of which was a little village of itself. A large mud-built fort in the centre protected the whole. The cattle had been driven in, the milking hour was past, and all the inhabitants were enjoying themselves; the grown-up people, seated upon charpoys outside their doors, were chatting together, while the children were sporting about in the open space in front of the houses, and the thoughtless happy laugh of the young men and maidens caught our ear. We inquired for the Malik. He soon appeared, and led us to the mosque, the usual sheltering place of the way-faring stranger. It was already occupied, so we took up a position in the open air in its front. The boys now took our horses by the bridles and led them about till cool, whilst others procured us charpoys, water, firewood, and fire. The Hakim brought us a large bowl of milk, and a vessel to boil our tea water. He communed with the guide for some time, and seeing we were in need of rest, very considerately withdrew. It was late ere I could get to sleep, and even to that hour parties of women continued sauntering about, apparently enjoying a quiet walk and friendly converse, after the labours of the sultry day. Though we reached Gumut very much fatigued, no sooner had we dismounted before the mosque than the guide, and another horseman who had joined our party, went a little apart, unbound their kammer-bands, spread them out, knelt and said prayers. The Koran, though it teaches much that is wrong, contains also a large proportion of good. Often since that time have I observed that the Mohamedans, both old and young, however worn out by fatigue, or suffering from hunger and thirst, have postponed all thought of self-indulgence to their duty to their God.

It is not with them the mere force of habit; it is the strong impression on their minds that the duty of prayer is so important, that no circumstances can excuse its omission.

Among Mohamedans there is much kindly feeling. Their religion knits them as it were into a general fraternity, in which every member, rich or poor, is, though a stranger, always affectionately received. Much of this charitable disposition is no doubt to be traced to those causes which make the inhabitants of thinly peopled districts so generally hospitable. More, however, is attributable to the precepts of the Koran. Nor are the followers of Mohamed exclusive in their benevolence, for all strangers share their charities; and though the Christian be not met with the open arms that welcome a brother Mussulman, he is courteously received, and treated with kindness and respect. A Mohamedan looks upon Christians in the light of benighted and misguided men; but yet people of "the Book," who, though not heirs to the high destinies of Mohamed's followers, are nevertheless, from the sacred character of Isau (Jesus), entitled to the commiseration of the faithful.

We learned from the Malik of Gumut, that the Mullah had that day been praying for rain; and that on the morrow all the villagers, headed by their aged priest, would again in the open air, and in the face of heaven, supplicate their Maker for that nourishment to their ground, without which the fields of the Kuttock may be tilled, but can never be reaped. On similar occasions the Hindu makes prayers and offerings to his favourite idol, and seeks by the frivolous mummery of unmeaning ceremonies to obtain the object of his wishes. How infinitely more beautiful and pure is the Mussulman's humble and pious acknowledgment, that in Jehovah's hands rest the destinies of all flesh.

At an early hour on the following morning (Wednesday, 16th,) we were in the saddle and on the road to Kohat. Before emerging from the rough hills and broken gullies that bound the plain of Kohat to the south, we passed several graves by the road-side. A heap of stones thrown carelessly together marks the spot where the rahgeer or traveller lies. In former years many Afghans resorted to Hindustan, where they took service in the independent states, and after a stay of some years returned to their native land, carrying with them their scanty but honourable savings. These poor fellows were, it seems, often cut off by cool-blooded miscreants while upon their homeward road. These cairns are, therefore, melancholy memorials, each of which is connected with a tale of violence and blood.

As we neared Kohat, our horses were completely knocked up. That of Gholam Khader Khan had been flagging for some time, and he now beat the poor beast so unmercifully about the head, that I felt compelled to interfere. On my lecturing him on the cruelty and impropriety of such conduct, he assured me that the horse was a haramzada (a rascal), that a kote or spirit had taken possession of the beast, and that the plan he adopted was the only one calculated to expel the demon. The magic process proved, however, somewhat too successful, as the poor animal died the next day.

This little excursion gave me an opportunity of mingling somewhat among the Kuttocks, and of gleaning a good deal of information regarding them.

The tribe is now broken into two parts, known as the Kuttocks of Akora on the Kabul river, and the Kuttocks of Tiri in the province of Kohat. Hussein Khan, whom I met at the sulphur mines, is the head of the Tiri division, and one of his cousins governs the other. Both are, however, subject to Runjit Sing, and are under the immediate rule of Sultan Mohamed Khan, his viceroy. They are much exasperated against the Seiks, and no less partial to Dost Mohamed Khan of Kabul. Hussein Khan showed me a letter from the Kabul chief, detailing his defeat of the Seiks at Jamrad. He told me how much he regretted Sultan Mohamed Khan's engagements with the Maharajah, and added that it was entirely owing to the former's influence with the tribes that the Kalabagh boats had been permitted to ascend the river to Attock. The Kuttocks can bring into the field about 1,000 fighting men, all foot soldiers. The lands are the property of the cultivators, who pay a nominal duty to their chief. For example, the village of Gumut pays yearly eighty rupees, but the revenue of Hussein Khan is principally derived from a tax on merchandise and the sale of salt. It is estimated at 30,000 rupees; but I greatly doubt its reaching to that amount. The Kuttock lands are too arid for pasture, and the flocks owned by the tribe are therefore few.

The lands of the Bungush, of which Kohat is the capital, are very fertile. They are said to yield a revenue of 80,000 rupees. The governor of the district keeps a small force in pay for its defence, amounting to 100 horse, and about double that number of infantry. Kohat has been given by the Seiks as a jagger to Sultan Mohamed Khan, who has confided the government of it to his nephew, as I have already mentioned.

Next day, having completed the necessary observations for fixing the position of Kohat, I went to durbar and got my rukhsut, or permission to quit the place. Kheirulah Khan, the governor, was seated in his Kutchery, or justice hall, hearing and answering the complaints of his people. The room was filled by respectably attired Mussulmans, each of whom in turn stated his grievance. I was surprised at their freedom of speech, and their bold, manly, nay, almost boisterous manner, so different from the slavish cringing of a Sindi to his Amir, or the supple accommodating tone of an Hindu before his chief.

Two individuals who had been in disgrace were this day again admitted into favour. A piece of cloth as a nazar or present, was wrapped round the head of each, in token that their past offences were forgotten. The poor men seemed to feel the graciousness of the act, and as they left the hall amidst the whispered gratulations of their countrymen, were unable to restrain their emotion.

At six o'clock in the evening of the next day we commenced our night journey, escorted by Agha Maheide, and long before the morning dawned had emerged from the defiles of the dividing mountains upon the plain of Peshawur. As soon as the increasing light enabled me to pick out my way across the plain, I left the staid old gentleman to pursue his more leisurely pace; and giving my horse the bridle, set off for the town, where I arrived in time for an excellent breakfast with Captain Burnes, rendered doubly agreeable by the

[111]

cordial welcome which he gave me.

In closing these brief memoranda of my journeyings in Kohat, I should indeed be ungrateful were I to omit making honourable mention of my cicerone, Agha Maheide Khan. Old, nay, almost decrepit, as he was, his exertions to afford me every comfort and accommodation possible were unintermitting. There was a cheerful kindness in his manner which could not but excite my gratitude; although I well knew that his conduct was dictated by his respect for the government I served, and not for myself individually. I parted from the good old man with feelings of respect and friendship.

The day succeeding that of my arrival at Peshawur I started for the Kabul river, with the intention of descending it to Attock, where I wished to to take another set of chronometric observations to determine its longitude. This river bounds the plain of Peshawur on the north, and though there called the Lundi, the stream, from its source to the Indus, is better known by the appellation of the "Kabul."

On the 21st I reached Attock, much pleased with the scenery on the banks of the Kabul river. The following day was devoted to taking the necessary observations, and on the succeeding one I rejoined the mission at Peshawur.

This town has suffered much at the hands of the Seiks. In fact everything, both in Peshawur itself and the surrounding plain, bears the stamp of violence and oppression. In whatever direction the eye is turned, it rests upon uncultivated fields and half tenanted villages. No sooner do you pass Akora on the road to Peshawur, than signs of the ravages of war may be discerned. The groves of large tamarisk trees which used to shelter the traveller, have been levelled, and small forts erected in their place. The fine caravansery of thirty-two cells aside, where the foreign merchant stored his goods, and the wayfarer found an asylum, has been converted into a residence for the commander of the garrison, and the adjoining mosque has been pulled down, because it was a bone of contention between the subjugated Mussulmans and their haughty oppressors. To soothe the irritated feelings of both creeds, Monsieur Avitabile, the governor of Peshawur, has built a mosque for the one, and a temple for the other, within the walls of the square. Where the Bala Hissar, or palace of the Afghans, stood, the Seiks have built a substantial fort, in the erection of which they recklessly destroyed a large portion of the Bagh-i-shah, or King's garden, and disfigured the rest.

While we were at Peshawur the Seik forces were reviewed. There were upon the field three brigades of infantry, numbering 8,000 men, besides 12,000 irregular cavalry. On reaching the parade-ground, we rode down the infantry line; and though I am no soldier, I could not help admiring its materiel. The men were tall, slim fellows, well set up, with a fine soldierly bearing. They were neatly dressed in well cut uniforms, and all their accoutrements clean, and in the best order. Their bright gun-barrels, however, I could not approve. After this inspection, we took our seats in a small lodge erected for the occasion, when the brigades manœuvred singly in its front. They were first marched past the lodge in review order. This over, they were formed into line, and exercised with blank cartridge, firing from flank to centre alternate volleys, by whole companies. They were next ordered to prepare to receive cavalry. A square with a gun at each corner was immediately formed by each brigade, when a file firing opened, which was much better sustained by one of the three than by the other two.

As the cavalry were not expected to perform any evolutions, they merely rode past in front of the lodge. The chiefs at the heads of their respective contingents were all clad in chain or plate armour, and had their helmets ornamented by heron feathers. The troops wore so great a diversity of colours, that a Seik chieftain present, as he looked down upon these moving masses,

[113]

likened them to a flower garden. Side by side were to be seen the grim steel-clad warrior on his henna-dyed charger, and the gaily attired lancer upon his gorgeously caparisoned steed, waving his small pointed banner. Onward they moved, cheering as they went, and shouting the national battle cry, "Wah guruji ka fatteh!"—may the Guru be victorious!

On the 28th of August the mission moved forward to Jamrud, a Seik fortress at the west end of the Peshawur plain, commanding the entrance to the Khyber Pass. A few days were spent here negotiating with the Khyberies for the passage of this defile, during which these people showed their deep-rooted hatred of the Seiks, by cruelly murdering two defenceless grass-cutters, and making off with a herd of camels. Instant chase was given, and the camels were recovered, but the same hills that enabled the animals to be recaptured favoured the escape of the ruffians. The bodies of the murdered men were brought into camp, one with the throat fearfully cut, the other a headless trunk.

Chapter X

On the 2nd of September we took a friendly leave of the Seiks, and very soon after we had bade them "Wah guruji ka fatteh," or constant victory, we heard the well-known salutation "Wussulam alaikum," or peace be with you, of their adversaries the Khyber Maliks, welcoming us to the country of the Afghans. We had been under the protection of the former people ever since our first meeting with them at Mittun-Kote, and their conduct towards us had been, with few and unimportant exceptions, invariably kind. It was gratifying to perceive that in spite of their opposite creeds and hostile feelings, the presence of a British agent was equally acceptable to both parties, Hindu and Mohamedan; and though the poverty of the Afghan would not permit him to be more than hospitable, yet his sobered, trustworthy deportment was infinitely more pleasing to us than the ostentation and arrogance of the Seik. The relative situation in which these two nations are now placed may have a considerable effect on their behaviour to others, but for my own part, I could not help thinking that I saw truth in the gravity of the one, and much of varnished artifice in the polite and studied attentions of the other.

Nor was the change we had just made, in other respects, less calculated to arrest attention. To the emanations of Baba Nanak had succeeded the revelations of Mohamed. The Grinth or holy book of the former had given place to the Koran of the latter, and on the precepts of this book were based the laws of the land we had entered, its moral code and social system, its government and its commerce.

To the Christian there was much in this change to excite a painful interest, whilst seeing around him one gross superstition taking the place of another, and he is led to pray, in the pure spirit of his own benevolent creed, for the accomplishment of David's prophecy;—"When all kings shall fall down before the Lord; all nations shall serve him."

Dost Mohamed had ordered Agha Jan, the governor of Jelalabad, to meet the mission at Khyber, and escort it with all honours to Kabul. But Agha Jan was not forthcoming, and the Maliks of the Pass seemed inclined to detain us until his arrival. On this, Captain Burnes told them that he wanted no other escort than the Khyberies, and no better security for his baggage than the presence of themselves. Without more ado, we threw ourselves on the honour of this thieving community, and although the act might be a rash one, we had no reason to repent it.

A short distance from the entrance of the Pass several Seik scalps were seen in the middle of the road, partly covered with earth; trophies of the field of Jamrud, where some months before our arrival the Afghans had routed a considerable body of Seik troops, and slain their leader Harri Singh.

We wound up the Pass to the fort of Ali Masjid, and were there received by its commandant, an ill-conditioned, dissipated-looking Englishman; slipshod, turbaned, and robed in a sort of Afghan dishabille—having more the look of a dissipated priest than a military man. His abode was a cave in the mountain, from which he and his hungry followers levied black-mail on the passing Kafilas. The Seik fortress of Jamrud was at this time dependent for water on the stream that runs through Khyber, and the chief occupation of the young Lieut.-Colonel, for so he styled himself, was to stop the supply, and again to permit it to flow on being bribed to do so.

Lieut.-Colonel Battray received us at the head of his column; which, drawn up for the occasion, had something approaching to a military look; but no sooner did the commandant attempt a manœuvre, than a most ludicrous scene ensued. In utter hopelessness of restoring his scattered legion to order, he disbanded it forthwith, and then the Lieut.-Colonel commenced whacking his men with a cudgel; but he was soon overwhelmed by numbers, and compelled to desist. In the evening he came into the tent to inquire, with all military formalities, what were the orders for to-morrow's march; when he took occasion to point out to Captain Burnes an error in his Narrative, assuring him that although forty bottles of wine might formerly have been procured in Kabul for a rupee, nothing like that number could be now obtained. Before retiring, he requested, with a degree of quiet impudence, which was really meritorious, a loan of 50l. to defray the expenses of the march, for which he gravely tendered an order on his regimental pay-officer in Kabul. Failing in this attempt, he hit upon the expedient of quartering his men upon the mission; and to accomplish this, issued a General Order, which, as a specimen of bombast, was quite a curiosity. A captain's guard was ordered to one place, a subaltern's to another, until the whole of the lean crew was disposed of. No sooner had these cormorants taken up their stations than they piled arms, and asked for food. The result was, that the Soorsat (provisions) Dost Mohamed had intended for the mission was made over to these hungry soldiers.

When Mr. Rattray became aquainted with our different pursuits, he made the round of the camp and waited on us individually, proffering, for a consideration, to put us each in possession of the information he had amassed during a long sojourn in these countries. To Dr. Lord he promised an account of the rivers in Karakorum, and the site of all the valuable ores between the Indus and Kabul. To Lieut. Leach, the military resources of kingdoms and states, from Lahore to Mushid, from Sind to Kashmir. To me, a map of half the continent of Asia, in which should be delineated every river and mountain chain, every town and route. He borrowed from Captain Burnes the volumes of his travels and those of Forster and Elphinstone, and from these sources and his own fertile imagination, he would, had we encouraged him, have furnished us with a full and particular account of countries he had never seen, and tribes, the very names of which he had not before heard. Some time after this, when we were in Kabul, this man became a convert to Mohamedanism, much against the wish of Dost Mohamed Khan, who thought him a disgrace to any creed, and expressed in strong terms the contempt he felt for men who could change their religion to improve their fortune. The Khyber commandant was altogether a singular character; void of all principle, but clever and well informed. His autobiography, written at the request of Captain Burnes, affords another proof how often the real events of life exceed in interest the wildest conception of fiction.

As the fort of Ali Masjid is perched high up the mountain, we encamped in the bottom of the pass, which from its mouth to that station, is a steep, walled, but not rugged mountain ravine. For some distance beyond the fort, it assumes more the character of a deep defile; its north side being a mural precipice, rising many hundred feet in height, while the opposite side, on which the fort hangs, falls back as it rises, but is nevertheless steep. In the afternoon the gathering clouds betokened rain, and we were engaged removing the baggage from the dry bed of the torrent, when it began to fall. The Khyberies rendered us efficient aid; but for which, much property would have been lost. So quickly did the waters come down, and the little rill swelled so rapidly into an impassable stream, that our party was divided, some having sought shelter upon the right, and others on the left bank. The rain continued, and innumerable cataracts came pouring over the mural cliffs, which in contrast with the blackened rocks, looked like streaks of silver. The roaring torrent now filled the bottom of the ravine, while we, unhoused and drenched to the skin, sat terribly out of humour among horses and baggage, watching its fierce struggles among the opposing rocks, and wondering when the tumult would be over. The rain cloud was at last emptied, and an hour afterwards the little brook meandered as quietly down the ravine as it had done before the storm.

A day's halt was necessary to dry our wet tents, and to repair damages; after which we passed safely through the Khyber mountains, and debouched upon the Kabul river at Dhaka. The pass on this side of Ali Masjid is wider than the portion already described, and has more the character of a valley than a ravine.

In our last march one of those "topes," or mounds of masonry, which are so numerous in Afghanistan, was seen occupying the summit of a small hill on the north side of the valley. These solid structures which have so long defied "time," and which the apathy of the natives left undisturbed, have at last fallen before the enlightened curiosity of Europeans; and as the entire deposits of many, consisting of coins and relics, are already in the East India Company's Museum, and other cabinets of the learned, we hope soon to hear that modern research has, by deciphering their inscriptions, dispelled all doubt of the purpose for which these singular piles were originally erected.

Before we left Dhaka, the Maliks of Khyber were assembled to receive from Captain Burnes the reward of their praiseworthy forbearance towards us whilst we were among the mountains. The presents made them were of very trifling value, but derived a higher worth from the kind, yet impressive, and dignified manner in which they were bestowed. The Khyberies left the camp in high glee, promising that our kasids, or letter-carriers, should be made "free of the pass;" a declaration which, all things considered, has been tolerably well kept.

From Dhaka we journeyed along the fertile valley of the river to Umber Khana, where a branch road leads to Jelalabad. It is usual for merchants going to Kabul to take this route as being the safest; but escorted as we were by Agha Jan (who by this time had joined us), we had no occasion to make so useless a détour. Leaving, therefore, the Jelalabad road to the right, we held on nearly due west over the rough broken ground that skirts the range of Spenghur, or Sufeid Koh (snow-clad chain). Beyond the Kabul river towered the giant Himalaya, while close to us, on our left hand, rose the range already mentioned, clad in a mantle as pure as its more elevated neighbour. The result of some trigonometrical observations at the village of Synu, when combined with our barometrical measurements, gave 14,000 feet for the height of Sufeid Koh above the level of the sea, and 20,248 for that of the highest part of the Himalaya in the meridian of 70° 50' east.

The hoary head of one mountain has given its name to an entire range; for though it be known throughout its whole extent as Sufeid Koh, or the white mountains, yet the only portion of it which reaches the line of perpetual congelation lies between the meridians of Synu and Gandamuk. Its outline is broken and irregular. The chain is formed by a succession of parallel ridges that rise like steps into the region of eternal snow. The two nearest ridges are covered with pine forests, in which are trees of a large size. The timber is of the best quality, and is brought in large quantities to Kabul, where the frame of every house is made from the fir tree. I do not remember to have before seen so highly resinous a wood. In one species of tree which resembled the Scotch fir, the pitch actually oozed out and dropped from its cones.

Among the many advantages that will unquestionably accrue to western India from the opening of the river Indus, the European inhabitants in the Bombay presidency will not consider as one of the least important, the prospect of a constant supply of ice. This article is sold in Jelalabad, a town situated under Sufeid

Koh, and on the bank of the Kabul river. From Jelalabad to Akora on the same stream, there is a raft navigation, and from the latter place to the sea, there is no impediment to river boats. The ice should be embarked at Jelalabad between the 1st and 5th of September, so as to be carried down the stream by the latest freshes of the swell, by which arrangement the sea-going vessel (which should be waiting in the river) will catch the last breathings of the monsoon in her voyage to the presidency. The time which the combined river and sea voyage would occupy may be thus stated:—

Segment	Days
From Jelalabad to Akora	3
From Akora to Kalabagh	1 1/2
From Kalabagh to Mittun-Kote	5 1/2
From Mittun-Kote to the sea	9
River voyage	19
Time for transfer of cargo	3
Sea voyage	8
Total	30

In carrying out the details, there will at first he some difficulty, but none that a very small outlay will not overcome. The fir-wood of the raft, and the boat herself, would bring a handsome profit in Sind; and surely ice and fresh English-looking apples, pears, plums, and cherries, the far-famed, seedless pomegranates, besides all descriptions of dried fruits, would render the traffic profitable.

Though the general appearance of the country lying under Sufeid Koh is remarkably barren, there are, nevertheless, among the inequalities of its stony, sand-coloured surface, many sweet valleys, which, like islands in the desert, appear only the more beautiful from the sterility that surrounds them. The name of this province is Nanjhnehar, derived from a Pushtu word signifying nine rivers, the supposed number of rivulets that intersect the district. It has a length of fifty-nine miles, and a mean width of about fifteen. It is bordered on the north by the fertile plain of Jelalabad, while to the south it gradually slopes upward towards the snowy chain, among the roots of which its higher valleys insinuate themselves. The tribes of Nanjhnehar are, it is said, addicted to robbery, and their fortlike dwellings are certainly not the best signs of a settled country; yet on our route we saw the inhabitants industriously and, as it appeared, contentedly, occupied in the cultivation of their fields. Though quiet and respectful in their demeanour, there was a dash of the mountaineer in their mien; but men so singularly situated, that they can look to the hills above them and proclaim them to be Yaghistan or rebel land, while a rich plain studded with villages skirts the lower edge of their own bleak domain, must be expected to exhibit traits of character and temperament peculiar to themselves. From Khyber to Kabul there is no waste land; every spot capable of cultivation has been turned over by the plough or the spade; and so great is the command of water, that even the acclivities of the hills which enclose the small circular valleys are successfully cultivated. It is here no uncommon thing to see a stream of water conducted along the face of a hill forty feet above the fields below; and when rivulets are wanting a running stream is procured from kharaizes or tunnel-wells. In these secluded valleys orchard, garden, and field are beautifully blended together. They abound in mulberry, pomegranate, and other fruit trees, while the banks of the small streams that meander through them are edged with a fine sward enamelled with wild flowers and fragrant with aromatic herbs. These delightful spots seem little fitted for the abode of the robber and assassin. A love of country and of home must be engendered by them; and after having seen the Afghans in their snug valleys, I am not surprised at their disinclination for travel: stern necessity, however, often drives them abroad. In Afghanistan, as in all other Asiatic nations cursed with an unstable government, the population of the several districts is perpetually varying; in some it has diminished, in others increased; whilst the census of the entire nation must show a progressive augmentation. The lands that yield a ready return, that is, the well-watered valleys, are already occupied; but in those districts where water has sometimes to be brought from a distance of four and five miles, at very great expense, it requires considerable capital to attempt the cultivation of waste lands. If the hills will feed sheep, the surplus population become pastoral; but if, as is the case with Nanjhnehar, they present a naked surface, many of the dwellers among them will, it is feared, as their numbers increase, be compelled by actual want to resort to a life of violence and rapine; and although we must blame, we cannot but pity them.

The road continued full of ascents and descents over larger tracts of barren surface, interspersed with small fertile valleys, till we reached the Surkh Rud or Red river. The bed of this stream is here narrowed by two ridges of blue slate, that rise like walls on each side of its deep cut channel. In 1606 a fine arch was thrown across by Ali Mardan Khan: it still remains, after a lapse of two centuries, in good preservation, a monument of his public spirit.

I have already mentioned that Nanjhnehar has the Jelalabad plain to the north, and Sufeid Koh to the south, but I omitted to say that its east and west extremes are bounded respectively by the hills of Khyber and Karkatcha. After crossing the Red river we neared the latter ridge, over which there are four different roads. That of Lattabund, the most southerly, had been traversed by Capt. Burnes in 1832. The others were now to be examined, and that of Karkatcha, the highest and most northerly, was allotted to me. Parting with my companions, I turned off to the left, and having passed through the vale of Hisarak, noted for its seedless pomegranate, entered the bed of a stream tributary to

[123]

the Surkh Rud river. Up this we wound our path to near the summit of Karkatcha. On entering among the mountains, the bed of the stream contracted to a narrow defile not more than ten feet in width, the sides of which were naked, craggy, and precipitous, while its bottom was encumbered by the trunks of huge fir trees, and here and there crossed by ledges of rock. On nearing the ridge of the pass, we quitted the defile and kept to the right, along the face of mountains which here assume a more open character. On the top of the pass are the ruins of two windmills, said to have been erected by Mahmud of Ghizni, and on a clear space a little below them some slight traces of buildings, together with remnants of brick and pottery, mark the place where a town had been situated. The Pass of Karkatcha has an elevation of nearly 8,000 feet; and from it we looked down upon the various mountain and hilly chains that intersect the country about Kabul. The hills forming this pass have both their east and west faces covered with almond trees: there is also plenty of the uzulzus or wild indigo, and numerous wild flowers and fragrant plants. The mountains are of blue slate; and though they have soil upon them to their summit, they have no grassy covering. The black wolf (Gurgh-i-Siah), the fox, and the leopard are met with here, and these, with many other animals, are said to be numerous upon the adjacent mountains of Sufeid Koh.

At Bhut-khak I rejoined the mission, which entered Kabul on the 20th, escorted by Mohamed Akbar Khan, the favourite son of Amir Dost Mohamed Khan. He brought out a large cavalcade with him; but though scarcely twenty-one years of age, he was the largest man in the cortege. He conducted us at once into the Bala Hissar, and introduced us to his father. Dost Mohamed Khan is about forty-five years of age, and looks worn out and aged before his time. His frame is large and bony, and all his features strongly marked. There is a sternness in the general expression of his features, which is increased by his flowing, jet-black beard, but his countenance is lighted up by eyes of peculiar brilliancy and intelligence: when he fixes them upon those by whom he is addressed, they actually seem to flash with approbation or dissent. From the ease with which he ran over the names of places visited by Captain Burnes in 1832-3, it is evident that his memory must be a good one; and the various subjects on which he spoke, the good sense of his remarks, and the readiness of his replies, proved that his conversational talents were of no mean order. When any one of us addressed him, he sat with his eyes rivetted upon the speaker, and his whole soul appeared absorbed by the subject; when he himself spoke, though he did not resort to Persian gesture, nor assume the solemnity of a Hindu rajah, there was that in his manner and tone of voice which enforced attention.

Our welcome had been cordial; and as we left the apartment I could not help contrasting the audience we had just quitted with the scene in a Haiderabad durbar on a like occasion, and the bearing of the blunt, homely Afghan with that of the vapouring Beluche. Dost Mohamed's reception of the mission was less warmly expressed than that of the Sind Amirs, but the ruler of Kabul felt what the others only feigned. He deemed himself honoured by the arrival of a British mission at his capital; while on the contrary the potentates of Sind, when they grant an interview to a British agent, affect to think that the condescension is on their part; they consider only the servant who is sent to them; but the more intelligent Afghans view in the servant the government which he represents.

Chapter XI

One of the objects which Captain Burnes had greatly at heart was to obtain materials for the construction of an entirely new map of Afghanistan, in which actual survey should supersede hearsay information. In prosecution of this design, we had not been long in Kabul before he obtained its ruler's permission to visit the Koh Daman; and I shall venture to give a brief description of this fair province, although it will somewhat interrupt the narrative of my travels.

The valley of Koh Daman lies north of Kabul, from which it is separated by a low creeping ridge, not far from the town. At the upper extremity of this valley rises the snowy peaks of Hindu Kosh, while those of Pagman overlook it on the west. To the east it is bordered by a lower range, which decreases in height as it goes south, until it sinks into the low ridge crossing he bottom of the valley. So enclosed, the Koh Daman has a length of thirty-one miles and a medium width of seven. The western side of the valley is much higher than the eastern, along which the drainage of the opposite mountain flows. From the base of the Pagman much débris, splintered rocky fragments and heavy boulders, are strewed over the plain, having been loosened by the winter's frost from the granite peaks above. The sides of these mountains are split by numerous ravines, down which come tumbling rills of the purest water. The slopes of their rugged channels are thickly planted with the mulberry, and every moderately level spot is clad with fruit trees or the vine. The mountains at the head of the valley throw out three streams, which are named Ghorbund, Parwan, and Panchshir. The latter issues from the north-east corner of Koh Daman, and the Ghorbund from its north-west. The Parwan, which flows between the other two, unites about four miles below the hills with the river of Ghorbund, which, thus augmented, joins the Panchshir at Ali Burj on the north-east end of the Begram plain, in latitude 34° 59' 46" north. A few miles east of this junction the Bari-ke-ab falls in from the south, and the drainage of the valley thus collected into one channel flows through an opening in the eastern hills to join the Kabul river, of which it is the northern fork. That portion of the Koh Daman watered by the northern streams is a basin lying full forty feet below the level of the south part of the valley. The latter is a stony and comparatively infertile tract, whose principal produce is fruit, for which both soil and climate are well suited. The former yields grain, cotton, tobacco, artificial grasses, and vegetables, but scarce any fruit besides the mulberry, of which, however, there are innumerable plantations.

Koh Daman is a favourite country residence of the wealthy inhabitants of Kabul, and is almost as thickly studded with castles as with gardens. They are strongly built, and are, in fact, mimic representations of the old baronial residences in our own land. Life and property are here very insecure; and I really believe it would be difficult to find any two neighbouring castles, the owners of which are not either covert enemies or at open feud with each other. This, and the exactions of Dost Mohamed Khan, have forced a number of families across the Hindu Kosh, where I afterwards met many natives of this valley whose hearts still yearned for the pleasant home of their youth.

On the 14th of October we set out upon our excursion. In the environs of Kabul the roads lead by the side of brooks, and are usually edged by willow trees. Many passages both in the Old and New Testament have been made familiar to our minds by an attention to the customs still prevalent in Eastern countries; and the circumstances under which we here find the willow illustrates Isaiah 44:4—"And they shall spring up as among the grass, as willows by the water courses."

Half an hour's walk from the Bala Hissar brought us upon the Kabul race-course, a fine, straight, broad road, nearly three miles long. It is belted on both sides by vegetable gardens, beyond which lie those of fruit. Nowhere have I seen better cauliflower and cabbage than were now growing here. Quitting the race-course, the road led over cultivated fields to the base of the low ridge that separates Kabul from the Koh Daman. About ten o'clock in the forenoon we stood upon its crest, and after enjoying the beautiful prospect that was spread around us, descended its northern slope, and arrived a little before noon at Shukur Durah. This is a delightful village; and whilst rambling over its gardens, climbing its grassy slopes, or lounging under the fine foliage of its stately walnut trees, I felt that Koh Daman deserved all the praise which the Kabulies bestow upon it. We scrambled some distance up the barren side of the Pagman ridge, and from our elevated position had a noble view of the whole mountain-girt valley. In the plain were green fields and corn lands, while every ravine that gave passage for a rill from the mountains streaked their sterile surface with foliage of a mingled hue. The castles of the nobles might be seen peering through the trees—at one moment gleaming in the sunshine, and the next darkened by the passing cloud. The leaves had not begun to fall, but, like old age, autumn has its heralds; and amidst the healthy foliage of many a tree signs of the "sear and withered leaf" were not wanting.

From Shukur Durah we continued along the base of Pagman to Danow and Istalaf. The orchards at both these places had more of a wintry look than those we saw at Shukur Durah. The season, however, had been backward throughout the valley. The grapes in some of the gardens were still unripe, though the other fruits had long been gathered in. The hedges in this neighbourhood bore the common haw and a description of cranberry; beneath them shot out the burr-thistle and the stinging-nettle, while the "wee modest daisy" spotted every bank where the ear detected the gurgling sound of water. These sweet districts, full of clustering hamlets, here and there stretching up the side of a barren and forbidding mountain-chain, though rich and fertile in themselves, derive much adventitious beauty from their peculiar situation. In the plain they would be but "green fields and fruitful vineyards," but here they are gems of fertility set off by the desolation that surrounds them. The thermometer at sunrise indicated a temperature of 43°; nor did it at any subsequent hour of the day range higher than 68° in the shade. This to an Indian is a bracing temperature; and buttoning close my surtout, I was uncertain whether most to admire the scenery of the valley or its invigorating climate.

A stranger cannot be long in Kabul without hearing of Istalaf. Its gardens are famous throughout Afghanistan, and were so in the days of the Emperor Baber.[1]

Those, however, who have been accustomed to trace perfection in the regular arrangements of our botanical gardens might feel dissatisfied with the rugged charms of Istalaf. Though its gardens are not laid out with square and line, to me the varying outline of the ground

---

[1] In his pleasingly written commentaries, he thus speaks of the place:—"Few quarters possess a district that can rival Istalaf. A large river runs through it, and on either side of it are gardens, green, gay, and beautiful. Its water is so cold that there is no need of icing it. In this district is a garden, called Bagh-e-Kilan (or the Great Garden), which Ulugh Beg Mirza seized upon. I paid the price of the garden to the proprietors, and received from them a grant of it. On the outside of the garden are large and beautiful-spreading plane-trees, under the shade of which there are agreeable spots finely sheltered."—Memoirs of Baber.

they occupy gave them a charm which all the skill of Repton himself could never have equalled on the plain.

As we approached Istalaf by a road leading over the wavy ground about the base of Pagman, we saw nothing of the town or its suburbs till we gained the south bank of the hollow in which they lie; the whole then burst on view with panoramic effect. Seating ourselves upon the grass, we contemplated at leisure the lovely scene. A row of white bark chenar trees (the plane trees of Baber) edged one side of the ravine, and bending their aged boughs over the chasm, occasionally shed a withered leaf that might be seen circling into the depths below. On the opposite bank stands the town, piled house upon house stretching up the shoulder of the mountain that overlooks the valley. The sunny slopes around were now tawny with the vine and the broad ravine for a mile and a half along its course was one mass of chequered foliage. A considerable stream holds its way in the bottom of this valley, which, chafed and torn by a rocky bed, produces a noise which, when heard beyond the ravine, sounds like a long-continued moan.

The greater portion of the fruit brought by the traders into Upper India is from the Koh Daman. Here are grown grapes of a dozen different kinds, apricots of six sorts, mulberries of as many, besides endless varieties of apples, pears, peaches, walnuts, almonds, quinces, cherries, and plums. Though the vintage this year was late, the grapes were very plentiful. The only two descriptions that will bear exportation are the Huseini and Saibi, and these could be bought at the gardens for twopence a-pound, while others, too luscious for export, were selling at very little more than a halfpenny.

In the bottom of the valley nearly east of Istalaf is the plain of Begram, the locality where such numbers of old coins have lately been disinterred. It contains about twenty-four square miles, and, except some slight ridges, the rubbish apparently of dilapidated buildings, it is a perfectly dead level, on which rain stagnates as it falls. Though many thousands of coins have been collected, the hoard is by no means exhausted. During the few hours of our stay, some children sent out in search of them, returned with thirty-five copper pieces. When gleaning the surface is attended with such a result, what splendid success may be expected to crown the systematic and assiduous researches of Mr. Masson, the British Agent at Kabul!

Baber, when he conquered Afghanistan, located a number of his countrymen in Koh Daman, the descendants of whom are now among the most prosperous in the valley. When addressing each other, they still speak the Turkish language, though Persian is the medium of communication with their neighbours. On the road to Begram we passed several of their castles.

At the upper end of Koh Daman, on its eastern side, the face of the hills, at one particular spot, is covered with fine sand, called Reig-Rawan, or the moving sand. To this the natives of the valley ascribe the utterance of strange unearthly sounds, and by their marvellous relations induced us to visit the spot. The moving sand rests upon a base of 100 yards wide, and stretches up the face of the rock for 250 yards, with an acclivity of about 45°. At 3p.m. the temperature of the sand on the surface was 103°, while at the depth of ten inches it was only 75°. Looking down from the top of this sandy, inclined plane, it is seen to lie in a hollow of the rock fronting west-south-west. The formation of the adjoining rocks are limestone, and a loose, conglomerate sandstone. The first is both fractured and calcined, and the same appearance is observed at other places along the side of the valley; but is always local: that bordering the moving sand is strictly so. From Reig-Rawan there is no other sand deposit visible, though further south, and on the east side of the valley, there are one or two smaller stripes, but which are not asserted to be vocal. The west side of Koh Daman is composed of granite, and the prevailing wind is from the north, but no sand is likely to come from either of these directions. From the known propensity of the ignorant to exaggerate every thing connected with supposed supernatural agency, we did not come to the place very confident believers in the current tales of Reig-Rawan. However, we did as we were directed, and sent six men to the top of the sandy stripe, while we took up a position in the most favourable place to hear any noise that might be emitted. The party above came trampling down, and continued their march to the foot of the inclined plane; but without eliciting the slightest sound. This was repeated again and again, but only once with any success. The sound then heard was like that of a distant drum, mellowed by softer music. The secret of Reig-Rawan is, I should imagine, that of the whispering gallery. The slightest indentation in the sand is immediately filled up by the fall of the particles above. Moving waves are thus produced by the heavy tramp of a descending party; and the rustle of the dry sand is condensed and reverberated by the circular conformation of the rocks around. Not far from the moving sand is an artificial cave of small dimensions, within which reposes the body of a holy man who came thus far from Arabia in search of a resting-place. Fastening his steed to a tree hard by, he descended into the earth, from which, like the spectre of Loch Awe, he has never again appeared to mortal eye. In this valley there are many such places of pilgrimage, with similiar legends attached to them; and I may here mention Dost Mohamed Khan's opinion of them. When we returned to Kabul from this excursion, he inquired, amongst other things, what we thought of the ziarats in Koh Daman, and added, although the Mulvi was present, that for his part he was no believer in such absurd vanities; and that those who were, differed little from Kaffirs.

From Reig-Rawan we visited the month of the Panchshir valley. A short distance within its gorge, it contracts so as not to leave a foot-path between the stream and its steep, black sides. But before quitting the mountains, the water expands to a width of eighty-seven feet, with a depth of twelve. Here it is crossed by a wooden bridge, and from the centre of this rickety fabric the best view is obtained. Looking upwards, a snaky line of intermingled white and green water is seen leaping and twisting among the huge stones that pave its narrow bed. Presently it enters the basin over which the bridge stands, where the quiet, unruffled surface of the stream pleasingly contrasts with the turmoil above. The current here is hardly perceptible, and so beautifully transparent is the stream, that the stones at the bottom can be counted. The water glides slowly onward till it reaches the lower lip of the basin, when it pours down with a headlong fury, tumbling and foaming as violently as ever, until it is lost sight of in the extensive mulberry plantations of Gulbar, a straggling village on the banks of the Panchshir, just without the valley.

While employed mapping the Koh Daman, I was unexpectedly recalled by Captain Burnes to Kabul, for the purpose of accompanying Dr. Lord, whom he was about to send into Turkistan.

Chapter XII

Towards the end of October an officer on the part of Murad Ali Beg of Kunduz arrived in Kabul with presents for its ruler. A dozen good horses obtained him an honourable reception, and enlisted the warmest sympathy of Dost Mohamed Khan in the object of his mission. Mohamed Beg, the brother of the Uzbek chief, had long been a martyr to ophthalmia in its severest form. Shrines had been invoked, and charms essayed, but all in vain, and the faculty in Turkistan had pronounced the case to be hopeless, at the very time when the news of a British mission being at Kabul reached Kunduz. At this welcome intelligence, the flagging spirits of the patient revived, and Mirza Buddi, the physician and confidant of Murad Ali Beg, was deputed to bring, if it were possible, the Firingi hakim or English doctor over the Hindu Kosh.

Mohamed Beg is described as having been in his younger days a hard-hearted and deliberately cruel man, the ready tool of his tyrant brother. But age and infirmities had now softened his disposition; and whether the chief felt pleased or otherwise at the change, he showed himself grateful for former services by the interest which he took in his brother's recovery.

Captain Burnes was greatly pleased at this opportunity of securing for his government, on such easy terms, the friendship of Murad Ali Beg, with whom he was already personally acquainted, and determined at once to send the medical aid requested. Accordingly on my return from Koh Daman, I found the Uzbek, ambassador in high good-humour at the successful termination of his mission. Dr. Lord was at this time absent on a geological tour, and Captain Burnes only waited his arrival to despatch us both to the court of Kunduz. Mirza Buddi, under whose guidance we were to travel, was an honest, warm-hearted, old man, of about sixty. His bland and winning manner contrasted singularly with his large figure and harsh Tartar features. Dr. Lord and myself became greatly attached to him; nor was any visitor so welcome to our little bechoba as the mild, friendly, and simple-minded Uzbek, the leading feature of whose mind appeared to be an anxiety to do good to all around him.

It was necessary to decide by what pass we should cross the Hindu Kosh. There are four; and the caravans make their selection according to the season of the year and the more or less peaceable state of the country which borders them. The most direct lead through the plain of Koh Daman, where, diverging as they enter among the mountains at its head, they wind up the course of the streams described in the last chapter, and from which the several passes take their names of Ghorbund, Parwan, and Panchshir. The fourth road makes a considerable detour to the westward, and crosses the chain by the Pass of Hajikak. It remains open longer than any of the others; besides which advantage, the road by Bamian, although circuitous, rewards a stranger with a sight of its colossal idols, caves, and other records of the existence of a race of men unknown either to history or tradition. But this route had been travelled by several of our countrymen; and, therefore, although the season was late, we resolved to make trial of the Parwan Pass.

To protect our Indian servants from the sleety blasts of the snowy chain, each of them was provided with a posteen, or coat of sheep's skin, having the woolly side next the person; and on the 3rd of November, all the necessary arrangements being completed, Doctor Lord and I started for Turkistan, escorted by Mirza Buddi, and accompanied by an Elchi or ambassador from Dost Mohamed Khan to Murad Ali Beg of Kunduz.

Though only a fortnight had elapsed since I quitted Koh Daman, the frosty mornings had made sad havoc among the foliage of its groves. The wintry wind now rustled through the dry leaves, and everything looked bleak and desolate.

On the 5th we reached Charekar, the largest town in Koh Daman, and situated at the mouth of the Ghorbund valley. The Kafila Bashi, or leader of the caravan, forgetting that we had selected another route, brought us here by mistake. We were, however, told that a good cross-road connected the two valleys, and that by it we should reach the river of Parwan on the morrow.

While here the Afghan Elchi thought proper to separate his party from ours, and without imparting to us his intention, continued his route up the Ghorbund valley. The fact was that the Elchi had left Kabul without money, or at least pretended he had done so, and wished us to advance him a sum for his travelling expenses. This being peremptorily refused, the Elchi felt so annoyed that he revenged himself by deserting us.

Next morning we clambered up the shoulder of the mountain forming the eastern side of the Ghorbund valley, and kept across the hills for Parwan. The whole of this day and the next was spent in painful travel, toiling up steep acclivities and descending their opposite slopes. The hills took the conformation of horse-shoe crescents, detached from each other for some distance below their summits, but connected at the base. The good cross-road promised us by the Kafila Bashi was nowhere to be found; and we experienced the usual fate of those who follow short cuts, and were soon bewildered among the mazes of the mountains. The man who had got us into this dilemma was, however, to be pitied. Not a yabu or baggage pony cast its load or lost its footing, but its irritated driver consigned to all manner of punishments, not only the Kafila Bashi himself, but his whole race, especially his father; and all this in language by no means complimentary nor characteristic of Persian politeness.

Late in the evening we arrived, very weary and somewhat disheartened, at the bottom of a deep dell, along which was scattered a village named Sambala. Its male inhabitants, armed to the teeth, as is customary with these mountaineers, kept hovering about the encampment, wistfully eyeing the baggage, but restrained from any act of violence by the knowledge that we were guests of both Kabul and Kunduz. Nothing but this kept the savage crew from considering our property a lawful prize—a waif brought by dame Fortune to their very doors. We were early astir next morning, and anxious to quit what was rightly considered a dangerous neighbourhood. My companion would not leave the camp till he had seen everything off the ground, while I rode ahead to reconnoitre. None of the villagers were stirring; and our long Kafila moved slowly forward, winding along the sides of the mountain till we reached a shallow ravine, on the opposite bank of which stood a tower commanding the ascent on that side. On approaching the foot of the tower, we saw that it was full of armed men; and others quickly made their appearance from all quarters. We were soon surrounded. By this time many of the baggage ponies had descended into the ravine, and those which had not were in equal peril from robbers in the rear. Three men came out of the tower, with whom a parley was held; and we were given to understand that we must pay certain taxes before the Kafila would be permitted to pass. On our arrival at their village the preceding evening, the Kafila Bashi had given their chief what was customary; but he, seeing so much baggage so ill protected, deemed it expedient to revise his scale of charges, and now asked for more. Matters were on the point of being amicably adjusted, when fear seized upon the kirakush or mule-drivers, and in the tumult that ensued a hair-brained

Persian levelled his musket at a mountaineer. The party with whom we were conferring immediately fled into the tower, and in an instant matchlocks were seen in every direction pointing into the ravine. We were completely in their power. It was a trying moment; for had the Persian drawn his trigger, we should have been massacred. He had, however, but time to point his musket when it was wrenched from his hand by one of his companions, who was fortunately cooler-headed than himself; on perceiving which, an old woman stepped forward to the edge of the ravine and stayed the hand of her highly offended countrymen. A war of words now ensued among the incensed and disappointed band, in which the shrill piercing voice of the woman rose high above the rest. Her garments hung in tatters, and her manner and gesticulations were fierce and wild. One moment pointing with her half-bared arm towards our party in the ravine, the next fiercely turning upon the men, she appeared to be loading them with reproaches. One of the party, and one only, she deigned to intreat and caress, and we discovered that this favoured individual was her son. At length her eloquence was successful, and we were permitted to move on.

A few of these vagabonds continued to dodge the caravan throughout the day; they molested us, however, but little, their depredations being limited to snatching a turban from the head of an uususpecting mule-driver. Presuming that our road into Turkistan was to be by a usual Kafila route, we had not stinted ourselves in baggage and servants, and our party, though large and encumbered, was for the same reason comparatively unarmed; the weapons it could muster being only two crazy matchlocks, the imprudent Persian's musket, and our own pistols and fowling-pieces. We were, besides, entangled among the folds of the mountains and uncertain of the road. It was therefore with no small pleasure that we emerged, a short time after sunset, into the Parwan valley, at the village of I-angheran.

Next day we reached the head of the valley, and though the hour was yet early, pitched our tent at the foot of the pass, that we might have an entire day to cross its ridge. The place is called Sir-i-lung, an appellation which is also given to the inhabitants of the valley who dwell in a few straggling hamlets. The chief of the tribe soon presented himself, and we arranged with him to procure us guides for the morrow.

The ground where we had encamped was covered to the depth of a foot with snow, and our eyes suffered severely from the dazzling reflection of the sun's rays. The Indian servants, who had never seen snow before, surprised at the warmth thus produced, tauntingly observed that blankets and woolly coats were useless in such weather. The stories they had heard of the severe cold in England could not, they said, be true, for here there was snow all around, and yet the cold did not equal that of the winter months in Hindustan.

The morning of the 9th broke in clouds and gloom. More snow had fallen in the night, and this, combined with the lowering weather, made us hesitate to start. The guides, however, now presented themselves, with huge boots and straw trussings on their legs, a short skin jacket belted close to their body, and also the usual posteen, the latter being tied behind their saddles ready for use. They all rode mares of a small size, but remarkable for strength and endurance. Both men and horse looked as if, under any circumstances, they would doggedly do their duty. Dr. Lord was very desirous of proceeding, and felt annoyed at the delay which had already been caused by the mistake of Hyat, our Kafila Baslii. The appearance of these men decided us, and in a short time the Kafila was again on the road.

Dense white clouds, which looked like hills of snow, were rolling along the mountains' summit from the north-west, in which direction lay the pass. The breeze rose as the day advanced, and came sweeping along the hollow up which we marched, driving before it a sleety drift more like ice than snow. When about half way up the ascent, Dr. Lord, Mirza Buddi, and myself, sought the shelter of a friendly cliff, and there awaited the arrival of the Kafila, which had fallen some distance in the rear. Joined by Norrudji Ferdonji and Kassinath our Munshi, we again set forth; but it was only to struggle unsuccessfully against the storm. The wind had lulled, but the snow on the hill was too deep for our horses. The guides now took the lead by turns, and for a considerable distance their hardy little ponies made a track, in which our larger but less active horses managed to follow. At length even the ponies of the guides gave in, and the snow again falling heavily, their riders were at fault, and we lost the road. It was now judged prudent to retrace our steps whilst return was still possible; and this decision, under the blessing of a kind Providence, saved us from the fate of the poor recusant Elchi, who, with four of his attendants, perished in this day's snow-storm in the Pass of Ghorbund, several miles to the westward of Parwan.

This rough march had nearly proved fatal to our Indian followers. Their terrors and complainings now were a perfect contrast to their elated feelings of the day before. All of them had slunk to the rear except Norrudji and Kassinath, who were cheered on by Mirza Buddi and ourselves. They, too, at last gave in, and with tears in their eyes entreated us to return. All the poor fellows sat on their horses more like logs of wood than living men, and were dismounted by every stumble the animals made. Whenever the Indians found themselves sprawling in the snow they became perfectly helpless, and often did the kind-hearted Uzbek dismount and extricate them from their perplexity. Some of them, afraid of being left behind on our return, invoked the aid of the Sir-i-lungi to help them down the mountains, promising them money for so doing. That vagabond fraternity, seeing the children they had to do with, readily assented, but did not fail to make the most of so good an opportunity, and pilfered the poor fellows most unmercifully.

We now gave up all hopes of being able to enter Turkistan by any of the eastern passes at so advanced a season of the year, and next day saw us marching back on Kabul, where we arrived on the 13th, with the intention of taking the route by Bamian.

From the foot of the pass to the village of I-angheran the Parwan valley is a narrow, rocky defile, with either high bluffs for its sides, or mountains rising with steep acclivities; but after passing that village assumes a softer character, the mulberry-tree rising in terraces up its scantily earth-clad sides. The valley is here very tortuous, and at every turn a portion of the mountain projects into the stream. Upon these outlying shoulders there are always patches of level ground, upon which are erected the castellated buildings of the Sir-i-lungi.

A violent wind throughout the cold season blows in the lower half of the valley. The trees fronting the gorge in Koh Daman take the direction of this prevailing wind and slant to the south. Where the cultivated soil is so very limited, the question naturally arises, how so many inhabitants are fed. The mulberry-tree is what the date is among the Arabs, and a flour made from its unripe fruit is the principal support of these Kohistanees or hillmen throughout the year. Thus even the biting north wind is beneficial; for were the mulberry to ripen on the tree, it would not be so well adapted for a staple article of food.

Chapter XIII

Our experience of the eastern passes taught us the importance of not tarrying long in Kabul. We allowed ourselves, therefore, only one day for repose and for reducing our baggage to light marching order; and having got rid of the useless Hindustani servants, now as anxious to remain behind as they were formerly solicitous to go with us. At an early hour on the 15th of November, we set out by the Bamian route for Kunduz, and that night slept at Rustam Kyl, a village twenty-five miles west of Kabul, and the second stage on the Turkistan road. Proceeding onwards, we wound up the valley to Sir-chesme, one of the sources of the Kabul river. We had now entered the country of the Hazara, many of whom passed us on the road, wending their way to Kabul in search of employment.

On mustering our party at Rustam Kyl, it was found that sundry travellers had attached themselves to the Kafila for greater security on the road. Among these was an unfortunate Mussulman, whose story clearly proved, that despite all Mohamed's enactments in support of the husband's authority, the wife in Mohamedan countries sometimes rules the roost. This votary of Hymen had, if he spoke the truth, been in reality sacrificed at the altar, for ever since he entered the connubial state, his spouse had rendered his life miserable; and to make matters worse, his children as they grew up sided with their mother. On the day we left Kabul he had been soundly drubbed by the fair lady, and in a fit of despair joined our Kafila, resolved on a separation, and to place the twelve thousand feet barrier of the Hindu Kosh, between himself and his Xantippe. How frequently these matrimonial disagreements may occur in Kabul, I know not, but it is very seldom indeed that a Mohamedan parent has to complain of disobedient children. Among both Afghans and Uzbeks, such conduct is of very rare occurrence.

Quitting Sir-chesme, we crossed the Pass of Hunai and the Plain of Urt. This latter, though undulating and hilly, is an elevated table-land of about six miles broad, dividing the water of Kabul from those of Herat and Kandahar. Along the north face of this table-land runs the Helmand, which rises at a place called Fazindaz, in the neighbouring mountains of Pagman. Where we crossed the stream it was twelve yards wide and less than a foot in depth. The current was brisk, and in the morning the stream was laden with young ice. The Ab-i-Siah, or black water, is a feeder of the Helmand, and up its valley we journeyed to Gulgatui, a hamlet on the southern side of Hajikak. In the summer season the upper waters of the Helmand are a favourite resort with the pastoral tribes of eastern Afghanistan.

Every day we encountered parties of half famished Hazara, abandoning their inclement mountains for the less rigorous winter of the plains. Some of the groups presented sad objects of compassion; their torn garments ill protecting them from the cold. To see the aged of both sexes, ill clothed and scantily fed, toiling on through the snow, and exposed to all the asperities of the season, might almost induce one to tax Providence as partial in the distribution of its gifts. But to the honour of these poor people, though hard pressed by misfortune, and lacking even the common necessaries of life, they viewed their lot with another eye and in a better spirit. Though not cheerful, they were resigned, and if the destitute condition of his children did sometimes cloud a father's brow, could it be wondered at, for can any trial of a parent's fortitude be more severe than to hear his offspring call upon him in vain for bread? The early fall of snow this year, had, they told us, destroyed the crops, and as they had been unable to pay the usual tribute to the Amir of Kabul, Dost Mohamed, their sheep had been seized. Without the means of passing the long dreary winter now closing in upon them, they were compelled to emigrate to the plains where the wealthy would employ them in keeping the roofs of their houses free from snow, clearing the foot paths, bringing firewood, and in the other drudgery of the household. This is a misfortune that often overtakes the Hazara, and yet so improvident are they, that they never think of providing against it. The Hazara and Eimaks occupy the whole of the mountain belt, extending from Kabul to Herat. The former live on the eastern part of the, belt, but do not extend in that direction beyond the Ghorbund valley. They are quite a Tartar race, and even more marked with the disagreeable features of that nomade people, than the Uzbeks in the valley of the Oxus. They strongly resemble the Kirghiz of Pamir. Among individuals of the same nation, the mere differences of locality produce a strong effect on the physiognomy. A low-lying plain smooths and tames down the characteristic features, which, in mountainous regions, are seen in their full sharpness and strength. The following is a list of the Hazara tribes:—

Eastern Tribes		Western Tribes	
Names	*Number of Families*	*Names*	*Number of Families*
Da Murda	2,000	Da Murda	N/A
Durbi Ali	1,000	Dal Timur	N/A
Ism Tunur	1,000	Deh Kundi	N/A
Dia Zungi	5,500	Durghan	N/A
Dowlat Pai	2,000	Jakuri	N/A
Marak	1,000	Naur	N/A
Kuptseom	3,600	Badaws	N/A
Yarkhana	500	Syud Dan	N/A
Zhalek	200	Tazak	N/A
Tejuk	100	Sugh Pah	N/A
Die Murza	300		
Deh Zingi	5,000		
Sheikh Ali	3,000		
Tatar	1,000		
Jurghai Burjeghai	1,000		
Diah Pollah	2,000		

The first of these lists contains the eastern tribes, and the other those of the west. The number of families is roughly stated, but will in some degree show the comparative strength of the eastern tribes, and their relative importance among themselves. Estimating the ten western tribes, the strength of which I had not the means of ascertaining, at 10,000 families, we shall obtain for the aggregate of the Hazara nation, inhabiting the Paropamisian chain, a population of about 156,000 souls.

Of these tribes the most powerful are the Deh Kundi, Dia Zingi, Deh Zingi, and Sheikh Ali. Sometimes they are subject to Kunduz and at other times to Kabul. They now own allegiance to the former, and annually send Murad Ali Beg a tribute in slaves. In paying this inhuman tax, the custom is for a certain number of houses to join together, and when the value of a slave is collected, he is furnished by them. In years of great scarcity, such as that in which we visited this people, it is not unusual for a Hazara family voluntarily to dispose of one or more children. It is a sacrifice to which they are compelled by necessity. But generally they speak with detestation of the practice of man-stealing, and never mention the Uzbeks, who enslave them, but in terms of loathing and hatred.

Hucksters from Kabul visit the Hazara country, and are enabled advantageously to barter white and coloured coarse cotton cloths, Peshawur lungis, and the poor fabrics of Koh Daman, for carpets, felts, and ghi. A very durable, brown-coloured chogha or pelisse, much worn in Afghanistan, is also obtained of the Hazara. They have fine sheep of the Dhumba or large-tailed species, and a small but hardy breed of horse, well adapted to their mountains. The country abounds in lead and sulphur.

The Hazara females go unveiled. They are much softer featured than the men, and have a healthy florid complexion. Their figure is delicate, and would appear but ill fitted to brave so severe a climate. All out-door work is, however, performed by the men. The women are by no means shy of strangers; but, I believe, that what in a Mussulman country appears a want of modesty is only a freedom of manner resulting from the liberty in which both sexes are reared, and not any laxity of morals. The Afghans brand the race as immoral, and all agree that the tribe of Jakuri is notorious for a singularly depraved species of hospitality, which compels the host to transfer his wife to the embrace of his guest. The Hazara are Shiahs—heretics—in the eyes of Suni Mohamedans; and those orthodox detractors assert that such a creed is a cloak for every crime.

We passed the night at Gulgatui, under the roof of an Hazara family. The house was of stone, low, flat-roofed, and contained a considerable number of apartments, in one of which the females slept, and in another the men of the family and ourselves. The fire-place in the kitchen or sitting-room was merely a hole scooped in the earthen floor, while the smoke found a vent through two apertures in the roof. On the top of the house was piled, in bundles, the winter's store of fuel. On the whole, an

Hazara house, with a cheerful fire on its hearth, is a snug berth enough, could custom but reconcile one to its smoky atmosphere. The head of the family was a hale, hearty old man, who had been married thirty years, the last twenty of which he had lived in this house. The whole stock on his farm consisted of two cows, as many calves, and a few sheep. For the little spot of ground which he occupied, he paid to the ruler of Kabul a portion of the village tax of sixty rupees. He told us that in this bleak region the men, for seven months out of the twelve, have little other employment than to bring fuel from the hills. We retired early to rest; and when they imagined us to be sleeping, the whole family cautiously entered the room in which we were lying, and which adjoined the kitchen, lit the candle, and minutely examined such articles as had been left upon the table. A plated candlestick, in particular, astonished them; and after handling it over and over, a young woman, casting a furtive glance at Doctor Lord and myself, deposited the treasure in a corner of the room. Having finished their survey, a large basin of water was brought in, from the half-frozen stream before the door. This and a few mouthfuls of coarse barley bread formed the frugal supper of the family. The fire was now extinguished, and all retired to rest. Next morning, when we were prepared to start, the fair thief inquired if we missed nothing; and we, wishing to discover the motive that led her to secrete the candlestick, pretended a total ignorance of the scene we had witnessed the preceding night. The secreted treasure was now produced; but whether the laughing culprit had hidden it for better security, or merely to frighten us with the loss of so costly an article, we could not well determine. To these simple-minded people it must have appeared of immense value. At all events it was evident that no dishonest motive had prompted the conduct of the Hazara maiden: and we left the house well pleased with our reception.

On the morning of the 19th we commenced the ascent of Hajikak, which we accomplished with great ease, and encamped in the afternoon at the village of Kalu, in a narrow valley bearing the same name. Hajikak is geographically remarkable as dividing the waters of the Afghan country from those of Turkistan. South of this pass the streams join the river Helmand, and those on its northern side the Oxus. It has just been remarked that the chief employment of the Hazara through the long winter is to collect fuel. This fuel consists of a description of furze commonly called buta, and sometimes "Kollah Hazaras," or the Hazara's cap. It grows luxuriantly on the highest mountain, and there is considerable risk in getting it into the valleys. Towards evening the gatherer collects the produce of his day's work on a convenient point of the range overlooking his home. The large bundle is then launched, when it slides down the mountain's side in a zigzag line between the jutting crags, and sending up a volume of dust like that caused by the brisk passage of a troop of cavalry along a dusty road. The sides of the mountain are in this neighbourhood furrowed by the tracks of the buta collectors.

We had followed the direct Kafila route thus far, but it now became necessary to make a small circuit to avoid the Pass of Kalu, which was covered with snow to a depth that prevented our attempting its ascent. Continuing, therefore, our route along a valley, having the range of Hajikak to our right and that of Kalu to our left, we made a considerable détour and doubled the latter range; thence we were conducted to Bamian by the precipitous defile of Pimuri and the volcanic valley of Zohawk.

The Pimuri defile is of a pecularly wild character. The mountains that wall this narrow ravine have evidently been rent asunder by some tremendous subterranean convulsion. Their bases nearly join, and their sides rise almost perpendicularly. Beetling crags threaten the traveller from above, whilst immediately below his insecure pathway, a brawling stream cascades through the length of the chasm. At one place the stream is bridged over for a distance of 200 paces by a portion of the mountain that has fallen across the ravine.

The ruins of Zohawk occupy the corner of a volcanic wall, which separates a valley so named from that of Bamian. They are scattered over a considerable extent of surface, but there is nothing grand or imposing in their appearance. The light style of the architecture would lead one to fix the era of Zohawk's erection in an age less remote than is generally assigned to it by popular tradition. Geographically the site of these ruins is remarkable, as being the junction of the two streams which form the south-west fork of the Kunduz river. On quitting Bamian we crossed the Pass of Akrobat, and arrived at a small valley on its north side. Our reception at this place, where we first entered the dominions of Murad Ali Beg, was not very cordial; for the governor of this elevated and ungenial district, on hearing of our approach, quitted his fort and left Mirza Buddi to look elsewhere for supplies. Before reaching this valley we saw on the way-side a very remarkable stone, known by the name of Juring-juringi. It is a cube of eight feet and of a green colour. When struck by any hard substance it rings like bell metal. To Akrobat succeeded the valley of Sykan, inhabited by Tajiks, being the first of that race we had seen north of Hindu Kosh. The Hazara are now no longer met with in distinct societies, but are incorporated with the Tajiks, whose protection they purchase by an outward compliance with the orthodox religion. Sykan stands in a fruitful vale; its mountains also yield large quantities of assafœtida, and the districts where it grows are as regularly apportioned out to individuals as the corn-fields in the plain, and the property in it as carefully guarded. The produce of this plant is usually bought up by the chiefs, and sold at a monopolising price to Kafilas in their transit through the country.

At Sykan we met a man of the Deh Kundi tribe, bringing part of the yearly slave tribute to Kunduz. The able-bodied slaves were chained together; the aged, who were too infirm to walk, rode on donkeys, and behind them were bound children, whose extreme youth rendered them happily unconscious of the home they had left and the liberty they had lost. They all of them were squalid and dirty, and the ragged pieces of clothing that hung from their shoulders were but a poor substitute for covering. One haggard old woman, on whose lineaments Time had traced many a wrinkle, presented an appearance scarcely human; she was a humiliating sight.

From Sykan we descended by the Pass of "Dundan Shikun," or the "Tooth-breaker," into the valley of Kamrud, and remained during the night with a Tajik chief named Rahmutulah Khan, the same drunken old man who so piteously bewailed his empty flagon to Captain Burnes's party in 1832. Kamrud supplies a large body of water to the Kunduz river. Under its fort this stream had a width of twenty-four feet, a mean depth of two, and an average current of four miles and a half an hour. Its source is at the head of the valley, where it issues from an aperture in the rock. Here is the Ziarat of Khaji Abdullah, much resorted to in the hot months, but now rendered inaccessible by ice and snow. Summer and winter, the volume of water of this mineral spring is unaltered in bulk. It now had a temperature of 48°, that of the air being 34°. The fort of Kamrud is 5,600 feet above the sea.

In very mountainous regions, the occasional violence of the streams is adverse to the employment of water as a moving power; still, throughout the Paropamasian chain, both east and west of the Indus, corn mills driven by water are very frequently met with. The mountaineer, taking advantage of his situation, erects that simplest of machines, the water wheel, and is enabled to grind his corn with ease and at little cost, an operation which, when performed by manual labour, is the severest tax on the cultivator of the ground. In many localities this water power could be vastly increased, and streams, portions of which are now only employed to turn a few corn-mills, might be made subservient to the production of those articles of clothing, which, at present, after they have half circumnavigated the globe, are purchased by the inhabitants of the very regions where the raw material is produced. For such a purpose, few places are more favourable than the valley of Kamrud; but radical must be the changes wrought in the habits of these people before the man-seller will betake himself to so honest an employment, and the blood feuds of centuries be quenched. Still such blessings may one day attend the march of civilization; some powerful chief, fixing himself on one or the other side of the snowy chain, may have strength to control these turbulent sons of the mountain, and give a direction to their energies more favourable to civilization. Glens that now only echo the matchlock's report, may then as closely resemble Switzerland in the moral character of their peasantry, as they do in their scenery and local advantages. As we continued our journey by the road familiar to all travellers into Turkistan, I need not particularize its stages; they have already been frequently described. On the 28th we reached Khurm, the estate of Mirza Buddi. His son and some of his tenantry came a few miles to meet him, and welcome him back; and no one who witnessed his warm reception could have suspected that under this show of affection ranked the deepest animosity; yet such was the case, for shortly after we quitted the country, poor Mirza Buddi was barbarously murdered in his own house.

In the Khurm valley we overtook another slave party from the Hazara country. The owners, to the astonishment of our party, were men of Kabul. They appeared greatly mortified at being seen by us, hung down their heads, and wished, but in vain, to escape notice. The Khirakushes recognised them as inhabitants of Chardeh, a plain in the vicinity of Kabul, and at once charged them with carrying on a traffic, as degrading to an Afghan as it is accounted honourable in an Uzbek. They were asked how they could face their clansmen after such disreputable conduct. In extenuation of their conduct, they stated, that after trading to a considerable extent with the Hazara, and waiting twelve months for a settlement of their claims, they had been unable to obtain payment. The correctness of the demand was readily acknowledged, and slaves, valued at its full amount, offered in lieu of all claims. At first they refused this mode of payment, but were at length induced to comply. Unable after such a description of compromise to return direct to their own country, they were now proceeding to the Uzbek mart of the Khurm, or Tash Kurghan, there to realize by sale the proceeds of this discreditable barter.

Nothing surprises one so much, nor is more difficult to be accounted for on rational principles, than the marked shades of difference which often, as in this case, are exhibited in the moral character of neighbouring nations. Here we have two races of men, professing the same belief, whose habits in many respects are alike, and whose location and pastoral pursuits offer many points in common, yet differing in almost every feeling that marks the man, and which in their combined influence constitute the peculiar genius of a people. Of the freedom enjoyed by the Afghans, the Uzbeks know nothing. The liberty of the slave they capture is not more at their disposal than their own life is in the hands of their chief or Beg. To love of country, a feeling dominant in the breast of an Afghan, and which glows with more or less intensity in the soul of every other people from the Zahara to the Esquimaux, the Uzbek is almost a stranger. The custom of man-stealing appears to have smothered every better feeling, and the practice of trafficking in human beings extends even into their domestic arrangements; for their wives are as much articles of property as their slaves, and are bought and sold with the same callous indifference. Again, among the Uzbeks though the tribes are numerous and distinct, we do not detect that attachment between individuals of the same clan, or that devotion to its common head which has ever been the bond of union in all countries where this primitive arrangement of society prevails. When the Kattaghan, indeed, mentions his tribe, it is with a conscious feeling of superiority, but Murad Beg, the ruler of Kunduz, is a Kattaghan, and the pride of the Kattaghan is founded on their belonging to the tribe of their chieftain, and not on their own ancestral lineage. I never knew an Uzbek of any of the other tribes boast of his descent. The truth is, that among this people, as with other semi-barbarous nations, the most honoured tribe is always the one headed by the strongest chieftain; for he who can make himself dreaded, is sure to be respected.

A little below the village of Khurm, we struck off to the right for Kunduz, and despatched Kassinath to Khurm, together with those supernumeries of the party who had attached themselves to our Kafila for protection on the road. Most of these were pilgrims on their way to the shrine of Hazrat Ali of Mazar. The sanctuary stands about twelve miles from the old city of Balkh, and twice that distance west of the modern town of Tash Kurghan. It is famous on both sides of the snowy chain, for its sanctity, and for the miracles performed by its patron Hazrat Shah. Once in the year a fair is held, during which the blind, infirm, halt, and maimed of many a distant region crowd to Mazar, and encamping round its shrine, watch day and night for the saint's interposition in their behalf. Of this numerous band, some few are restored to health probably by the change of air and scene; a considerable number die on the spot, and the larger proportion return as they came, bewailing their want of faith, and their sins, but never questioning the potency of Hazrat Shah. From Tash Kurghan to Mazar the road is much infested by highwaymen, but while this holy fair lasts, robbery is unknown, although at other seasons it is unsafe to pass between these places without an escort.

The plain between the streams that water Kunduz and Khurm, has a wavy surface, and, though unsuited to agriculture, affords excellent pasturage. The only village

[153]

on the road is that of Hazrat Baba Kamur, where we halted for a night. On the eastern side the plain is supported by a ridge of hills sloping down from the mountains to the south. We crossed it by the Pass of Archa (so called from the fir trees that cover its crest), from the top of which we had a noble view of the snowy mountains to the east, the outlyers of Hindu Kosh. Next day we forded the river of Kunduz, and continuing to journey along its right bank, through the swampy district of Baghlan and Aliabad, reached the capital of Murad Beg on Monday the 4th of December.

Chapter XIV

The day following that of our arrival at Kunduz, we were invited by Mirza Buddi to accompany him to Durbar. Our reception was most gracious. After exchanging the usual compliments of an eastern court, Murad Beg expressed himself highly gratified with our visit to Kunduz; and turning to his Mirza or secretary, directed him to read Captain Burnes's letter aloud. When the Mirza had concluded, Murad Beg exclaimed, "Khoob Khoob," good good. A piece of Russian loaf sugar was then placed before us, and the few presents we had brought were produced. A spying glass and some bottles of essential oils, with other restoratives, particularly pleased him. Each bottle was separately examined, and he requested Dr. Lord to communicate through the native medical assistant, a knowledge of their contents to his secretary. This was done; and in the chief's presence the bottles were labelled. The apartment in which we were received measured about thirty feet by fifteen, with a portion of its floor elevated more than a foot, and well carpeted. The Begs were seated in rows on one side of the room, and below them on the less elevated part of the floor stood grouped the Mir's personal attendants and household slaves. Opposite the Begs, his legs carelessly stretched on a coloured felt, and leaning back on a large silken pillow, was Murad Ali Beg. The head of the room was reserved for us. The number of Begs present was large, and all of them old men. This is not to be reconciled with the known insalubrity of Kunduz. We may presume, however, that having such mature advisers prudence guides the councils of the chief. But if, as an Algerine once hinted to a British Admiral, the wisdom of a people is to be estimated by the length of their beards, but little of Solomon's mental superiority is inherited by the Uzbeks.

Kunduz, though the capital of Murad Beg, is one of the most wretched in his dominions. Five or six hundred mud hovels contain its fixed population, while dotted amongst these, and scattered at random over the suburbs, are straw-built sheds intermixed with the Uzbek tent or Kirgah. Gardens and corn fields alternate in its suburbs and extend even into the town. Nothing, in short, can be imagined less resembling a metropolis. Overlooking the east end of the town is the fortress. This is merely a mound, of an oblong figure and considerable extent, strengthened by a mud wall, and a dry ditch. The wall is in a dilapidated state on all sides but the south, on which is the principal entrance by the bazar gate. On the north-east end of the fortress is the citadel, the winter residence of Murad Beg. It is an irregular structure of kiln-dried brick, surrounded by a moat. It has many loop-holes for matchlocks; there are also guns within it, but none are mounted on the walls. The dry ditch which surrounds it, though now laid out in gardens, can be filled should occasion require it. Inside the fortress the inhabitants are either Uzbeks, or Hindus connected with Atmah the Dewan Begi, or steward of the chief. The appearance of Kunduz accords with the habits of an Uzbek; and by its meanness, poverty, and filth, may be estimated the moral worth of its inhabitants.

Murad Beg, the head of this Uzbek state, is one of those prominent political characters that unsettled times, and a disorganized state of society produce. Such were Mohamed Ali in Egypt and the late Runjit Sing in Hindustan. Men whose fortunes were based on mental superiority; and though Murad Beg cannot be ranked with either of these remarkable men, the Uzbek will not suffer by comparison with them, when we take into account the rudeness of the material on which he had to work. Little craft enters into the character of his chieftain, but to his splendid talents he unites what does not always accompany them, strong common sense. His forces, composed entirely of cavalry, are well adapted to predatory warfare, for which neither infantry nor guns are essential. The horses though small, have great power, and will endure much fatigue for ten successive days; carrying grain for themselves and their rider. The habits of his subjects are equally well fitted to this mode of life; and the absolute authority which he has over them, places their services at all times at his disposal. There is not a man in his dominions, let him possess what authority he may, but must yield it up at the nod of the Mir. His own tribe are devotedly attached to him, and seldom mention his name without exclaiming, "May God add to his riches." He is not equally popular with the Tajik mountain states, which he has subdued; but among these all spirit of resistance is so completely crushed, that while Murad Beg lives, there is no chance of their attaining freedom unless aided by a foreign power. Still these people, though indignant at the Mir's arbitrary rule, do not deny his great abilities, and especially his talent of quickly penetrating into the counsels of other men.

But with all his high qualifications Murad Beg is but at the head of an organised banditti, a nation of plunderers, whom, however, none of the neighbouring powers can exterminate.

Able as he is to bring together, in a surprisingly short space of time, a body of 15,000 horsemen, inured to predatory warfare, and to those stealthy attacks for which Turkiman and Uzbek are equally celebrated, he feels himself perfectly secure from the assault of any of the chieftains by whom he is surrounded, nor, indeed, were they to league together could they successfully oppose him. The only people who, though occasionally chastised, have hitherto escaped subjection are the tribes on the north bank of the river Oxus. Murad Beg, aware that his description of force was ill-calculated to retain conquest when made, razed every hill fort as they fell into his hands, but reserved the Uzbek strongholds in the plain. These, Tash Kurghan excepted, are held by members of his family, or by men whose interest is identified with his own. The conquered experienced more favourable treatment than was to have been expected at the hands of the Uzbeks, in whose character clemency is no ingredient. If the chief himself be not wantonly cruel, his conduct is often needlessly severe; but of this more hereafter. Not the least remarkable trait in the character of this man is the contrast afforded by his well ordered domestic government, and the uninterrupted course of rapine which forms the occupation of himself and his subjects, whose "chuppaws," or plundering expeditions embrace the whole of the upper waters of the Oxus, from the frontier of China on the east, to the river that runs through Balkh, "the mother of cities," on the west. His government is rigidly despotic, but seldom is absolute power less misused. The rights and property of his subjects are respected, merchants are safe, and trade is encouraged. Punishment for crime, whether against individuals or the state, is most summary; for theft and highway robbery, if the highway be in their own country, for that makes a wonderful difference, the only award is death. An offender, when detected, never escapes punishment, and sentence is no sooner pronounced than executed. This prompt procedure is little in accordance with the beautiful maxim of English Jurisprudence, that it is better many who are guilty should escape than that one innocent man should suffer; yet the certainty of punishment has lessened the commission of crime. Countries in former times closed to the traveller, may now, with Murad Beg's protection, be as safely traversed as British India.

The Uzbeks are a tribe of Tartar, or rather Scythian origin, which, in a comparatively modern era, crossed the Jaxartes and fixed themselves in Transoxiana. The descendants of the ruthless Jangez Khan then occupied that country, but were soon forcibly dispossessed. Their chief, the renowned Baber, after vainly endeavouring to stem the torrent of invasion, yielded to its strength, and led his forces into Hindustan, where he established the Mogul empire called after Mogul Khan, the founder of his line. Those of the disinherited nation who neither submitted to the Uzbek or accompanied their chief, retired across the river Oxus; and in the Turkimans of that locality I think we may recognise their descendants. In the early part of the sixth century, the Turks of the Altaian chain first emerged into notice. In a few years after their first appearance, among their other conquests, was that of Nephthalites, or white Huns of Soghdiana—that is, Samarkand and Bokhara, the countries from which the Uzbeks expelled the Turkimans. The beauty of the latter race has long been celebrated by Persian poets; and as the name of Turkiman is otherwise obscure, we may perhaps be justified in supposing them the mixed progeny of Huns and Turks. The Turkimans boast of having founded the Ottoman empire, and, moreover, point to the mountains of Imaus as the original seat of their ancestors; and tradition goes far to establish the consanguinity of the Osmanlee and the Turk of the Oxus. Though the languages of the various hordes that now roam over Central Asia are different, there is reason to believe that the Huns of antiquity are the prototypes of them all, whether designated Kalmucks or Kirghiz, Uzbek or Turkiman. Most of their names have had a personal origin, such as Tartar, Noghai, Uzbek, and Moghul. The first, corrupted to Tartary, has now become a generic term for the Scythia of the Roman historians, though I do not remember to have heard it used by the Uzbeks of Khunduz. From this custom much ambiguity has resulted. It is, however, foreign to my purpose to descant more at large on the wandering hordes that now occupy these wilds; yet so interesting is all connected with these

[159]

shepherd tribes, which more than once have overrun Europe and Asia, that I could not omit giving the subject a passing notice.

The Uzbeks of Khunduz have genuine Tartar features, though the physiognomy of their chiefs is becoming softened by intermarriage with the Tajik, a Caucasian race whom I believe to be the indigenous inhabitants of Persia, and perhaps of Transoxiana also, and who are now found widely scattered on both sides of the Paropamasian chain. A Tajik is not permitted to marry the daughter of an Uzbek; but this unjust distinction is the only social difference that now exists between them. The Uzbeks are Suni Mohamedans, and consider an intolerant persecution of the other sect as the best evidence of the sincerity of their own faith and of their attachment to the Prophet. They are much fettered by their priests, or Ishan Kajahs, to whom they yield implicit obedience in all things, temporal and spiritual. Whatever may be thought of the effect produced by this influential class on Mohamedan society generally, I do not hesitate to say, that among the Uzbeks it is the reverse of good. These mullahs, or priests, are the most notorious slave dealers in the land, and encourage the odious traffic among their disciples, by readily purchasing of them whatever victims of the Shiah creed they may entrap. The good of the soul is assigned as ample extenuation, and religion here, as but too often has been the case elsewhere, becomes a cloak to crime instead of a guide to virtue.

It is rare to find an Uzbek of Kunduz who can read and write; so that the Tajiks, who are less illiterate, and the Hindus also, frequently rise to consequence among them.

They are as firm believers in predestination as the Turks. I remember that, having on one occasion deplored the untimely end of a chief whom Murad Beg had put to death, an Uzbek in company called out "his time had come—spare your pity;" for "Be nusseeb"— nothing happens that is not ordained. The Uzbek never utters a sentence which has the slightest reference to the future, however certain the events spoken of may be, without the prefatory words "Nusseeb bashud," or, if we have luck; and were the subject of his discourse the probability of the sun's rising the next morning, it is ten to one that he would introduce this saving clause. With the Afghan it is the same; and were we to judge of their piety by their frequent repetition of the supplicatory words "Inshallah," or please God, it would be difficult to rate it too high.

All ranks in Kunduz eat twice a day—at "Chasht," or about nine o'clock in the forenoon, and at "Nimaz Akhur," or twilight; pillaw and soup, with good leavened wheaten bread, constitute the repast; mutton is the flesh in general use. That of the horse, though eaten, is not often exposed in their markets; it is too expensive for the generality of the people. On the banks of the Oxus the pheasant is very plentiful, and is a delicacy greatly esteemed by the inhabitants. A meal is never concluded without tea; it is also drunk at all hours of the day; but this beverage, says the Uzbek, "goes for nothing." Yet tea in this country is not the meagre unsubstantial fare it is with us; it is termed "Keimuk chah" or cream tea; and the cream is so rich and clotty as to give one the idea of its having been mixed with oil. Fat is sometimes added, and salt is the uniform substitute for sugar. The tea is made in a large iron pot, from which it is baled out with a wooden ladle, and handed round to the company by the host in small china bowls. After a few trials Keimuk chah has rather an agreeable flavour.

When an Uzbek on horseback meets a chief or other superior, he forthwith dismounts and makes his salam. One foot, however, remains in the stirrup, and so rapid are his movements, that he has regained the saddle and set off at a canter almost before you are conscious of his having touched the ground.

The Kunduz breed of horse is very inferior to that of the Turkiman, or even to that which their countrymen rear about Shehr Sabz and the environs of Bokhara. The animal to suit Murad Beg and his subjects, must be small and hardy, adapted to the hilly country as well as to the plain. Speed is a secondary consideration; endurance everything. Their fore and hind quarters are remarkably large. One year from the day on which a colt is foaled, it is mounted and ridden by a light weight for a considerable distance at full speed, after which for two years it is not again saddled, and at three years old it is regularly broken in. Shoes are used only upon the fore feet, and in shape are a perfect circle. Like the rest of their race, the Uzbeks are extremely fond of horses and racing. Many idioms in their colloquial language have reference to them. For instance, if you inquire how far any particular place is distant, you are answered "ek doweedah" (a gallop); or if you ask what time any operation will require, the answer is still the same— "while you may gallop so many miles."

The dog in Turkistan, although not elevated to so important a rank as the horse, is still as useful and as highly esteemed as in more civilised communities; and here we have an example of those caprices and contrarieties which everywhere distinguish man. To ask an Uzbek to sell his wife would be no affront, but to ask him to sell his dog would be an unpardonable insult, "Suggee ferosh," or dog-seller, being about the most offensive epithet that one Uzbek can apply to another. In speaking of the Uzbek ladies, I must not omit recording that they are admirable housewives; so that though they lack beauty they have a more enduring claim on the affection of their lords. Like others of their sex, they strive to dress well, and as is too frequently the case with our own fairer country women, they disfigure their natural beauty by vain attempts to improve it. The sleeves of an English gown look as if they were intended to conceal a couple of small barrels instead of two slight and delicately proportioned arms; and in Turkistan the fashion leads to equal absurdities. Like the mantilla of Spain, the gown of the Uzbek lady envelopes the head, as with a hood, and from about the ears are suspended the sleeves, long narrow slips of cloth that sweep the ground, and which, dangling to and fro as the portly beauty rolls along, bring to mind the stories told by Ptolemy and the elder historians, of a long-eared race of men. The gallants of Kunduz love to show themselves off clad in scarlet or some equally bright and glaring colour, while the ladies, on the contrary, wear dark clothes, or dress in pure white, with only a showy silk handkerchief bound round the head or held in the hand.

Those who like myself have resided in a country village, and trod the green sodded churchyard every Sunday, cannot but feel displeased at the little attention which the Uzbeks pay to their cemeteries. While all around is grassy, the burial-ground remains naked and unattended to. Situated without the suburbs, the heaps of red and brown earth, like mounds carelessly raked together, are painful to the eye, as indicating a spirit callous to the obligations of friendship, parental affection, or conjugal love. Still more revolting is it, when obliged to thread our way amongst these cities of the dead, to observe on many of the graves signs that the jackal has been burrowing there. South of Hindu Kosh more attention is bestowed upon the burial grounds. Slabs with appropriate inscriptions are common among the wealthy; and the great, both in India and Afghanistan, have mausoleums erected to their honour with the splendour of which nothing in Europe can vie.

The very first visit to the patient, Mohamed Beg, enabled Dr. Lord to decide on his unfortunate case. The sight of one eye had gone for ever, and the visual ray of the other was fast waning. So elated, however, were the hopes which the poor man had conceived of the Firingi's superior knowledge, that the task which now devolved on Dr. Lord of undeceiving him, as to his power to work miracles and restore the blind to sight, was one of great delicacy and of some hazard. Mohamed Beg was told that all which the utmost skill could achieve would be exerted to preserve the remaining eye, but that cures were in the hand of God, and he must trust to

Providence for a favourable result. Predestination here favoured the doctor's moral lessons, of which he was not sparing, and Mohamed Beg from this date was more of a Mullah than an Uzbek chief. We had now been a week in Kunduz, and as there was every probability of our being compelled to remain the winter, the question arose how we could most profitably employ this sojourn in Turkistan. The great object of my thought by day and dreams by night had for some time past been the discovery of the source of the river Oxus, and, thanks to my fellow traveller's tact and Mirzá Buddi's good-will, Murad Beg on the 10th of December conceded his permission to me to trace the Jihun, an appellation by which this river is better known among the Uzbeks.

Chapter XV

Monday the 11th of December was fortunately a market day in Kunduz; so that the articles required for our expedition were at once obtained; and least Murad Beg might recall the permission he had given, we started that same evening for Badakhshan and the Oxus. We adopted the costume of the country, as a measure calculated to smooth our intercourse with a strange people, and we had little baggage to excite cupidity or suspicion. Coarse clothes to barter for food with the inhabitants of the mountains, was our stock in trade; and my chronometers and other instruments the only articles of value which I took with me. Dr. Lord accompanied us for the first few miles, and parted from us with cordial wishes for the success of our expedition.

The most important of my fellow travellers was Gholam Hussein, Munshi, cook, and "servant of all work," in whom were more sterling good qualities than I at one time believed it possible to find in the breast of a Hindustani. More intimate acquaintance with Eastern countries has considerably modified my unfavourable opinion of their inhabitants, and taught me to dissent from those wholesale terms of abuse which Europeans too often lavish on the native population. It will generally be found that our opinions of a people rise as our acquaintance with them increases. Vice in every community is sufficiently prominent to be seen without being sought after; but the wise and good shun notoriety, and it is only when we probe society deep that they are discovered. Gholam Hussein was a native of Jaysulmir, but had been from a lad in the army of Sind, where, after a faithful servitude of sixteen years, he had attained the rank of Jemidar, and a salary of twenty rupees a month. While the Seiks continued to threaten Sind, this pittance was regularly disbursed; but no sooner did the Indian Government come forward and avert the impending invasion, than the Amirs, relieved from their personal fears, displayed their accustomed avarice; and orders went forth to reduce the pay of all "Pardesi," or foreign troops. At this juncture the mission entered the Indus; when Gholam Hussein, with whom I had become acquainted during my previous sojourn in Sind, left the service of the Amirs and entered mine. Of a swarthy complexion, and diminutive height, his frame was thick set, strong, and active. On horseback the rotundity of his figure and his consequential air obtained for him, from my witty and mirthful companion Dr. Lord, the soubriquet of Joss. Luckily the meaning of the word is, to this day, unknown to the Munshi. A disclosure must have been attended with unpleasant consequences, since few followers of the Prophet could be more strictly orthodox than this honest little fellow; and the slightest hint of a resemblance between himself and a Chinese idol, would have been a deadly affront. Gholam Hussein's failing was a naturally irascible temper, but this fault he admirably, subdued, and never suffered it to appear save where the ebullition was productive of good to his master. He possessed a fund of anecdote, and was, besides, tolerably skilled in Eastern lore.

Another of our small party was Abdul Ghuni Yesawal, a Tajik by descent, but at heart a genuine Uzbek. He had been educated for a Mullah, but had long ago renounced the cloister for the field, and was now, as the affix "Yesawal" implies, an officer of Murad Beg's household. He was a jocund, good-hearted soul, though, perhaps, a little too susceptible of the tender passion. After a day's march, when a glowing fire, and the enlivening cup of tea had mellowed his rugged nature, I have listened to him expatiating on what he termed the three best friends of man, and what, next to life, should be most cared for. These were the Koran, a horse, and a sword. The first he would uncase from its numerous clumsy leather coverings, kiss the volume, and holding it out to the Munshi, swear by Khoda there was no book like it. A good horse, he would sagely remark, was a great blessing, it was invaluable; for what did it not do?—it procured a man his livelihood, and obtained for him his wives. That, in fact, without the horse, it would be impossible to steal, and then the Kattaghan's occupation and glory would be no more. His sword was a very poor one, but that mattered nothing. His imagination could revel in the superb weapons possessed by the Mir; while to prove the keen edge of his own, he would step beyond the threshold and with superabundant flourishes, hack away at the willows, the almond bushes, or whatever trees stood near. Had his affections been always as platonic as in these three instances, he would have saved himself a world of disquiet, as the sequel will show. There was a gravity in the man's appearance which contrasted strongly with his absurdities of conduct, and added point to the good-humoured jests in which he freely indulged. This man's home was at Talikhan, and he was deputed by the Kunduz chief to accompany us thither, and through the remainder of our journey. Ibrahim a Sindi, and Mohamed Cassim from Hindustan, carried the chronometers. Three Kabul men had the charge of the yabus, and two other Afghans that of the horses.

Before proceeding further, I must call the reader's attention to the travels of Marco Polo, the distinguished Venetian, who, towards the close of the thirteenth century, startled and delighted Europe with a description of civilized communities, then perfectly unknown. For a very long series of years this interesting work did not meet with the attention it deserved. The learned suspected it to be a fictitious narrative, or at best a mere compilation from hearsay authorities. Some, however, there were, and these men of profound and original minds, who amid the ignorance and bigotry which characterized the middle ages, perceived the real importance of the work. Among such stood pre-eminent, Christopher Columbus. Though the writings of the Venetian tended to mislead that great man on many points, there is little doubt but that they were principally instrumental in stimulating him to attempt reaching India by sailing in a direction due west. Columbus failed in this object, but added a New World to the geography of our globe. In latter times the genuineness of the Travels has never been seriously impugned, though the exaggerated statements of their credulous author continue fit subjects for pleasantry. The perusal of Marsden's "English translation of Marco Polo," a work illustrated by copious and most erudite notes, first impressed me with a conviction of the authenticity of the narrative; and this has been strengthened by my subsequent travels through countries described by the Venetian. In this neighbourhood we first come upon his track; but I shall reserve my observations on the old traveller and his work for another occasion, since they would lead me into dissertations ill suited to this narrative.

The day was far advanced when we left Kunduz. The afternoon had been cloudy; but as the sun went down, the moon, near her full, served to show the path. As night advanced the sky cleared, and we could then trace the shadowy outline of the mountains that look upon Kunduz; and we congratulated ourselves that on the morrow we should be above the gloomy atmosphere of the fens, and enjoy, what, at this season, is a rare occurrence in these plains—a pure sunshiny day.

The open plain we were now crossing is encircled on all sides by mountains, except on the north, where the river Oxus flows; and is intersected by the rivers of Kunduz and Khana-a-bad, both tributaries of the Oxus. The country strongly resembles the delta of the Indus, but is more moist and unfavourable to human life. The jungle grass is here taller and more dense. We saw but one village, though the number of rice mills at work and the continued barking of dogs proved that the region must be populous.

As we neared the river of Khana-a-bad the ground gradually rose and became drier; but before reaching the stream we had to cross four canals and as many rivulets, and from the velocity with which the water flowed in these, I infer that the upper portions of this plain might be easily drained.

During the whole of this march a veil of mist kept flitting before us. It vanished as we approached; but no sooner did one gauze-like screen disappear, than in succession another and another was discovered. The vapour cloud was seen against the clear azure sky, struggling to gain the higher regions. But not a breath of wind shook the long grass jungle, and the marsh miasma, if such it were, rose but to a certain height and there became stationary, floating above the spot where it had risen. At nine in the evening we forded the river, and immediately afterwards arrived in Khana-a-bad, the summer residence of Murad Beg. The stream abreast of the town runs in two channels. That on the west bank, though only three feet deep, was so rapid as nearly to unhorse me. With some difficulty, however, I escaped; but the Munshi was less fortunate, and got a complete ducking. Its width did not exceed fifteen yards, but its velocity was fully five miles an hour. The other branch had a width of sixty yards, and ran immediately under the walls of Khana-a-bad. It now discharged but little water, for though the principal course of the river, the stream had lately been led into another channel, while the bridge across it was under repair.

It was late when we entered the village, and to the hospitality of some of the students in its Madrasa, or colleges, we were indebted for shelter and for firing. Our horses were soon stabled in a corner of the court-yard, and, having seen that their provender bags were not empty, we entered as snug a berth as the most fastidious traveller could desire. A march of seventeen miles through a thick grass jungle often knee deep in water, performed in a keen winter's evening, had prepared us to welcome rest and shelter wherever found; and as we stretched ourselves upon the comfortable warm felts, and sipped our tea, I felt a glow at my heart which cannot be described. A calmness of spirit, a willingness to be satisfied and pleased with everything around me, and a desire that others should be as happy as myself. How often must every worn-out traveller have experienced this; and why is it that we should no sooner be restored to our wonted vigour than this placid temper leaves us, and we suffer ourselves to be ruffled and disturbed by every trivial occurrence?

Our kind entertainers were from Badakhsban, and the present state of that country became the subject of conversation. As the young men recounted what it had suffered under the iron rule of Murad Beg, they all but shed tears. There are here two institutions dignified with the name of colleges for the education of youth. One owes its existence to the governor of this district, and the other to the Kunduz chief. The latter, which is by far the largest, contains forty apartments. They are very poorly endowed; but should the reader smile at the following details, let him recollect that we are speaking of an Uzbek tribe on the outskirts of even Tartar civilisation.

The annual revenues of the two establishments are as follows:—

	Mir's College	Governor's College
Cash	144 rupees	150 rupees
Wheat	30 sacks	50 sacks
Rice	10 sacks	20 sacks
Mash (pulse)	2 sacks	5 sacks

The students pay no fees, but support themselves by labour. Divinity and law are the only branches of learning strictly taught; and these, with a sprinkling of the Persian poets, constitute the entire system of scholastic acquirements. The Koran and its commentators are the source from which he draws his ethics, and a work entitled the Babool Kismut his law.

Khana-a-bad stands upon the east bank of the river of that name. The stream is crossed by a stone bridge, now undergoing repair. Behind the town rises Koh Umber, an isolated mountain remarkable as dividing the plains of Kunduz and Talikhan. Khana-a-bad contains a large, ill constructed fort, and 600 mud-built houses; but the two colleges and the governor's residence are the only buildings entitled to even a passing notice. A large portion of its inhabitants are Badakhshies. The town is governed by Musa Yesawal, a household slave of Murad Beg, deservedly high in favour with his master. He was then just returned from the western frontier, whither he had been with a considerable body of troops to protect it from Bokharian aggression. The climate of Khana-a-bad is superior to that of Kunduz.

After a good night's rest we awoke completely refreshed; and cordially thanking the poor, but kind-hearted students for their hospitality, were soon on the road to Talikhan.

There was a fresh, cold breeze, but the thermometer indicated a temperature of 42°. Had we not been provided with the means of measuring it, I should, from the degree of moisture in the atmosphere, have supposed it to be at least 10° lower. A cloudy morning ushered in a gloomy day. Clouds floated low about the mountain sides, and the course of the river far onwards could be traced by the heavy masses of fog that hung over its surface. These put in motion by an easterly wind, came rolling down the valley like circling clouds of smoke from the muzzle of some enormous gun. For the first ten miles we followed the banks of the Khana-a-bad river, upon an excellent road, although slippery from the effects of yesterday's rain. This brought us to the spot where the waters of the Bungi join the Khana-a-bad, which is here called the Talikhan, and which we forded just above the point of junction. Then leaving the Bungi river to the right, we proceeded for a further distance of four miles, through low rounded hills, which on both sides met the river, and among which the road assumed a worse character, though at no part of it is a horseman obliged to dismount. The boundary line of Kunduz and Talikhan is in this rugged part of the road, a fact of which the traveller is apprised by a custom-house on the road-side. In this neighbourhood the hills rise about two hundred feet above the river. All of them are grassy, and the slopes of some are under cultivation. Koh Umber towers full 2,500 feet above the surrounding level, and a large portion of its bulk was now encased in snow. This mountain is central to the districts of Talikhan, Kunduz, and Hazrat Imam; and its pasturage is common to the flocks of the three plains. We were told that it had not always stood where we saw it, but had been placed there by a holy man, who transported it from Hindustan; as a proof of which, our informant assured us that upon the mountain's side might be gathered every herb indigenous to India. Koh Umber, as seen from these plains, forms a grand and remarkable object: it therefore it is not to be wondered at, that an ignorant and superstitious people should borrow from the marvellous to account for its somewhat peculiar position.

Above the hills numerous eagles were seen soaring, and large flocks of the white-backed or hooded crow. During summer the latter frequent the hilly country, but when winter sets in, they come down into the plain. Emerging from the hills, we drew up for some time at the entrance of the Talikhan plain, and I went a little distance from the party to get the bearings of a remote range of hills, which here first came into view.

On returning, I found Abdul Ghuni in earnest conversation with a stranger on horseback, behind whom was sitting a very handsome female slave, and it was evident from his manner that the Mullah was waxing wroth. He seemed anxious to detain the horseman, who, on his part, insisted upon proceeding. On my nearing the disputants, the stranger rudely gave his horse the whip, and struck off at a brisk pace along the Khana-a-bad road.

Abdul Ghuni gazed on the receding couple for some time in silence; then turning to me and sighing most piteously, he said, "Alas, alas, my lord! when I left my house in Talikhan, the very last order I gave was, that she whom you have just seen should not be sold. My other slaves were all for sale: but this one! this favourite one! I had thoughts of taking to wife!" and here the sighs began again. It appeared that in the Mullah's absence at Kunduz, a Khurm slave-dealer had visited Talikhan, and made a tempting offer for the favourite. The sum was large, and Abdul Ghuni's brother at once concluded a bargain. Unspeakable, therefore, was the Mullah's astonishment and grief, when she, the object of his tenderest affections, whom he had pictured to himself as already at the door to welcome his return, was thus unexpectedly encountered, seated behind a burly stranger, on her way to the Bokhara market. He raved and swore that the transfer was illegal, and that the dealer should give her back. He would be revenged, he would appeal to the Mir. But the thought of the twenty-six golden tillas (about 17l. sterling), for which the fair lady had been sold, by degrees calmed his grief, and in a resigned, but melancholy tone, he exclaimed, "She is too cheap, too cheap: the villain will get forty tillas for her in Khurm."

As a drizzling rain had set in, we crossed the plain, a distance of about ten miles, at a canter: and by three o'clock in the afternoon, when it began to pour in earnest, we had reached Talikhan, and were comfortably lodged in our conductor's Mehman Khana, or house for the reception of guests.

Chapter XVI

The 13th December was passed in Talikhan, awaiting the return of a messenger from Kunduz. As the weather was ill suited to travelling, we had no reason to regret this detention; more especially as we were admitted to an interview with the governor, and had a visit from a still more interesting individual; from no less a personage, indeed, if his own account were true, than a lineal descendant of Alexander the Great.

Ataluk, the son of Murad Beg, bears a close resemblance in personal appearance to his father, and his subjects add in character likewise. He is entrusted with the government of Talikhan, which, after Hazrat Imam, is next in importance to Kunduz. The Prince occupies a larger and better fort than his father, and is surrounded by at least equal state. He appears to be a sensible young man, but has the selfish and repulsive look common to his countrymen.

Mohamed Shah, our other visitor, was portly and well favoured; but there was nothing in the lines of his good humoured countenance that bore out his bold assertion, that the blood of Sekander Zool-Kurnein ran in his veins. Fifteen years ago, his father, the reigning prince of Badakhshan, was defeated by the Kunduz chief and banished his country, on which, Mohamed Shah and his two younger brothers were placed here by Murad Beg, under the surveillance of his son. Though poor and unfortunate, the family is much respected by their countrymen, among whom, Mohamed, the head of the house, is still honoured with the title of Shah, or king.

Talikhan is not so large a place as Khana-a-bad. I should not suppose it contained more than from three to four hundred houses, which, like those of the latter place, are merely hovels. Its inhabitants are chiefly from Badakhshan. The town stands about three hundred yards from the river, and is a most disagreeable place in rainy weather—the streets being then scarcely traversable. Here, as at Kunduz, the sparrow builds its nest in the most exposed situation; but no one thinks of injuring the confiding bird, and in this respect, the habits of Uzbek children are superior to those of Britain. These birds here associate in larger families than I remember to have seen elsewhere.

Among the slaves of Abdul Ghuni, who was still disconsolate for the loss of his favourite, were two Kirghis from Pamir. Although their features were Chinese, their complexions were fair, and even rosy. One, a good-looking young woman, had a child at her breast, and cried bitterly when detailing the circumstances attending her capture. The other was more advanced in years, and did not seem to feel the loss of liberty so acutely.

The following day a market was held in Talikhan. In all the principal towns of Murad Beg's dominions, it is customary to hold them twice a week. Though we left Talikhan at an early hour, the thronged state of the roads leading into it, soon apprised us that the day was no ordinary one. Troops of horsemen were hurrying in to market, many riding double. Gaudily painted cradles, toys, bird-cages, skins of animals, and white and striped cotton cloth, were the articles forming the stock in trade of most of the dealers. All whom we met were blythe and jocund; and but for the difference of dress, and the large proportion of those who rode, I could have fancied them my own countrymen hastening to some merry fair in old England. We counted the horsemen on our line of march, and found there were two hundred and ninety.

At least twice that number rode donkeys, and there might be a hundred individuals on foot. Admitting the three other approaches to the town to have been equally crowded, the influx from the neighbouring districts into Talikhan on market days, will he nearly four thousand souls. The circle of country supplied by this town, may be considered as having a diameter of eighteen miles.

On our route, and at the distance of a few miles from Talikhan, resides Mohamed Cassim Khojah, the Sayid who treated Moorcroft, the traveller, so well. I made a point of calling on the good man; and had prepared myself to meet a decrepid old chieftain, but was agreeably disappointed. The Sayid has either but little passed the meridian of life, or the corroding cares of this world have not made their usual impression on his face or figure. I thanked him in the name of our countrymen for the protection he had afforded the traveller. When he heard that the fame of this good act had reached Firingistan he was silent, but his eye spoke joy. Such instances of benevolence are not of every day occurrence; and when we remember where it took place, and that the favoured party was of our own creed and nation, it surely is the duty of those in power, to send the Sayid some written acknowledgment, if only to show that the British can appreciate virtue.

Bidding farewell to this worthy man, we struck off to the left, and were soon at the base of a mountain ridge, beyond which lay Badakhshan. The road through this barrier is by the Pass of Latta-band; and by noon we reached its entrance. For an hour we kept winding through a defile called An-durah; and towards its summit, where the ascent became more abrupt, we first met the snow. The road, however, continued good, and at about 3.30. p.m., we gained the crest of the pass. From this spot the prospect was glorious. In every quarter snow-clad peaks shot up into the clear sky. Looking towards Kunduz, Koh Umber, with its hoary summit and regular outline, stood pre-eminent in the plain. To the east, where our road lay, the horizon was bounded by the

[176]

high snowy range of Khoja Mohamed, which, crossing the country in a north-east and south-west direction, divides Badakhshan, and is the eastern barrier of Darwaz and Shagnan. Between us and this range, and seemingly at our feet, the Kokcha, or river of Badakhshan, rolled its green waters through the rugged valley of Duranah; while to the north could just be discerned, the blue hills of mountainous Karatagin. The summit of Latta-band is wide and level: we travelled along the top of the pass for an hour and a half, before we commenced the descent on its eastern side. Here we picked up the carcase of a black eagle; a noble bird, which had been recently shot, and from which the claws, beak, and wings had been cut off. The two first of these, tied round the necks of children, are thought to keep off the evil eye.

At the foot of Latta-band, on the Badakhshan side of the mountain, is Ak-bolak (or white springs), a thriving village, the property of Mohamed Cassim Khojah. We left it on the right hand about sunset, and pushing along the plains, soon reached our halting place in Kila Afghan. The length of this day's march was thirty miles, and we were little more than nine hours upon the road. We had left Talikhan with a slight hoarfrost in the morning, but here snow covered the ground, and the thermometer had fallen to twenty-eight degrees. Everything spoke a difference in the level of the two places, and by observation, I found Kila Afghan to be nearly a thousand feet more elevated than Talikhan. Mohamed, the governor, came to the door of his castle, and bade us welcome in the Mir's name. A large fire was soon kindled in the open air; seated round which, we received and returned the salutations of his people. After some time spent in this friendly manner, we retired within doors, and amid a more select company quaffed

" The cup that cheers, but not inebriates."

As the night wore on, we began to feel uneasy af the prolonged absence of my attendant Mohamed Cassim. He had fallen behind the party about sunset, and had not yet come up. The governor, who dreaded wolves, sent out several men to look for him. These animals are here both numerous and daring; as a proof of which, our host mentioned what had occurred to himself some years ago. He had been to Kunduz on some urgent business for the Mir; and on his return reached the Kotul or Pass of Latta-band about midnight. The pass was cleared without accident, but on proceeding through Ak-bolak, the wolves gathered on his track, and but for the timely assistance of the villagers, would have eaten both horse and rider. So daring and close were their assaults, that they had already torn away with their teeth the saddle-cloth, and his own mantle. Some of the wolves repeatedly went ahead of the horse, and by scratching with their hind feet threw up snow so as to frighten the animal, and bewilder its rider. Had three minutes more elapsed before succour reached him, his doom would have been fixed. It was now near midnight; but before going to rest I walked out into the open air, expecting the arrival of the missing man, or the return of those sent out in search of him. A halo full thirty-five degrees in diameter encircled the moon, though otherwise the sky was beautifully clear. It was, however, bitterly cold, and there being no signs of the party's return, at length we all sought our felt couches, and were soon asleep.

Kila Afghan is famous for its springs, of which there are said to be 450 in the neighbourhood. Its fort, with every house in the village, was thrown down by the earthquake of 1832, and by that fearful calamity many lives were lost. Next morning we were agreeably surprised at Mohamed Cassim's return. After losing our track he had the good sense to make at once for Ak-bolak, which village was in sight when he parted from us. In consequence of the detention occasioned by this man's absence, the sun was high in the heavens before we left Kila Afghan, but by making a forced march we reached Taish- khan, distant twenty-six miles, before dark.

Here, in 1823, the Badakhshies, under Miryar Beg Khan, made their last stand for independence against the power of Kunduz. The forces of the latter, consisting of 10,000 horsemen, were led on by Murad Beg in person. The opposing army was less numerous by 1,000 men, and partly composed of foot soldiers. After skirmishing with various success, the Uzbeks made a general charge, and put the Badakhshies to flight, killing and wounding 300 of them, with a very trifling loss to themselves. The conquered army fell back on Fyzabad; but though the troops of Murad Beg were flushed with success he was unable at this time to follow up his victory, and Badakhshan, for two years longer, retained her waning independence.

Quitting the plain of Karabolak we crossed a rough waste, four miles wide, and entered the narrow and pretty vale of Meshid, through which meandered the largest stream we had yet forded in Badakhshan. This valley is reported to have been extremely populous in former times, and the Badakhshies assert that of hardware artificers alone it once contained 10,000 workmen. The kings of Badakhshan passed the winter season at Meshid, and the summer at Fyzabad; and there is a legend current here that in former days the valley was sadly infested by scorpions: to avoid them a certain king, named Suliman, had a residence built on the summit of the mountain which now bears his name. His meals were prepared in the valley, and transported to the Takht, or throne, by a line of men, placed side by side, who passed them on rapidly from one to another. His timid majesty, however, at length met his death from the insect he had been at such pains to avoid, and which, concealed amongst a bunch of grapes, found access to his person, in spite of all his precautions. These traditions are at least evidence of the populousness of these countries in olden times. The valley does not now contain a hundred families.

[179]

From the valley of Meshid we ascended a steep hill, called Agur-durah, on the further side of which runs the small stream of Nahwi. From this to our halting-place at Taishkhan, a distance of nine miles, the road led over a hilly country. In most places the ground was covered with snow: but the steep sides of the vallies showed us that the whole of this wavy district was pastoral. Taishkhan is governed by Mirza Muksud, a relation of the deposed Badakhshan family. It is a secluded valley, little more than a musket-shot across, and is washed by a fine stream, along the margin of which are some large and aged mulberry trees.

No sooner had the day dawned than we saddled, and commenced the ascent of Junasdurah, a huge mountain-ridge that rises immediately beyond the Taishkhan valley. On gaining its summit we found, by the boiling point of water, that we had reached an elevation of 6,600 feet. Steep, however, as this pass is, Murad Beg, with his accustomed dogged perseverance, dragged a heavy piece of ordnance over it; and in more than one place we came upon the traces of its wheels. From the crest of the ridge we had a view of some fine mountain groups, and I took the bearings of Khoja-Mohamed, Argu, Takht-i-Suliman, and Astanah, the most remarkable among their peaks. Descending the eastern side of Junasdurah our march was rendered less fatiguing by following hog-tracks in the snow. So numerous are these animals that they had trodden down the snow as if a large flock of sheep had been driven over it. At the foot of the pass lay Duraim, a valley scarce a bow-shot across, but watered, as all the vallies in Badakhshan are, by a beautiful stream of the purest water, and bordered, wherever there is soil, by a soft velvet turf. To Duraim succeeded the plain of Argu; but, though once the happy home of 6,000 families, its surface was now desolate, and neither man nor beast was visible. Beyond this plain is the wavy district of Reishkhan, a name associated in the mind of a Badakhshi with all the misfortune of his country. About

[180]

a century back Khan Khojah, a Mohamedan ruler of Kashghar, and Yarkand, eminent for his sanctity, having been driven from his dominions by the Chinese, took shelter in Badakhshan, bringing with him 40,000 followers. He was wealthy, which circumstance, added to the beauty of his harem, excited the cupidity of Sultan Shah, who, at the time of the khaja's arrival ruled in Badakhshan. This coming to the knowledge of the ex-ruler of Kashghar he, with his people, fled down the valley towards Kunduz; but were overtaken by Sultan Shah, at Reishkhan. The khaja's adherents were defeated, and he himself made prisoner. He sued for life, but in vain; on which the holy man cursed Badakhshan, and prayed that it might be three times depopulated—that not even a dog might be left in it alive. Already has the country been twice bereft of its inhabitants; first by Kohan Beg of Kunduz, about forty years back, and again by Murad Beg, in 1829.

Descending Reishkhan we entered the valley of the Kokcha, and, traversing an open plain, reached a small hamlet, named Chittah, where we halted for the night.

Since crossing the Pass of Latta-band we had travelled along the left or south bank of the Badakhshan river, over a succession of steep ridge-like hills and deep narrow glens, occasioned by numerous lateral shoots which the chain of mountains to the south throws out towards the Kokcha. In this ridge the most conspicuous peaks are Kishm and Takht-i-Suliman; but these, though lofty, were now lost in the superior chain which diagonally divides Badakhshan, and at the foot of which we had arrived. This range is pierced by the river Kokcha, and at the gorge of its valley, on the right bank of the stream, opposite to our encampment, were the ruins of Fyzabad, the former capital of Badakhshan.

Since quitting Talikhan we had been journeying through a depopulated country. The dreary appearance of winter was not enlivened by the sight of man or beast, for not a single wayfarer did we meet on the road, and, except the partridge, which was very plentiful, and the hog-tracks before mentioned, there were no indications of animal life. It was certainly no season for travelling; but scanty indeed must the inhabitants of that country be, in which a journey of eighty miles can be performed without meeting a human being, except in hamlets thirty miles apart.

Of Fyzabad, once so celebrated throughout the East, scarcely a vestige is left save the withered trees which once ornamented its gardens. Its fort, the dilapidated walls of which are still standing, occupied a rock on the left bank of the river, commanding the entrance of the upper valley, which is here 400 yards wide. Behind the site of the town the mountains rise in successive ridges to a height of at least 2000 feet. Before it flows the Kokcha, in a rocky trench-like bed sufficiently deep to preclude all fear of inundation. Looking up the mountain-valley, the ruined and uncultivated gardens are seen to fringe the streams for a distance of two miles above the town; while in an opposite direction the Kokcha winds through a grassy plain, which, sweeping out from the base of Khoja Mohamed, is encircled by swelling hills alike fitted for agricultural or pastoral purposes. The town could not have been substantially built or its ruins would be more prominent. Although but a few years have elapsed since its walls were levelled, its site can only be recognised by the appearances I have described. Murad Beg must have had evil councillors when he destroyed Fyzabad, and forcibly removed its inhabitants to Kunduz, a place only fit to be the residence of aquatic birds. He has lost both in men and revenue by the measure. It was impossible to behold the desolation of so fair a scene, without commiserating the unfortunate exiles and execrating their tyrant, or without shuddering to think, that one man, as ill-advised as cruel, should have the power to work so much mischief and to make so many of his species miserable! But, alas, the history of every age presents us with a catalogue of similar atrocities, nor will they cease until education and pure religion are diffused over the entire world. From Fyzabad to Jerm, the modern capital of Badakhshan, towards which we now directed our steps, there are two roads; one along the banks of the river, the other somewhat more to the south by the Pass of Kasur, and the high-lying glen of Kash. The latter, though the most toilsome, is the shorter of the two, and as we were not encumbered by baggage, I resolved to take it. After getting a meridian observation of the sun, we set out up the valley which, though it rapidly narrowed, continued to present traces of terrace cultivation. Five miles beyond Chittah we crossed the rivulet of Ishpingow, and shortly after passed Karacka, a hamlet embowered in fruit trees. Beyond it are the ruins of Mobaruk and Childokhturan, connected with which are legends too gross for notice. Here we left the Kokcha, and turning to the south, commenced the ascent of the mountain of Kussur. The road wound along its face, and being rough and slippery, from the combined effects of frost and snow, the summit was not gained without considerable labour. Midway we encountered a flock of 1,400 goats and sheep coming down the pass, and had to stand with our backs to the rock till they had filed by. Towards evening we gained Kasur, a small village situated at the entrance of the glen, at an elevation of 6,600 feet, and thirteen miles distant from Fyzabad. The latter place is 3,500 feet above the sea. When we left it the ground was free from snow, but in Kasur it was full a foot in depth.

Next morning, the 18th of December, we set out for Jerm, with the thermometer at 7° of Fahrenheit. The breeze was fresh and pierced us to the very bone. Several springs occur in this glen, all of which had a temperature of 53°. On arriving at the bottom of the Kasur mountain, we turned off to the left and held our way down the course of a brawling torrent which led us into the valley of the Kokcha, close to Jerm. On arriving at that town, our first applications for food and shelter were unsuccessful, but, after repeated disappointments, we at length prevailed upon an honest Tajik to receive us as his guests, and had soon wherewithal to appease our keen appetites, sharpened by cold and a twenty-four hours' fast. The town of Jerm, although the largest place in Badakhshan, is little more than an extensive cluster of scattered hamlets, containing at the very utmost 1,500 people. The fort is substantially built, and is the most important of any we saw in Murad Beg's dominions. Both it and the town are situated on the left bank of the Kokcha river.

Chapter XVII

I lost no time in delivering to Mirza Suliman Khan, the governor of Jerm, my credentials from the Khunduz Mir, apprising him at the same time of my desire to trace the Amu or Oxus to its source, and also to visit the ruby mines and those of lapis-lazuli. He readily promised me every assistance, but said that it was now too late in the season to perform the first two journeys, and that a month ago a Kafila had been compelled to return to Badakhshan, after having reached Wakhan; hut that the road to the mines of ladjword (lapis-lazuli) was still open, and if I decided on an excursion thither, he would be happy to furnish me with a guide. I consented, although with regret, to this arrangement, and as it was quite uncertain how long the road might remain open, I resolved to visit the mines forthwith, and accordingly we set forward the next day. The valley of the Kokcha, in the neighbourhood of Jerm, is about a mile wide; but not far above the tow it contracts, and the mountains having suffered from earthquakes, the road is rugged and the land uncultivated. Passing on we had to climb an irregular mass of earth of great extent, that completely blocked up the road on the left bank of the stream, and which had evidently slipped down from the mountain above. On the summit of this slip stands the village of Firgamu, around which the uneven surface of the ground is laid out in fields. It would therefore appear that the catastrophe which brought this immense mass into the valley is not of very recent occurrence. Beyond this the bed of the Kokcha becomes so narrow, that a man without risk can leap across its stream, which runs about seventy feet below the surface of the valley, pent in by rocky walls. After passing the Khustuk rivulet, which joins the Kokcha by a cascade of twenty feet drop, we reached the village of Senna.

We had got but little way from Jerm, when it was discovered that our guide was ill-qualified for his task, and was, or affected to be, crazy. To every question he replied by a quotation from Hafiz, the purport of which was, that a man in love was the laugh and sport of his acquaintance. Had it not been for the venerable looks of the reciter, I should have been inclined to think that he himself had left his first love behind him in Jerm. He was escorted back, and in his stead Mirza Suliman sent us a much more competent guide. I may here remark that on our return to Jerm the governor's mirza, in the course of conversation, gravely asked me whether I had not conjured the spirit of the poetical guide into a jackass, for, added he, the man is now discovered to be a fool for the first time in his life, and it is known in the bazar that you left this place with only four donkeys and have brought back five. Murad Beg's letter had introduced me to his representative in Badakhshan as a Munujam, a term in Turkistan equivalent to astronomer or alchymist; so that the secretary, although from politeness he acquiesced in all that was said to expose the absurdity of this and similar stories, evidently had his doubts on the subject, and I daresay retains them to this day.

On the road we saw a party of sportsmen hunting partridges which is here a very common diversion with both Uzbek and Tajik. The irregularities of the valley appeared to me to be unfavourable to the amusement, but this evidently gave to these fearless riders a keener appetite for the sport.

Abdul Ghuni had escorted the crazy guide back to Jerm, and in his absence our reception by the natives was less cordial than usual. After many refusals we at last took possession of an untenanted building standing apart from the rest, and consisting of a small room about ten feet square. The floor was damp and muddy, but a little dry straw remedied these evils, and heartily glad we were to get screened from the piercing cold without. We had not been long here when some of the villagers entered, and taking a corner to themselves, quietly said their prayers, and then departed without asking us any questions. It was clear that we had got possession of a mosque, the most appropriate shelter for strangers where there is no Mehman Khana. As soon as it became generally known that a Yesawal was of our party, the male part of the inhabitants deserted their homes, but were induced to return by the assurance that the officer they dreaded would only tax their hospitality in a very moderate degree. We were now conducted into the best house in the village, and had set before us Ashbakola, or pea-soup, thickened with wheaten flour, and flavoured with kroot, a kind of cheese, making altogether a most excellent dish in cold weather.

On starting in the morning it became necessary to retrace our steps for some distance, as we had to cross the Kokcha, and the best ford lay below Senna. Hitherto we had been following the left bank of the river, but the mountains now pressed so close upon the stream that further progress on horseback on that side became impracticable. The width of the river was here forty-three yards, with a depth of two feet and a half, and a medium velocity of four miles and a half per hour. The temperature of the air was 33°, that of the water 36°. The bed of the stream was about sixty feet below the surface of the valley, and the section of its banks thus exposed showed thick masses of conglomerate resting on thin horizontal strata of sandstone. In the early part of the forenoon the sky was cloudy, and the thermometer down at 23°; but as the day advanced the sun shone out, and by noon we were suffering from heat. Numerous parties from the head of the valley passed us on the road, carrying to Jerm their yearly tribute in kind.

Continuing our journey up the right bank of the Kokcha, we crossed various mountain-rivulets, and saw others which flowed into the river on the opposite side. The Ziarat of Shah Nasr was the first inhabited place we came to on this day's march, and here we spread our felts for the night.

A little below the Mazar the mountains are highly ferruginous, and, at one particular spot, a small hill, almost wholly composed of iron-ore, protrudes through the. surface of the valley in the very path of the traveller. As the formation actually crosses the road, its existence must have been known for a very long period; and yet so tedious are the processes here resorted to for obtaining and smelting the ore, that the progress hitherto made has been slow in the extreme. The surface of the hill bears evidence indeed of having been battered in every direction with sledge-hammers, and at one place it is pierced by a shaft, six feet wide, to the depth of eight feet. It must not, however, be imagined that the inhabitants of these parts are ignorant of the value of the ore; on the contrary, the Badakhshies smelt iron more successfully than any people in the East, and with the articles they make carry on a profitable trade with Eastern Turkistan and the tribes on their southern frontier; but they possess neither sufficient capital nor skill to work their mines advantageously, and the unsettled state of the government keeps back everything like mining enterprise. The deficiency of wood for fuel is another disadvantage.

Shah Nasr Khusrau, whose remains are here interred, came originally from Mecca, and died in the year of the Hidjrut 393.

We heard, for the first time, in this Astanah, that the earth is supported on the shoulders of four holy men, of whom it need not be added that the saint of Badakhshan, the before-mentioned Shah Nasr Khusrau, is one. His companions are—Sultan Yar Khoda Ahmed, of Afraziab; Sheikh Fureed Shukkur Gunge, of Hindustan; and

Imaum Ali Mooza Raza, of Khoristan.

Shah Nasr is the patron saint of the Kohistan, and much revered by the inhabitants of the Upper Oxus. For the support of this Ziarat a tract of land was assigned at the time the buildings were erected; and in return for an indulgence which has been confirmed by the subsequent rulers of Badakhshan, the Mazar is bound to furnish the wayfaring man with food, water, and a night's lodging. Its inmates complained that wheat will not grow upon their land, though it does on that of their neighbours. The grain, they said, springs up and forms an ear, as in other fields, but no wheat is in it, and the straw alone will not repay them the labour of cutting it down. There must be something in the soil inimical to the growth of this grain; but the inhabitants of the Ziarat have found a better reason, alleging that the saint in compassion to human frailty has kept wheaten bread from them, that their passions might be easier kept under, and their tendency to sin be the less. The white dome of this Mazar is visible a considerable distance down the valley. Leaving a trifle at the shrine in return for the hospitality we had experienced, we went on to Firgamu, a village eight miles farther up the valley, and on the opposite or left bank of the Kokcha. We were now approaching the haunts of the Kaffirs, a nation of unbelievers occupying the most inaccessible portion of the Hindu Kosh. Fearful tales were related of their hatred of Mohamedans. Our last halting-place had often suffered from their vengeance. In one of their night attacks, which was yet but too well remembered by the inhabitants of the Mazar, the Kaffirs, surrounding a neighbouring flour-mill, cruelly butchered eight of its inmates.

Towards sunset it blew strong; a gloomy mist darkened the heavens and canopied the narrow valley: the wind, veering from point to point, swept in violent gusts, threatening some fine old walnut-trees under which we were lodged. This was the shortest day of the year, and, as we listened to the warring elements without, my thoughts reverted to Scotland and the social gaieties of her winter.

Firgamu stands at the head of the fertile portion of the Kokcha's valley, which, south of this, takes the name of Koran. Beyond Firgamu the mountains rise immediately from the bed of the river; and there the scanty population live in glens opening on the Kokcha, but none in the main valley itself. Our hardy yabus, though accustomed to rough roads, were here useless; and exchanging them for those of the country, we left them at the village to await our return. As the greater portion of the distance from Firgamu to the ladjword mines had to be performed on foot, we bartered our Uzbek boots for leather buskins (kumaches), and, with a willow staff to assist us in climbing, set out upon our expedition.

A party of countrymen had been sent forward to mend the road, to lay temporary bridges over chasms in the path, and to find a new tract where the old one had been defaced by the earthquake of 1832. The time allowed them was, however, too short for the performance of these several duties; yet, though they had not effected much as pioneers, they did us good service elsewhere. After a long and toilsome march we reached the foot of the ladjword mountains, but were too exhausted to visit the mines that night. One of the party, Hussein, an Afghan, had fallen on the road, and was too severely bruised to come on; but, with this exception, despite of the poet's warning, we arrived unhurt. Where the deposit of lapis-lazuli occurs, the valley of the Kokcha is about 200 yards wide. On both sides the mountains are high and naked. The entrance to the mines is in the face of the mountain, on the right bank of the stream, and about 1,500 feet above its level. The formation is of black and white limestone, unstratified, though plentifully veined with lines, thus:—

The summit of the mountains is rugged, and their sides destitute of soil or vegetation. The path by which the mines are approached is steep and dangerous, the effect of neglect rather than of natural difficulties. The mountains have been tried for the lapis-lazuli at various places; but the following is a section of the principal and latest worked mine:—

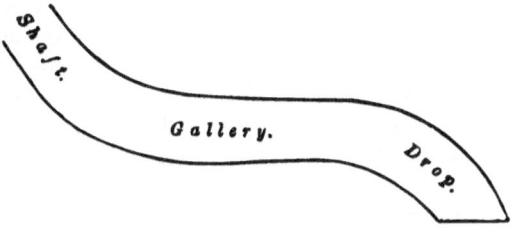

The shaft by which you descend to the gallery is about ten feet square, and is not so perpendicular as to prevent your walking down. The gallery is eighty paces long, with a gentle descent; but it terminates abruptly in a hole twenty feet in diameter and as many deep. The width and height of the gallery, though irregular, may be estimated at about twelve feet; but at some places where the roof has fallen in its section is so contracted that the visitor is forced to advance upon his hands and knees. Accidents would appear to have been frequent, and one place in the mine is named after some unhappy sufferers who were crushed by the falling roof. No precaution has been taken to support by means of pillars the top of the mine, which, formed of detached rocks wedged together, requires only a little more lateral expansion to drop into the cavity. Any further operations can only be carried on at the most imminent risk to the miners. The temperature at the further end of the mine was 36° of Fahrenheit, while in the open air at its entrance it was 29°.

The method of extracting the lapis-lazuli is sufficiently simple. Under the spot to be quarried a fire is kindled, and its flame, fed by dry furze, is made to flicker over the surface. When the rock has become sufficiently soft, or, to use the workmen's expression, nurim, it is beaten with hammers, and flake after flake knocked off until the stone of which they are in search is discovered. Deep grooves are then picked out round the lapis-lazuli, into which crow-bars are inserted, and the stone and part of its matrix are detached.

The workmen enumerate three descriptions of ladjword. These are the Neeli, or indigo colour; the Asmani, or light blue; and the Suvsi, or green. Their relative value is in the order in which I have mentioned them. The richest colours are found in the darkest rock, and the nearer the river the greater is said to be the purity of the stone. The search for ladjword is only prosecuted during winter, probably because, labour in the mine being compulsory, the inhabitants are less injured by giving it in a season of comparative idleness than when the fields require their attention. Perhaps, also, during the cold of winter the rock may be more susceptible to the action of heat, and thus be more easily reduced, than when its temperature is higher. Within the last four years Murad Beg has ceased to work both the lapis-lazuli and ruby mines; and the reason assigned for his altered policy is the small success which has hitherto attended the operations. The mines, the produce of which was exported to Bokhara and China, have been known from a very early period, and the ballast ruby of Badakhshan has furnished the poets of Persia with many a simile. I need scarcely add that the beautiful blue called ultramarine is obtained from the lapis-lazuli. After carefully inspecting the mines we set out in the evening on our return to Jerm, and put up that night at Robat, a deserted village seven miles down the valley. It stands at the mouth of a little stream on the right bank of the Kokcha, by the valley of which the Kaffirs usually make their inroads into Badakhshan.

Some time back the inhabitants of the village were attacked by these fierce people, and, contrary to their usual custom, the slaughter was indiscriminate; all perished, women as well as men. Since then there have been no permanent settlers in the valley above Firgamu.

As we moved among the lone hamlets it was some satisfaction to know that the passes between us and these barbarians were now blocked up with snow. Still they are as daring as cruel, and the bare possibility of a night attack from them did not tend to make our slumbers the more tranquil. There is a more than churchyard solitude about a region such as this, which has been rendered waste and desolate by the hand of the murderer and the robber, and every record scattered around of its former peaceful state comes with a crushing weight upon the heart.

The next morning ushered in Christmas-day; and at an early hour we continued our march down the valley. The journey, as before, was for the most part performed on foot. Abdul Ghuni, though a good horseman, was no pedestrian. He had never, he assured us, walked so far since he was a lad. Every two or three hundred yards he would sit down to rest, and give utterance to his grief in lamentations so prolonged and vehement as to be irresistibly ludicrous. It was Ramazan too; and hunger added to his other sufferings. It is true that, as a traveller, he might have eaten without infringing the Prophet's laws, but it was more meritorious to fast. Added to this, Abdul Ghuni, who prided himself upon being a good Mussulman, had up to this day kept the fast month most rigidly; and it was provoking, he said, to sin when only three days more remained to complete it. Eat, however, he did, and voraciously too; and quieted his conscience by vowing, as he concluded his repast, that he would expiate his offence by manumitting a slave on his return to Talikhan; a vow the performance of which I greatly doubt.

On the 26th we saddled at daybreak, and rode into Jerm, a distance of thirty miles. The latter part of the journey was performed in a heavy snow-fall: but whatever the danger in such weather from other causes, there is comparatively little risk of losing your road in a mountain valley, where the hills around you constantly point out the path.

Considerable fatigue and some danger had attended this journey; and had the only result been the examination of the lapis-lazuli mines, I should have thought the price paid for that gratification had been too dear: but I had also seen a country interesting in many respects, and very little known to Europeans; and on the whole, therefore, I returned well contented with the excursion.

Chapter XVIII

From the 26th of December to the 30th of January we were detained in Jerm by the inclemency of the season. The snow took the good people of Badakhshan completely by surprise. Not expecting so hard nor so early a winter, they had made no adequate provision for their live stock; and no sooner did the snow cover the ground than there was a cry for fodder and fire-wood. We took up our abode with Hussein, our former host, who, though at first suspicious of his guests, became ere long our warm friend and almost constant companion. It is customary in these countries for relations to live in the same hamlet, often to the number of six or eight families. An outer wall surrounds this little knot of friends, within which each family has its separate dwelling-house, stable, and cattle-shed; and a number of such hamlets form a kishlak, or village. In Hussein's homestead were four houses, one of which had been vacant ever since its former inmates perished in the earthquake of 1832. This was now our abode. The style of building does not differ throughout the country, and our quarters at Jerm may be taken as a fair specimen of them all. The site is the slope of a hill, and a rivulet is usually not many paces from the door. Its course is here and there impeded by large, whitened boulders, glassy-smooth from the constant action of running water; while its banks are shaded by a few gnarled walnut-trees, and the lawn adjoining planted in regular lines with the mulberry. Down in the bottom of the valley, where the rivulet falls into the larger stream, lie the scanty corn-lands of the little community. The mountains rise immediately behind the village, and their distant summits retain their snowy covering throughout the greater portion of the year. An enclosure is formed by running a dry-stone wall round a space proportioned to the size and wealth of the family. The space thus enclosed is divided into compartments, the best of which form the dwelling-houses, whilst the others hold the stock. These latter compartments are usually sunk two feet under ground, while the floors of the rooms for the family are elevated a foot or more above it: flat roofs extend over the whole. In the dwelling-house the smoke escapes by a hole in the middle of the roof, to which is fitted a wooden frame, to stop up the aperture when snow is falling. The rafters are lathed above, and then covered with a thick coat of mud. If the room be large its roof is supported by four stout pillars, forming a square, in the middle of the apartment, within which the floor is considerably lower than in the other parts, and the benches thus formed are either strewed with straw or carpeted with felts, and form the seats and bed-places of the family. The walls of the house are of considerable thickness: they are smoothly plastered inside with mud, and have a similar though rougher coating without. Where the slope of the hill is considerable the enclosing wall is omitted, and the upper row of houses are then entered over the roofs of the lower. Niches are left in the sides of the wall, and in these are placed many of the household utensils. The custom of relations grouping together has its advantages, but they are not unmixed. Many of the sorrows of the poor are thus alleviated by the kindness of friends: the closeness of their intercourse adds to their mutual sympathy; and when death occurs, the consolation which the afflicted survivors receive from those near around them is great indeed. But to the newly-married couple the benefits derived from this arrangement are frequently very dearly purchased; and the temper of the poor bride, it is to be feared, is often permanently damaged by the trials she has to undergo at the hands of a cross-grained mother-in-law. Thus it often happens that the bitterest enemies are inmates of the same house. Were I to venture an opinion on so very delicate a subject, it would be in favour of a separate establishment for all newly-married people; but in these barren Alpine lands it is poverty which renders it necessary thus to congregate together. Small as is the population in many of the valleys or narrow mountain glens, it is yet too great for the limited extent of their corn-lands. In Badakhshan, as elsewhere, marriage is a new era in life; and when both parties have health and strength, they would do wisely not to stay and increase the number of mouths where food is already scarce, but remove at once to those districts depopulated by the tyranny of Murad Beg, where means of support can be more easily obtained. The woman would readily give her consent to such a procedure, but pride or indolence, or the love of home, would make the husband adverse to it.

The domestic arrangements of these people are as simple as with other mountaineers. Whilst we were at Jerm a neighbour of Hussein's was married. This gave us an opportunity of learning at what outlay the peasantry of this secluded region can commence housekeeping. I will state the articles separately (following page).

The vessels for holding water are made from the fir-tree, and those for containing flour from the red willow; the latter are circular and hooped. Earthenware is scarce, though in some families very pretty china bowls are to be met with. The bread is baked upon a stone girdle: the lamp is of the same material, and its shape is nearly that of a shoe. The bullet-mould is also of stone. Besides the lamp a very convenient light is obtained from a reed called "luz," about an inch in circumference. It is pasted round with bruised hemp-seed, and bunches, thus prepared, are to be found in every house, suspended generally from the rafters over head. When it

[197]

	Tangas		Rupees
The purchase of a wife	0		25
Bedding	0		6
Antimony for the lady's eyes	3		
An iron boiler	0		2
A wooden bowl and spoons	3		
Flour-sieve	2		
Drinking bowl	1		
Table-cloth	2		
Dresser	2		
Knife for cutting beans	3		
Wooden ladle	1		
Frying pan	6		
A wooden pitcher	2		
Stone lamp	4		
Iron girdle for baking	2		
Culinary and other utensils	31	or	1 1/2
Lutta, or head covering	10		
Kurta, or shirt	40		
Pajamah, or trousers	20		
Kufsh, or shoes	20		
Wife's wardrobe	90	or	4 1/2
Lallah, or turban	6		
Takun	2		
Chukmun, or cloak	40		
Chamboor, or shoes	10		
Jurab, or stockings	6		
Kummer for the waist	40		
Pajamah	10		
Karid, or long sword	40		
Tufungh, or matchlock	200		
Matchlock furniture	22		
Husband's wardrobe and equipment	376	or	18 3/4
Total			57 3/4

or, 5l, 14s. sterling

is wished to extinguish the burning reed, a circle of the bark is peeled off, and the flame, when it reaches that spot, expires of itself. Throughout Badakhshan I remarked a great disinclination to extinguish a light by blowing upon it with the breath.

The hill-men always go armed, but the inhabitants of the open valleys very rarely do so. Nevertheless there is not a house in Badakhshan without its quota of rusty old matchlocks. In dress the people differ little from the Uzbeks. They wear the same peaked skull-cap, and when a turban is super-added, its colour is generally white.

At the season of our visit every man wore thick coloured worsted stockings, and warm woollen cloaks, or chukmuns. On the cold days three of these cloaks were not an uncommon allowance. The shoes in use resembled half boots, made from goats' skin, and mostly of home manufacture. Instead of the heavy kammerband, or shawl, round the waist, the Badakhshi ties a handkerchief, and no native of the country ever thinks of setting out on a journey without a staff in his hand.

In former times Badakhshan was noted for the social qualities of its inhabitants, and we could still discern indications of this generous spirit, but few have now the means of being hospitable; and poverty under a task-master has produced a selfishness that exists not among Tajiks who are free. Among those communities which were styled Yaghi, or rebellious, we always experienced a more hearty welcome than from their kinsmen in the lower vallies, who, though richer, were galled and irritated by their Uzbek oppressors. Where independence is wanting, it is seldom that man retains his generous feelings.

The stranger who now enters a Badakhshi village is not welcomed as he formerly was; now every one strives to get rid of the intruder by turning him over to his next neighbour. According to old custom, there is a Mehman Khana in each village, and the head man or Aksikhail (Elder) is responsible for the comfort of the guest, who, if he be connected with the government, will not have to complain of any want of attention; but the poor man will only be provided with a lodging, and, for a meal, he must look to the really charitable.

This season in Badakhshan is one of inactivity. Most of the inhabitants are husbandmen, ignorant of those handicrafts which, among the peasantry in other countries, give occupation for the winter's day. While snow covers the ground, they busy themselves about their court-yards, digging and re-digging little channels to carry off the drainage; now and then throwing in a wisp of straw to their cattle, or shovelling the newly fallen snow from the flat roofs of their houses. Thus idling away their time, they cheat themselves into the belief that they are busy, though the only really active members of the homestead are their thrifty wives, who may be seen bruising zoghur (oilseeds) for their lamps, attending to the cattle in the cow-houses, or superintending their culinary operations. Should there chance to be a loom on the premises, it gives animation to the entire scene, for besides the one who weaves at it, two or three others are at work preparing wool or cotton for the next web. The women are fair, tolerably good-looking, and do not veil themselves as is customary in most Mohamedan countries. Females of the wealthier families, however, do. They are modest, of pleasing manners, and are good housewives; though they speak of themselves as inferior in these respects to Uzbek ladies. Towards the end of our stay at Jerm, we were considered more in the light of old acquaintances than guests. Visitors of both sexes would occasionally drop in upon Hussein, and seldom failed to exchange friendly words with us. Seated in snug quarters, by a glowing charcoal fire, we heard the news, or, as they expressed it, the gup of the day. It is singular that throughout the whole of our sojourn in this region I was never suspected of being other than a Mussulman, though hundreds knew me to be a Firingi, a term which, by-the-bye, merely conveys to them the idea of superior intellect. It was the same with their chiefs; and even a holy man of Jerm, a native of Hindustan, who ought to have known better, contributed to the delusion. This saint, however, I was reluctantly compelled to undeceive on an occasion which I shall have to mention hereafter. Of course I did not contradict the current opinion to which I owed much of my easy intercourse with this unthinking and not very observant people.

On the last day of the year a partial thaw occurred, sufficient to clear the housetops of snow, and more closely to compress that, which now everywhere covered the ground to the depth of a foot, or more. The starved partridges, attracted by the dark roofs of the houses, entered the village in coveys in search of food. They were so exhausted, that when once they alighted, they could not, until they had rested some time, rise again on the wing, and every time they attempted to do so, their flight grew shorter and shorter. The whole strength of Jerm was on the alert, man and beast, so that if the poor birds escaped the hands of men, the dogs were certain to have them. The slaughter was great, and for many days afterwards partridges smoked on the table-cloth of every Jerm family. We lived on these birds during the greater part of our stay here. This partridge is the common bird of Afghanistan; its back and wings are brown, the sides black-barred, the feet and bill red, and the pinions short.

On New-year's day, 1838, we visited Ahmed Shah, the Pir, or head Mullah of Jerm, who had emigrated from Hindustan when the British mission of 1809 was at Peshawur. He had travelled much, and made a long abode in Eastern Turkistan, which country he entered by the road of Wakhan, and left by that of Kokan. The difficulties of the first of these routes he described as great, arising chiefly from the height of Pamir, the severity of its climate, and the almost total absence of inhabitants. Of that by Kokan he spoke more favourably. The Pir, was a large, stout, cheerful, old man, who looked much younger than he reported himself to be.

He told us that throughout his travels he had

[201]

supported himself, as all his class do, by begging; and truly to judge by the merry looks of the fraternity, the trade must be a prosperous one.

He was in Yarkand when the lamented Moorcroft's messenger arrived there to request permission for his master to visit that city; on which occasion, a mandarin of Ahmed Shah's acquaintance told him that the Chinese had determined not to admit Mr. Moorcroft, for, added, the noblemen, we are persuaded were a Firingi to enter the country some dreadful evil would befall us.

Of the jealousy which characterises the Chinese, their fear, and distrust of foreigners; the wakeful vigilance with which their frontiers are guarded, and the efficacy of their restrictive measures, he had many anecdotes to tell; while, like every other native of these countries with whom I conversed on the subject, he praised their probity and good faith. Yarkand is not included within the limits of China Proper, but is nevertheless subject to the emperor, and a neutral ground, where neighbouring nations are privileged to meet the subjects of the celestial empire for purposes of traffic. No one except its governor is permitted to enter China, and he visits the frontier town of Eela once a year. At the time Yarkand and Kashkar were wrested by the Chinese from the Mohamedan family who had previously held them, their inhabitants traded with Eela. The occasion of their subsequent exclusion, and the advance of the commercial entrepôt to Yarkand, was, according to my informant, as follows. A foreign merchant informed the magistrates of Eela that he had lost his Koorgeen, or saddlebags. The man was required minutely to describe them, and to make oath to their contents. He swore to the value of one hundred silver yambos, and was then dismissed after being told to come back on a given day, when, if the saddle-bags were not recovered, the State would make good his loss. On the appointed day the merchant presented himself, when, to his great chagrin, the Koorgeen was produced. It had not been opened, and much to the crafty man's annoyance, this was now done by the authorities; when, instead of the sum he had sworn to, the articles it contained were found not to exceed a few yambos in value. A circumstantial detail of the whole affair was transmitted to Pekin, and the emperor decided it to be for the benefit of his exchequer, and the moral good of his subjects, that the admission into the country of barbarous and unprincipled foreigners should forthwith be prohibited. This may, or it may not have been the case; but from the story, we learn the high estimation in which the Chinese character is held among those most intimate with them.

All our visitors spoke in high terms of Yarkand, and appeared delighted with its climate, and inhabitants. They expatiated on the peculiarities of the Chinese, and the contrast which they exhibit when compared with other nations. Many accounts of their customs and habits, which I received when at Jerm, were afterwards confirmed by a travelling Jew, who had tried, but failed, to accomplish a journey through their territories. This man was a Russian by birth, and had been for many years a traveller in the countries bordering the Caspian and the lake of Aral. Hearing that records of the missing tribes were to be obtained in Kashmir, or Tibet, he was journeying thither when my Munshi, Cholam Hussein, fell in with him at Balkh, This man's original plan was, to penetrate by the route of Kokan Kashkar, and Yarkand; but, though skilled in the various languages of Central Asia, and conforming to the dress and habits of its people, the cunning of his nation was no match for the honest zeal with which the public functionaries of Kashkar executed the orders of their emperor. Suspicion attached to his character; and after proceeding as far as that town he was forced to retrace his steps. A large guard, he said, was stationed in a tower above the city gate, from which all caravans could be seen, while yet distant. Before they are permitted to enter the city, each individual is strictly examined; their personal appearance is noted down in writing, and, if any are suspected an artist is at hand to take their likenesses. Interpreters for every current dialect are also present. To each of the persons subjected to this vexatious investigation the Chinese make a present of a few tangas.

The Jew traveller mentioned a singular, and I should infer, an efficient punishment for the crime of theft, inflicted in the Chinese cities through which he had passed. The criminal is not incarcerated, but made to walk the street with a clog attached to his feet, or a wooden collar suspended about his neck, of a size, and for a time, proportional to the offence.

I remember to have seen the same kind of punishment successfully resorted to on board ship. The delinquent, a Portuguese, had been so repeatedly convicted of theft, and so repeatedly punished, that at length the cat-o'-nine-tails fell powerless on his back, but what bodily pain failed to accomplish a sense of shame did. A black board was strapped to his back and upon it was written, in large white letters, the word "Ladrone," or thief. This pressed like an incubus upon the man, and effected a complete cure.

On the 5th of January we were agreeably surprised in our Jerm retreat by a visit from an Afghan, whom we had known in Peshawur. The reader should be told that in August, 1837, Captain Burnes employed a Hadji of Peshawur to travel into Chitral for the purpose, amongst other things, of ascertaining the truth of certain information he had received as to the existence in that country of idols, and inscriptions to which the natives ascribed a very remote antiquity. Our visitor was the Hadji's travelling companion, and his story was a sad one. As far as Chitral, every thing appears to have gone well; but there they unfortunately associated themselves wrwith a pirzada, or Mohamedan of a religious character, and to this friendship they attributed all their mishaps. On the road to Badakhshan sickness overtook the party, and on reaching Khyrabad, a village not far from Jerm, were hospitably entertained by the Pir of the place.

Unfortunately the poor Hadji was of a temperament more ardent than scrupulous, and, in his anxiety to get well, told his credulous host that he possessed the secret of making gold, and that if the Pir would cure him, he, in return, would impart to him the invaluable process. The host did his best; appointed a female slave to watch over the invalid, and, in fine, by his skilful treatment, succeeded in closing seven of the eight ulcers that had broken out on the Hadji's legs. When the cure was thus all but completed, the Pir pressed the patient to fulfil his contract. The Hadji's falsehood was now apparent, and at the recommendation of their pious and considerate fellow travellers, the Peshawur pirzada, both the Hadji and our visitant were imprisoned by the disappointed saint. Daily was the unfortunate man branded with a red-hot iron, for the Pir still believed that the philosopher's stone was in his possession, and that a proper degree of heat would bring it out. At length the Hadji's health gave way under this rough treatment, and death seemed about to relieve him from further suffering. His host fearing that his own character might suffer under such a contingency, released the prisoner from irons and discontinued his system of torture. But both the Hadji and his companion were still under serveillance. Without loss of time we extricated the poor men and sent the Hadji down to Kunduz, where, by the skill and kind attention of Dr. Lord, he speedily recovered the use of his limbs, and was at length restored safe and sound to his employer.

About this time I accompanied Mirza Suliman on a hunting excursion along the banks of the Kokcha. Partridges were the game. The whole landscape was one sheet of dazzling whiteness. In the sun's rays the silvery pearls of the snowflakes shone like grains of mica in the sand, with a brilliancy that pained the eye. The sky, which for the last ten days had been obscured, was now clear through its whole extent, save where a few small misty clouds streaked the pure azure. The weather was cold, but we were warmly clad, and a brisk canter through heavy snow on such a day gives a new impulse to the spirits, a new value to existence. I came to the ground prepared to enjoy the sport; nor was I disappointed. Parties of foot and horsemen lined the banks of the river, each accompanied by a number of dogs. The men on foot and the dogs occupied the rough and broken ground bordering the Kokcha, while the horsemen stood aloof and ran down the birds which the beaters and dogs disturbed. The partridges seldom took to either the mountains or the plain, but crossed and recrossed the river, to the great annoyance of the sportsmen. We bagged nearly 500 birds.

The next day and the following we were startled by repeated shocks of an earthquake. The sensation was that of a sudden wrench rather than a tremulous motion. The first shock took place at five minutes past four o'clock in the afternoon of the 7th, and was repeated with more violence towards midnight on the 8th. On both occasions the inhabitants left their houses, and, rendered cautious by the awful calamity which befell them in January 1832, would not re-enter them until many hours had elapsed after the shocks were felt. That visitation had been indeed awful.

In the very hamlet where we lodged, of the twenty-five persons it contained, twelve perished. In each of the four houses there was death, and in one of them not a single individual escaped. So general was the havoc which the earthquake caused, that on the following day the governor, as a means of estimating the total loss of life, caused an exact census of three large hamlets to be taken, and the result was, that out of 310 souls, 156 were missing. In the neighbouring valley of Sir Gholam, out of a population of 155 persons, only 72 were saved; nor were the shocks of this earthquake confined to the valley of the Kokcha, the vibrations extended through every lateral defile. The very mountains were shaken, and numerous landslips and torn strata remain the evidences of a convulsion, which reached from Lahore to Badakhshan, though its point of greatest intensity was the upper valley of the Oxus. In Wardodj, a portion of the mountain fell into the valley, and dammed up its stream for eight days, at the expiration of which time it found an outlet over the embankment. The stream has now cut down a channel to its former bed. The whole of the Wardodj valley has suffered at different times by earthquakes. At one spot, a part of the mountain half a mile in length had slipped down, leaving a large gap in the chain of hills. Upon this landslip grows the dwarf fir-tree, which, though unknown to the valley, is found upon the mountains from which the mass had fallen.

Of all our Jerm acquaintances none was more welcome to our fireside than one of those singular people, the Siah-posh or black-vested Kaffirs. He was an uncommonly handsome man of about 25 years of age, with an open forehead, blue eyes, and bushy arched eyebrows, his hair and whiskers black, and his figure well set and active. He would sometimes bring us a present of a few partridges, and returning the Mohamedan salutation with which we greeted him, take his seat at the fire without further ceremony. Cross-legged he could not sit, for in this respect the Kaffirs differ from all eastern nations, and like Europeans prefer a chair or anything raised to a seat upon the ground. He gave us an animated account of his countrymen, and pressed us to visit them when the passes opened. As an inducement to do so, he promised us plenty of honey and oceans of wine. His sister was married to Mirza Suliman; but though thus connected with Mohamedans, he bore them the most deadly ill-will, and even in their presence would recount the numbers that had fallen by the bow or spear of his countrymen. "The Mussulmans," he said, "were responsible for the blood thus spilt, for since they hunted down the Kaffirs to make them slaves, the latter had retaliated; for the loss of liberty was worse than the loss of life." The governor of Badakhshan had done much to assuage the fierce passions on both sides, and since his appointment truces of various length have existed between his people and the Kaffirs, during which the latter have been supplied with salt, in exchange for their honey and wax. A good understanding existed between him and some of the strongest chiefs in the Kaffir country, which was further cemented by the marriage I have mentioned. But in such a government as that of Kunduz, upheld solely by rapine, the lenient system of the Badakhshan governor was not likely to meet encouragement from Murad Beg. Mirza Suliman was told that he must make a yearly descent upon the Kaffirs or resign his government. Like an honourable man, he chose the latter alternative, and was succeeded, before we left the country, by some one more likely to act up to the instructions of the Mir.

The Mussulmans unwittingly give high praise to this people when they acknowledge, as they readily will, that one Kaffir slave is worth two of any other nation. They add that they resemble Europeans in being possessed of great intelligence, and from all that I have seen or heard of them, I conceive that they offer a fairer field for missionary exertion than is to be found anywhere else on the continent of Asia. They pride themselves on being, to use their own words, brothers of the Firingi; and this opinion, of itself, may hereafter smooth the road for the zealous pioneers of the gospel. Unlike the Hindus and Mohamedans, they have no creed purporting to be a revelation; but, as far as I could discover, simply believe in the supremacy of a deity, and that men who have been good and hospitable on earth will be rewarded in heaven. At present there are many and perhaps insuperable difficulties to their conversion to Christianity; but let us hope that the military operations now carrying on to the west of the Indus may in due time be instrumental in guiding the yet unsophisticated mind of the Kaffir to a knowledge of the true God.

Whether their claim of brotherhood to Europeans be founded on tradition, or be a mere assumption of their own, I have not the means of ascertaining. For my own part, I believe them to be of the same race as the natives of Badakhshan, that is Tajiks, and that on the invasion of the Mohamedans they fled into the fastnesses of the mountains, whilst the rest of their countrymen, submitting to the invader, were converted, and so retained their lands in the plain.

On the 27th we dined with the principal merchant of the place. There were nearly a dozen guests present besides Abdul Ghuni, Gholam Hussein, and myself. The first course consisted of pillaw, mutton, and partridge; for the second, we had tea without sugar, but rich in fat, and according to Uzbek custom, the leaves were handed round for dessert. Thanks were offered up both before and after the meal: the host himself remained standing, attending to the wants of his guests. From this man, who had often been in Yarkand, I obtained good information of the upper course of the Oxus, and he likewise mentioned the fact of coal being used for fuel in the Chinese city of Eela.

We were not the only feasting party in the village. It is customary in Badakhshan for a bride not to enter the house of her parents during the first year of her married life. On the anniversary of her wedding day she visits her mother with much formality, and receives a present proportioned to her parents' means: a cow is the gift usually bestowed. This ceremony over, a feast to her female friends is given under her husband's roof, at which none of the men are permitted to be present. One of these marriage feasts took place on this day.

Of all our visitors Mirza Sala was the most regular. He had always something to communicate: either how affairs were going on at Kunduz, or what the tribes in our neighbourhood were doing. He was, as his title implies, a secretary or writer; but, poor man, like the rest of his countrymen, he had had his vicissitudes. I liked his independence of character, and the frankness with which he expressed his sentiments. One day when speaking of the changes that had taken place in this country, he exclaimed with genuine energy, "Since Badakhshan has lost her independence, many of her

[209]

chiefs have gone to Kunduz, and are there sharing with the Uzbeks the fruits of the land. I know this, but for myself, my coarse cloak and my homely pea-soup have more attractions than the brocade dress and rich pillaw of the Uzbek, if to possess the latter, I must desert my native country and bow at the feet of a conqueror. No; they would be no pleasures to me."

In looking back to the days spent in Jerm, I must not omit making honourable mention of a worthy ironmonger, our next door neighbour. He was the sole iron manufacturer in the country; and the community being in a great degree dependent on him for that indispensable branch of manufacture, Ismael was truly a man of no small importance. The Russian pots, he said, were not to be compared with those he made, which always brought a higher price in the market. Nevertheless, in spite of our honest friend's assertion, I must remark, that the foreign ones are here in very general use, and that amongst the wandering Kirghiz of Pamir they are universal—there is not a Kirgah without one. One of Ismael's trading speculations was remarkable, inasmuch as it showed the natives of this region to be possessed of considerable energy and perseverance. With forty iron pots he loaded five yabus, and made his way into Chitral. Here he readily disposed of them, and after investing part of the proceeds in honey, started for the Chinese frontier. In crossing the Cuner river a mule was carried down by the stream, and to add to Ismael's ill-luck it was the one which carried his surplus cash. The animal was recovered, but its load had disappeared. On reaching Pamir he lost a mule by the cold of that elevated region. Still, nothing daunted, he pressed on for Yarkand, where he safely arrived and sold his Chitral investment to such advantage that he cleared fourteen times the value of his original venture—the forty cast-iron pots. Fascinated by the pleasures of the place, he stayed there three years, and finally left Yarkand a poorer man than he entered it.

The ore he uses comes from the mines of Arganjika, in the neighbourhood of the village of Khyrabad. In smelting it he employs charcoal for fuel, and limestone as a flux.

Having enumerated those persons to whom we were most indebted for friendly attentions at Jerm, I feel bound to make mention of a canine friend whom I procured here, and who was called Jermy in honour of his birthplace. In our subsequent wanderings he proved, like all his species, serviceable and faithful, and woe betide the stranger who, regardless of his warning bark, ventured after nightfall within the circle of our pack-saddles. When the day of parting came I tendered a small present to our kind host for the trouble we had occasioned his family; but Hussein, fearful it might be in return for the dog he had given me, refused to accept it until assured it was not so; for in this respect Uzbek and Tajik are alike prejudiced, and dread, above every other opprobrious stigma, the epithet of dog-seller.

The following is a register of the weather during the month of our detention in Jerm:—

Thermometer, January 1838

Day	Date	Sunrise	Noon	Sunset
Monday	1	31° snowy	48° clear	clear
Tuesday	2	23° clear	36° do.	29° do.
Wednesday	3	32° snowy	41° snowy	35° do.
Thursday	4	25° clear	46° clear	...
Friday	5	32° sleet	35° sleet	28° snowy
Saturday	6	14° clear	26° clear	24° misty
Sunday	7	18° do.	...	...
Monday	8	23° snowy	29° snowy	19° clear
Tuesday	9	10° clear	26° clear	18° clear
Wednesday	10	18° ...	...	...
Thursday	11	...	...	...
Friday	12	...	...	...
Saturday	13	...	...	...
Sunday	14	...	...	...
Monday	15	...	...	...
Tuesday	16	18° clear	40° clear	29° clear
Wednesday	17	25° snowy	39° do.	20° do.
Thursday	18	18° ...	39° ...	...
Friday	19	16° ...	39° ...	...
Saturday	20	26° cloudy	39° ...	...
Sunday	21	...	...	...
Monday	22	26° ...	39° ...	...
Tuesday	23	...	...	...
Wednesday	24	24° cloudy	39° cloudy	31° cloudy
Thursday	25	20° clear	40° ...	31° do.
Friday	26	28° cloudy	41° ...	32° do.
Saturday	27	26° do.	42° clear	34° snowy
Sunday	28	26° clear	40° ...	32° ...
Monday	29	24° do.	41° cloudy	33° cloudy
Tuesday	30	...	42° do.	36° snowy
Mean		23°	38°	29°
Maximum		48°		
Minimum		10°		

Chapter XIX

I have ventured an opinion that Badakhshan was originally peopled from Balkh, and I am led to this belief from its inhabitants being Tajiks and the language Persian: there is, however, neither record nor tradition in the country to support this conjecture. That its ruby mines brought Badakhshan into notice at an early period we may well believe; but of its condition prior to the Uzbek irruption, in the commencement of the sixteenth century, nothing authentic is known. That event planted a Mohamedan dynasty in Hindustan, during the palmy days of which the fate of Balkh and Badakhshan seems to have been one and the same; nor did the decline of that splendid empire sever this union, since on the rise of the Durani monarchy both of these dependencies lapsed to Kabul. This connexion is proved by a document still in the possession of a family in Munjan, a small village on the crest of a pass leading from Kabul into Badakhshan. This writing shows that the inhabitants of the country hold their lands on condition of giving shelter and food to the king's messengers.

If the remote and inaccessible character of Badakhshan paralysed the edicts of the Delhi emperors, and caused its dependency to be more nominal than real, we may readily infer that under the disjointed rule of the Duranis its subjection has been still more nominal. Accordingly we find that when the country was lately attacked by the Kunduz chief the circumstance passed unheeded in Kabul; and Badakhshan, till overrun by Murad Beg, has never known the real miseries of a conquered country.

None of the three great Tartar invaders, Jangez Khan, Tamerlane, or Shebani Khan, seem to have penetrated so high up the valley of the Oxus, though some of the followers of Baber, when expelled from the rich plains of Soghdiana by the Uzbeks, sought shelter here; and their descendants, not having intermarried with the Badakhshies, are still to be recognised both by name and physiognomy. My principal reason, however, for assigning a Persian descent to the inhabitants of Badakhshan is their creed. Prior to the Uzbek invasion their religion, like that of Balkh, seems to have been Shiahism. There is no absolute proof of this, but it appears a fair inference when the following facts are considered. The last Tartar invaders were Suni Mohamedans, all of whom conceive themselves bound to wage interminable war with the other sect, for the purpose of converting them to the orthodox belief; and of this privilege it is well known they have never ceased to avail themselves. What has been the result?— Shiahism, extirpated in the open country, has sought and found refuge in the most inaccessible depths of the neighbouring mountains, in cold and hungry glens, that can only be entered during the summer months. Accordingly we find that in the open valley of the Kokcha the inhabitants are Sunis, though every Tajik hill-state around it is of the opposite creed. Nor can the people of the vallies have been long of their present belief, since Murad Beg, in his chapows or forays has more than once accused certain districts of an inclination to lapse into heretical opinions, and as a preventive, marched off all the inhabitants to the slave-market of Bokhara.

The Tajiks are a numerous people, diffused over an extensive range of country both north and south of Hindu Kosh. They are a handsome race of the Caucasian stock; wherever found they in general speak the Persian language; and though some may now be met with beyond the limits of that once extensive empire, it is only under circumstances which tend to show that their destinies have ever been more blended with that monarchy than with any other. Yet the Tajik himself points to Arabia and to the country around Bagdad as the primeval seats of his ancestors; and as this belief is general it at least merits attention. Their name, they say, is derived from Tadj, an ornament for the head, and was bestowed on their forefathers, who stand accused of stealing this symbol of royalty from Mohamed's head; hut they are too numerous to be the descendants of the Arab warriors who during the first century of the Hijra overran so large a portion of Asia. The actual descendants of these first disseminators of Mohamedanism are still numerous in these countries, but they bear no proportion to the Tajik part of the population.

The word Tajik has been said to mean the descendant of an Arab born in a foreign country; but surely if this definition of the word were correct we should find Tajiks in Africa as well as in Asia. To many countries in the former continent the Arab bequeathed his language with his creed; and if the word Tajik had this original signification, it is not easy to conceive how it should have been bestowed on their descendants in one country and withheld from them in another.

I take the inhabitants of Kaffiristan and the other mountain regions whose solitudes have scarcely yet been invaded, to be of the same race as the Tajik, and the latter to be the indigenous inhabitants of the open country wherever they are now found. The mountain districts to which I here allude have peculiar dialects of their own; but there is a strong resemblance between their inhabitants and the Tajik of the open country, and those points in which they do differ are the result of physical causes, evidently not of blood. These societies are Kaffiristan, Chitral, Wakhan, Shagnan, and Roshan, and the most probable way of accounting for their peculiar dialects is by supposing them forced into their present fastnesses at a very early era, antecedent, or at least coeval, with the first spread of Islamism. Of these several states the Kaffirs alone have successfully held out against the progress of that religion. Possessing a country strongly fortified by nature, they continue to wage an interminable war with every true believer, and have repaid on the faithful with a tenfold vengeance the injuries their forefathers suffered when idol temples were razed to make room for the mosque.

The Tajiks make good companions, particularly the Mullahs, who have far more liberality of sentiment than their untravelled disciples. They were always pleased to be visited by us, and used to say we were no Uzbeks, but like themselves in features and complexion. Though their own temperament is grave, they delight in a lively associate. Keep talking to them, and no European, with such an audience, can ever want subjects of conversation—and you are sure of their good-will: look solemn and you make enemies. Nothing is more common at the close of a spirited conversation than for them to exclaim, "He is a good companion; he speaks well." On our quitting a party the Mullah would sometimes run a dozen yards after us, bellowing out,"We are friends, are we not? What need I say more?"

Nowhere is the difference between European and Mohamedan society more strongly marked than in the lower walks of life. The broad line that separates the rich and poor in civilised society is as yet but faintly drawn in central Asia. Here unreserved intercourse with their superiors has polished the manners of the lower classes; and instead of this familiarity breeding contempt, it begets self-respect in the dependant. A kasid, or messenger, for example, will come into a public department, deliver his letters in full durbar, and demean himself throughout the interview with so much composure and self- possession, that an European can hardly believe that his grade in society is so low. After he has delivered his letters he takes a seat among the crowd, and answers calmly and without hesitation, all the questions which may be addressed to him, or communicates the verbal instructions with which he has been entrusted by his employer, and which are often of more importance than the letters themselves. Indeed all the inferior classes possess an innate self-respect, and a natural gravity of deportment, which differs as far from the suppleness of a Hindustani as from the awkward rusticity of an English clown. Of this public manner of transacting business north of Hindu Kosh, I have seen repeated instances. When Murad Beg receives a letter he deliberately unfolds it, calling out all the while for a mirza, or mullah, to decipher its contents. This official, after scanning it over to himself, reads it aloud in a high sonorous voice; then, slowly folding it up, hands it back to the Mir, who tucks it under the folds of his turban.

Even children in Mohamedan countries have an unusual degree of gravity in their deportment. The boy who can but lisp his "Peace be with you" has imbibed this portion of the national character. In passing through a village these little men will place their hands upon their breast, and give the usual greeting. Frequently have I seen the children of chiefs approach their father's durbar, and stopping short at the threshold of the door, utter the shout of "Salam Ali-kum," so as to draw all eyes upon them; but nothing daunted, they marched boldly into the room, and sliding down upon their knees, folded their arms and took their seat upon the musnud, with all the gravity of grown-up persons. This precocity of manner is owing to their early introduction into the society of men; and though it does away with much that characterises youth with us, I doubt whether the system be not better than our own. On the 30th of January some natives of Shagnan arrived with letters from the chief to Mirza Suliman. From these men we learned that they had travelled upon the Oxus, which was frozen from Darwaz upwards. This was glorious news to us, who had been lingering in Jerm, hoping rather than expecting that such an occurrence would enable us to visit the ruby mines, which are situated in the valley of that river, and close to Shagnan. It was the only chance I had of reaching these mines; for when there has been a deep fall of snow, the only communication between Badakhshan and Shagnan is by the Oxus, and it is not every year that the route on the ice is practicable.

We lost no time in putting our plans into execution, and that day I waited on the governor, and got his permission to set out. Having embraced our numerous acquaintances, it only remained to take leave of the Pir, whose benediction, it was believed, would facilitate our enterprise.

Ahmed Shah had summoned together some of the persons of most consequence in Jerm to bid us a last farewell. On crossing the threshold of his door it unfortunately happened that Gholam Hussein's rosary was in my hand. This the quick-sighted man immediately perceived, and notified to the assemblage as an unerring proof of my orthodox belief, and that in fact I really was, what he had always suspected me to be—a good Mussulman. Now, though well inclined to favour such an opinion among the commonalty, I could no longer, when so directly alluded to, continue the deception. I at once told them that I was a Christian; nor could I avoid briefly stating to them what was the groundwork of that faith. This brought on what I had uniformly wished to avoid—a religious discussion, in the course of which I was told by Hazrat Ishan, the holy man, that the ascension of our Saviour took place 392 years antecedent to the commencement of our era, and that we ought to call our current year not 1838 but 2230. One of the company said that he had seen the Angeel, or New Testament, in the But Khana, or idol-temples of the Russians, for so he called the Greek churches from the number of pictures they contain; and that the volume was so large that it would take a yabu to carry it. "Now," added he, "as all that is needful for man to know is contained in the Koran, from which, as every body knows, both the Old and New Testaments were compiled, how much there must be in the Christian Bible that is useless." This observation of the merchant had great weight with the audience. In short, I was getting worsted in the argument, when it struck me to produce the book which our friend the traveller had seen in what he considered such bad company in Russia. With the Pir's permission it was sent for. It was the small Oxford edition, containing both the Old and New Testaments, elegantly bound, the present of a valued friend. The effect it produced was singular. All present kissed the sacred volume, admired the rich gilding of its leaves, and were surprised, I might even say awed, by the clearness and beauty of its type. The merchant was silent, but as several of the persons who were present had evidently warmed towards me, I took an opportunity of turning the conversation to another subject, and one in which Ahmed Shah was deeply interested—that of slave-dealing. I exerted myself to point out, in the most impressive terms I could use, the deep guilt of this degrading traffic, and how contrary it was to every principle of humanity and justice. I was listened to with attention: but I greatly fear that whatever impression I made was only transitory. Ahmed Shah, to whom all the others looked up as their example and guide, was the largest dealer in slaves of any one in the town. He had now thirty on hand, and has received from Chitral as many as a hundred in a single investment. It was not to he hoped that a few words from a stranger, and an unbeliever, would turn him from his established course of trade.

It is difficult to imagine any train of reasoning which can reconcile the conscience of a rational being to the atrocities of the slave-trade. The ready excuse among Mohamedans, that the captives are converted to Islamism, though it may have its weight with the crowd, is too shallow to deceive men whose minds are comparatively enlightened. They well know that the conversion is never real; that the poor wretches who assume Mohamedanism do so only to render their bondage less severe. For my own part I can perceive one and only one mode, by which the traffic in human beings may be done away with. It is in the general diffusion of knowledge. The time will come, though it may be still far distant, when the printing press shall perform as great wonders through the whole of Asia as it has done, and is still doing, in Europe. Then, and not till then, will man know what is his duty towards his fellow men. That slavery can continue to exist in any nation where instruction, moral and religious, is generally diffused, I hold to be impossible. Let all those who are anxious for the abolition of slavery, and the conversion of the heathen nations, exert themselves to diffuse education among them. Assuredly this is the broad foundation on which missionary exertions should be based. It is true that education alone will not make Christians; but we are firmly convinced that, under Providence, it is the best means to accomplish that end. But education, as we find to be the case in our own country, must commence at a very early age to be really beneficial.

On the last day of the month we set out on our journey, and crossed over to the right bank of the Kokcha, by a good wooden bridge in the vicinity of the fortress. From the centre of this bridge condemned criminals, bound hand and foot, are thrown into the dark pool beneath. No executions took place whilst we were resident in Jerm, but not many days prior to our arrival an unfortunate man perished in this barbarous manner. He had been heard to utter sentiments injurious to Murad Beg; and those in power, more anxious to show their zeal than to fill their office honestly and humanely, took advantage of a few unguarded words, and deprived the poor man of his life.

Continuing down the valley, which gradually widened as we advanced, and along the right bank of the Kokcha, we reached, after a ride of nine miles, the river of Wardodj. From this spot the Kokcha turns sharp round to the westward, after receiving tribute from the Sir Gholam and Wardodj valleys, both of which open to the eastward. Beyond this, and under a range of lofty mountains to the north, lay the little village of Khyrabad, the scene of the alchymist Hadji's sufferings. In the same range are the iron mines of Arganjika, the source of wealth to our Jerm acquaintance, the ironmonger. Here the Kokcha's valley is not more than three miles wide, nor does it exceed that width at any point south of Fyzabad.

After halting a short time, and viewing the wintry aspect of the snow-covered mountains around us, we turned our horses' heads in the direction of the Wardodj valley, and commenced our journey up the left bank of its stream. This valley soon narrowed, so that no belt of level land margined the river; but where patches did occur, they were cultivated. Shortly after entering Wardodj we passed the ruins of a Kaffir fortress. Evidences of earthquakes were frequent, especially of the one of 1832. On the following day a market was to be held in Jerm, and numerous parties passed us, bound for that place. There being but one market town in Badakhshan the peasantry come from a considerable distance to attend it, and are thus obliged to start a day or two before that on which it is held. Many of these people wore coverings of horse-hair before their eyes, to shield them from the ill effects of the snow. Some had them of network, and made after the fashion of our spectacles. About four o'clock in the afternoon we dismounted at Khosh Darow, a poor village, five miles and a half from the entrance of the valley. On starting from Jerm it was necessary to hire a man to lead my new acquisition, Jermy; for though we were great friends whilst under his old master's roof, neither coaxing nor threats would induce the dog to follow us one step beyond the threshold. We applied to several of the poorer inhabitants, but without success; and the man who at length volunteered his services was much better off than many of those who refused the employment. I have frequently observed that the poor of these countries are little inclined to make themselves useful, or to do an obliging act; nay, that men, in the last stage of destitution, prefer to sit idle rather than perform a trifling service that would bring them a reward.

On the 1st day of February we breakfasted much at our leisure, and the day was well advanced before we commenced our journey, for we found that in this cold bleak valley, whose sides rose from 2,000 to 2,500 feet above us, and which was only looked into by the sun at mid-day, the keen air of the morning was too much for our Indian servant, the only one remaining with us, for his companion, Mohamed Kassim had been nipped by the cold, in our trip to the Ladjword mines, and, on our return to Jerm, had been sent back to Kunduz.

We passed in the course of the day, three scantily-peopled villages, and put up at a fourth, named Yowl. The character of the valley remained unchanged, except that here we remarked indications of cultivation on ledges of level ground, several hundred feet up the face of the mountains. The wind that blows down this deep defile is called "Bad-i-Wakhan," or wind of Wakhan, noted throughout all Badakhshan for its severity. It is indeed piercing. It continues during six months of the year, from the end of autumn to the middle of spring, freshening as the weather clears, but lulling when the clouds gather. When it dies away you are told, "the wind has gone to sleep." These people, like the Uzbeks, deal largely in figurative expressions. With the Uzbek, everything is computed by the galloping of his horse; and here, if you inquire the distance between two neighbouring places, you will be answered, "While soup is preparing you may go the distance," drinking soup being as every-day an affair with the one people as riding is with the other. Yowl is but 6,600 feet above the sea, yet beans will not grow here, and its few mulberry trees look sickly. The walnut, however, flourishes, and the few varieties of stone-fruit, which are cultivated, succeed well. Wheat is the common grain.

Here, as elsewhere, the donkey is used for every purpose of drudgery. Almost every one of them you meet upon the road is maimed: one has his tail docked; another wants his ears, or has both of them slit; while a third combines in his mutilated person not only these blemishes, but has lost an eye, and is perhaps lame of a leg. All such animals are "bad characters," and these punishments have been inflicted for crimes committed. When a young animal first visits a neighbour's field, a good drubbing intimates to him its owner's displeasure. Should the ass again trespass, a slit ear quickens his exit. As he grows older he becomes more wary; but few attain to old age without carrying about them signs of their youthful indiscretions. If the ill deeds of their owners had been recorded by a similar process, the mutilation would probably have been much more extensive.

Next morning, when in the act of mounting our horses, the wail of a female drew our attention to the house adjoining that in which we had slept. I walked over its roof, and, looking down through the square hole in the centre, perceived that the room was filled with women weeping for the dead. Gholam Hussein made his way into the house, and to our grief and surprise, there lay the corpse of a fellow-traveller Mohamed Amin, a young man who had accompanied us from Jerm. The nails were much discoloured, and I at once suspected foul play. The poor fellow was the native of a hamlet among the mountains, at a short distance from Yowl, and had long been attached to a girl who lived at the latter place. Her parents were averse to the marriage; and Mohamed, thinking that his poverty was the ground of their objection, left the mountains for the plain, and was now returning, after a four years' absence, with his hoarded gains. He had served during this time with Ataluk Beg, of Talikhan. Prior to our reaching Yowl, he told us his story, and solicited Abdal Ghani Yesawal to procure him an interview with his betrothed. The poor fellow wished to stay the night at her village, but could not venture to do so, unless publicly invited by the Mir's Yesawal. Abdal Ghani, promised to befriend him. On reaching Yowl Mohamed came up to our party, and, in the presence of the villagers, requested the Yesawal's permission to go on, adding that his own home was close at hand; and after so long an absence he could not think of sleeping anywhere else. Abdal Ghani, in an authoritative tone, overruled his objection, invited him to sup with our party, and added that to-morrow he might go to his home. Mohamed, with feigned reluctance, consented. The melancholy sequel has been told. The grief of the poor girl was excessive, and her parents attributed his death to poison, and roundly denounced Mirza Suliman as the guilty person. They asserted that he was known to have dong borne ill-will towards the deceased. That the guilt rested with Mirza Suliman seemed improbable, as eight and forty hours had elapsed since the young man had left Jerm. It was, however, clearly ascertained that he had drunk of the governor's tea before quitting his presence. Others traced his death to the curdled milk of which we had all liberally partaken the previous morning. Everything tended to strengthen my conviction that the poor fellow had been intentionally poisoned; but regard for our own safety restrained me from expressing that opinion.

We had not proceeded far when an aged female was seen coming down the valley. She proved to be a near relation of the deceased. Having heard of her kinsman's arrival at Yowl, she was now hastening to greet him. The poor woman's grief excited the sympathy of every one.

During the march a lead-coloured mist streaked the mountains, about a thousand feet above their base. Eagles were seen sailing over our heads; but when highest they were still below the summits of the mountains, which, in this part of the valley, reach a height of nearly 4,000 feet. The wind blew so strong, that we were forced at some places to dismount. No snow lies long on the ground. All that falls is soon whirled into the stream. Great havoc has been made by earthquakes. The appearance of one landslip in particular was singular. Though it continued to bear the dwarf trees of its native mountain, yet its surface was dotted over with small cone-like swellings, which would seem to have been caused by convulsions subsequent to that which brought it down. A ride of six and twenty miles brought us to Robat, a hamlet of seven families, where we halted for the night. Its elevation is 8,100 feet above the sea, and the valley had here assumed a very bleak appearance. The red willow and white poplar appear to be the only trees which can stand against the blast of the Bad-i-Wakhan; and even in sheltered situations there were but few fruit-bearing trees.

The frontier of Badakhshan seemed to recede as we advanced. Since the day of leaving Kunduz, the invariable reply to Abdal Ghani's grumblings about the quality of his food has been "What do you expect to get when you reach the frontier?" In these poor districts Jerm is the capital; and in Jerm it is Kunduz.

The next stage was to Ze-bak, and a cold march we had to get there. The wind fortunately had changed, or we could not have accomplished this stage. As it was, the thermometer had sunk to the 6th degree above zero; and the effect of a violent wind at this temperature in regions so elevated, has only to be felt once, to be ever afterwards dreaded. At the fifth mile from Robat, the mountains on both sides fall back, and leave a level plain, varying in width from one to two miles. Three miles farther on, is a hamlet called Gowkhanah, situated in the middle of the plain, and fronting two openings in the eastern range of mountains, one of which leads to Chitral, and the other in Kaffiristan. The former is only two days' journey from this hamlet. At Gow-khanah we tarried for some hours to warm ourselves, and made a luxurious meal on newly baked bannocks, warm butter, and kurut. This latter dish I have already commended. Its flavour somewhat resembles cheese, and it is thus prepared: when the milk is taken from the cow it is curdled; and in this state is termed Joghrat. This is churned, and the buttermilk, which is called Doagh, after being well boiled is poured into a bag of not very close texture. The whey drains off, and the clotted residue is the kurut. If it be of peculiarly good quality, no butter is extracted from the milk. Kurut is a most indispensable article in the food of these poor people. It enters into all their culinary preparations. Their soup, whether of beans or wheaten flour, is flavoured with it; and we owed to it the relish of many a meal, which would otherwise have been very poor. An alderman himself, provided he had been as cold, fatigued, and hungry as we were, must have honoured it with his approbation.

Resuming our march, we crossed the plain to the mountains on the right hand, and rode through a tangled forest of red willow trees at their base, till we came opposite Ze-bak. At one point in this range, there is evidence of extensive volcanic action. Large deposits of sulphur are also in the neighbourhood, but they were then buried deep in snow. It was late in the evening when we reached Ze-bak, which is distant fourteen miles from Robat, and is next to Jerm, the largest place in Badakhshan. It contains about fifty houses. Its site is under the western range of mountains, and is slightly elevated. The houses here, instead of standing apart in hamlets, as is customary, adjoin each other, giving to Ze-bak almost the appearance of an English village.

It continued to snow throughout the night, and when we resumed our journey the next morning, the 4th of February, it was still falling heavily. The plain, which was over-grown with willow, was in many places marshy; and it was no easy matter to prick our way onwards through the thickly grown trees, burdened as they were with snow, nor did we reach the head of the valley, a distance of ten miles, without sundry mishaps. We then crossed the southern range of mountains on our right hand, and debouched on the plain of Ish-kashm. The pass is 10,900 feet above the sea; and its crest divides the valleys of the Oxus and Kokcha. Here the eastern fork of the latter river has its rise, while on the Ish-kashm slope, the drainage falls at once into the Oxus; which can be seen from the crest of the pass, but was hidden from our eyes by the snowy mantle which covered the landscape. The Ish-kashm plain has a width of about five miles. Behind it rise, though not abruptly, the towering mountains of Chitral, while in front flows the Oxus, along the southern face of a range of hills, less high but more mural in their aspect.

Not far from Ze-bak we encountered a way-worn traveller, with the skin of a horse wrapped round his body, forcing his way through the willow bushes. He was one of a party of Badakhshis, servants of Mirza Suliman, who had taken advantage of the Oxus being frozen, to visit Darwaz, whither they had been directed to carry presents from their master. On their return the river had burst its icy fetters, and could no longer be trusted. The steep mountain banks offered no safer road, and the party went back to Darwaz, where they would be obliged to remain till the summer sun opens the passes into Badakhshan. The individual whom we met, was, however, determined to persevere; and he succeeded, though at the expense of his horse, which he had been obliged to sacrifice to save himself.

Hardly had this singularly clad traveller passed us, when we fell in with a number of Ish-kashm horsemen, the chief of whom, when informed of our destination, reined in his horse, and told us that he and his companions were just returned from the ruby mines. He had been sent by Murad Beg to collect the annual tribute at Gharan, a place consisting of a fort and a few hamlets in the vicinity of the mines. On coming upon the Oxus at Ish-kashm, they found the river no longer frozen; and the road down its banks being impracticable to horsemen, they dismounted at that village, and performed the remainder of the journey on foot. The tribute was received in kind as usual, and they set out on their return. More snow had, however, fallen in the interim, the road was obliterated, and what was still

[227]

worse, avalanches repeatedly rushed down from the mountains into the river below. The party was separated into three divisions. One went forward to track out the road; a second carried the tribute and took care of the live-stock, while he himself with the third brought up the rear. Four days before we met him, and whilst at the distance of six miles from Ish-kashm, as they were proceeding in this order he saw, on casually looking upwards, what appeared to him a sheet of mist rolling down the mountain-side. He was not long left in uncertainty as to its real nature: down came the avalanche with the roar of thunder, carrying with it into the Oxus, the whole of the centre division. Nothing more was seen of them or their charge; every man, every animal, was in an instant overwhelmed and destroyed. The other land parties reached Ish- kashm in safety but several of the men had been severely frostbitten. One poor fellow who rode beside the chief, had lost an arm.

At Ish-kashm we crossed the Oxus, here thirty-five yards wide, upon the ice, or rather upon bridges of frozen snow; and upon these we attempted to continue our route down the river, but we had not proceeded far before the slender covering we trode upon, gave us warning of its instability. The river when lowest had been firmly ice-bound; but being already on the increase, it had burst its winter fetters, and though it might still be crossed, it was upon irregular masses of snow and ice heaped together, and not upon solid ice. The mountains in which the mines are situated, were in sight, but however much I regretted turning back when the object of my journey was so nearly attained, there was no alternative. To proceed by the river was impossible; and had I been inclined to attempt the road along its banks, which I certainly did not think myself justified in doing, the melancholy fate of the Mir's party had so dispirited the men of Ish-kashm, that no offers of remuneration, however large, would have induced them to volunteer their services as guides.

The ruby mines are within twenty miles of Ish-kashm, in a district called Gharan, which word signifies caves or mines, and on the right bank of the river Oxus. They face the stream, and their entrance is said to be 1,200 feet above its level. The formation of the mountain is either red sandstone or limestone largely impregnated with magnesia. The mines are easily worked, the operation being more like digging a hole in sand, than quarrying rocks. Above Ish-kashm the water of the Oxus is beautifully transparent, but after issuing from the mountains below Darwaz, it is of a dirty red colour. The galleries are described as being numerous, and running directly in from the river. The labourers are greatly incommoded by water filtering into the mine from above, and by the smoke from their lamps, for which there is no exit. Wherever a seam or whitish blotch is discovered, the miners set to work; and when a ruby is found it is always encased in a round nodule of considerable size. The mines have not been worked since Badakhshan fell into the hands of the Kunduz chief, who, irritated, it is supposed, at the small profit they yielded, marched the inhabitants of the district, then numbering about five hundred families, to Kunduz, and disposed of them in the slave market. The inhabitants of Gharan were Rafizies, or Shiah Mohamedans, and so are the few families which still remain there.

Chapter XX

Disappointed in one object of my journey, I turned with increased ardour to the other; and despite the remonstrances and croakings of Abdal Ghani, resolved to trace the Oxus to its source. The ease with which we had crossed the Pass of Ish-kashm, seemed to presage success; and the winter was now sufficiently advanced to enable us to determine with some degree of confidence whether it would be mild or severe. Appearances spoke favourably; and we resumed our upward march along the left bank of the river. The Yesawal, thinking to shake my resolution, refused to be of the party, left the house where we lodged, and took up his quarters in another. High words had before passed between us; and he chose this opportunity of showing his resentment. Our misunderstanding arose out of my anxiety to prevent as much as possible the system of extortion which he practised in every wretched hamlet on our route. He never entered a place without proclaiming his dignity, and demanding something in the Mir's name, threatening those who refused, and making large promises to others who were more compliant. I had often before remonstrated with him on this subject, and had even promised to indemnify him for any loss he might sustain by abandoning a line of conduct that could not fail to compromise our good name. For a time he appeared to accede to my request, but his self-denial was not proof against the temptation of a pair of worsted stockings, or a woollen cloak; things which the poor families who were his victims, could ill afford to part with. The secret system of plunder which he henceforward adopted, was even more detestable than the open one which he abandoned. I again remonstrated with him, but to no better purpose. It was, he said, the custom of the country, and with such I had better not interfere; that he knew his duty, and that I should find I could not do without him. Abdal Ghani spoke the truth: for no sooner was it known that we had quarrelled, than food grew scarce, and guides were not to be had. Without the Yesawal's consent, no man would take a letter which I had written to Mirza Suliman, detailing our difficulties, and soliciting that instructions might be given to the chief of Ish-kashm, to send a trustworthy person with us into Wakhan, to the chief of which district I was accredited by Murad Beg. Seeing how completely we were in this man's power, I deemed it prudent to compromise the matter, and we left Ish-kashm as good friends as ever; and likely to continue so, since beyond that town, the authority of Murad Beg is little reverenced; and I soon found that the Yesawal no longer dared even to hint at the perquisites due to his office.

Proceeding up the valley of the Oxus, with the mountains of Shakh Durah on our left hand, and those of Chitral on our right, both rising to a vast height, and bearing far below their summits the snow of ages, we arrived early in the afternoon at the hamlet of Ishtrakh, having before passed Kila Khoja and Pullu, the first inhabited places since we entered Wakhan. We reached the village in the middle of a heavy snow-fall; and its houses built amongst fractured pieces of the neighbouring mountains, must have been passed unnoticed, but for a Yak or Kash-gow, as the animal is here called, standing before a door with its bridle in the hand of a Kirghiz boy. There was something so novel in its appearance, that I could not resist the impulse of mounting so strange a steed; but in doing so I met with stout resistance from the little fellow who had it in charge. In the midst of our dispute the boy's mother made her appearance, and very kindly permitted me to try the animal's paces. It stood about three feet and a half high, was very hairy and powerful. Its belly reached within six inches of the ground, which was swept by its bushy tail. The long hair streamed down from its dewlap and fore legs, giving it, but for the horns, the appearance of a huge Newfoundland dog. It bore a light saddle with horn stirrups; and a cord let through the cartilage of the nose, served for a bridle. The good Kirghiz matron was not a less interesting object than her steed. She was diminutive in stature, but active and strong, and wore some half dozen petticoats under a showy blue striped gown, the whole sitting close to her person, and held there, not by ribbons, but by a stout leather belt about the waist. Her rosy cheeks and Chinese countenance, were seen from under a high white starched tiara, while broad bands of the same colour protected the ears, mouth, and chin. Worsted gloves covered her hands, and the feet were equally well taken care of. She chid her son for not permitting me to mount the kash-gow; and I quite won the good woman's heart by praising the lad's spirit, and hanging a string of beads about his neck. Strutting up to her steed with the air of an Amazon, she emptied the flour she had obtained at the village, into her koorgeens, took the bridle out of her son's hand, and vaulted astride into the saddle. The sight appeared to be new, not only to us, but to the inhabitants of Wakhan; for the villagers had thronged round to see her depart. They enquired if she would not take the boy up behind her? "O no," was her answer, "he can walk." As the mother and son left us, a droll-looking calf leisurely trode after its dam; and when the party disappeared amid the falling snow-flakes, the rugged, half-clad Wakhanis exclaimed, as if taken by surprise, "None but a Kirghiz boy could thrive under such rough treatment."

The yak is to the inhabitants of Tibet and Pamir, what the reindeer is to the Laplander in northern Europe.

Where a man can walk a kash-gow may be ridden. Like the elephant, he possesses a wonderful knowledge of what will bear his weight. If travellers are at fault, one of these animals is driven before them, and it is said that he avoids the hidden depths and chasms with admirable sagacity. His footing is sure. Should a fall of snow close a mountain pass to man and horse, a score of yaks driven a-head answer the purpose of pioneers, and make, as my informant expresses it, "a king's highway." In this case, however, the snow must have recently fallen; for when once its surface is frozen and its depth considerable, no animal can force its way through it. Other cattle require the provident care of man to subsist them through the winter. The most hardy sheep would fare but badly without its human protection, but the kash-gow is left entirely to itself. He frequents the mountain slopes and their level summits. Wherever the mercury does not rise above zero, is a climate for the yak. If the snow on the elevated flats lie too deep for him to crop the herbage, he rolls himself down the slopes and eats his way up again. When arrived at the top, he performs a second summerset, and completes his meal as he displaces another groove of snow in his second ascent. The heat of summer sends the animal to what is termed the old ice, that is to the regions of eternal snow; the calf being retained below as a pledge for the mother's returning, in which she never fails. In the summer, the women, like the pastoral inhabitants of the Alps, encamp in the higher valleys, which are interspersed among the snowy mountains, and devote their whole time to the dairy. The men remain on the plain, and attend to the agricultural part of the establishment, but occasionally visit the upper stations; and all speak in rapture of these summer wanderings. The kash-gows are gregarious, and set the wolves, which here abound, at defiance. Their hair is clipped once a year in the spring. The tail is the well-known Chowry of Hindustan; but in this country, its strong, wiry, and pliant hair is made into ropes, which, for strength, do not yield to those manufactured from hemp. The hair of the body is woven into mats, and also into a strong fabric which makes excellent riding trousers. The milk of the yak is richer than that of the common cow, though the quantity it yields be less. The kurut made from it is considered to be first rate, even superior to the produce of the Kohistan of Kabul, which has great celebrity in Afghanistan. The Kirghiz never extract the butter.

The first yaks we saw were grazing among the snow on the very summit of the rugged pass of Ish-kashm, and at the village of this name, I procured one for Dr. Lord, and despatched it to Kunduz in charge of two trusty men. But so cold a climate do these singular animals require, that though winter still reigned in the Kunduz plain, the heat was too great, and the yak died within a march or two of the town. In fact it began to droop as soon as it had passed Jerm. Some years back, an Afghan nobleman succeeded in bringing two or three of these animals to Kabul, but even the temperature of that city, though situated 6,000 feet above sea-level, is not sufficiently cold to suit their constitution. They declined as the snow left the ground, and died early in the spring.

At Ishtrakh, a rivulet from the Chitral mountain falls into the Oxus, by following up the course of which, a man on foot in the summer months may reach the seat of Shah Kittore, ruler of Chitral, on the third day. We now learned that the valley of the Oxus, for some distance upwards, was uninhabited, and the wind was too strong and keen for us to attempt to bivouac on its unsheltered surface unless compelled by necessity. So we set off at midnight, and reached Kundut, the residence of Shah Turai, after a cold ride of forty miles, and having been thirteen hours in the saddle. This monarch of fifteen families gave us a warmer reception than the poverty of his capital had prepared us to expect. A large fire soon blazed upon the hearth of the best house it contained, and his subjects being convened, I was paraded round it, to refute the assertion of a wandering callender (fakir) from Jumbo in the Himalaya

[234]

mountains, who, it seems, had persuaded the credulous Wakhanis that the Firingis were a nation of dwarfs.

The valley of the Oxus from Ish-kashm, where we first came upon the river, to Kundut, varies from a few hundred yards to a mile in width. As we drew near the fort and hamlet of Shah Turai, the ground became more and more level, and the river, dividing into many channels, meandered over a sandy bed, studded with numberless islets, which were thickly covered with an under-growth of red willow-trees. In passing through one of these copses, our dog started a hare, the only living thing we saw between Ishtrakh and Kundut.

The houses at Kundut are clustered about the fort like so many cells in a bee-hive. We discovered that the holes in their roofs, besides giving vent to the smoke, perform the office of sun-dials, and when the sun is shining indicate the hour of the day. Before the housewife begins to prepare the family meal, she looks not up at a clock, but round the walls or upon the floor for the spot on which his golden light is streaming. The seasons also are marked by the same means; for when the sun's rays, through this aperture, reach one particular point, it is seed time.

Taking leave of Shah Turai, we resumed our journey up the valley, but had not proceeded far when the barking of dogs and the sight of yaks, camels, and sheep, roaming over the plain, told of a pastoral people being in the neighbourhood, and soon after we came upon a Kirghiz encampment. Anxious to see this nomade race, we struck off towards their bee-hive looking tents, but the fierce dogs prowling round kept us at bay until we managed to out-howl them, and succeeded in making ourselves heard by their masters. As we entered among the kirgahs or tents, the spaces between them were seen to be thronged by ewes, children, and dogs. The horde consisted of 100 families, and possessed about 2,000 yaks, 4,000 sheep, and 1,000 camels; not the ugly-looking camel of Arabia, but that species known as Bactrian, and which, to all the useful qualities of the former, adds a majestic port that no animal but the horse can surpass. This was the first year of their abode in Wakhan, and the only instance of the Kirghiz having made this district their winter quarters. They had been solicited to do so by the Uzbeks of Kunduz, with whom the Kirghiz profess to he connected by blood. The two people are evidently of the same stock, though the effects of location, or, in other words, the difference between a temperate and a rigorous climate is observable in the well proportioned frame of the Uzbek and in the stunted growth of the Kirghiz.

The arrival of strangers was an important event to the horde. Each kirgah poured forth its male inmates, and all clustered round our little party to hear the news of Kunduz. More rugged, weather-beaten faces I had never seen; they had, however, the hue of health. Their small sunken eyes were just visible, peeping from beneath fur-caps, while the folds of a snug woollen comforter concealed their paucity of beard. The clothing of most of them consisted of a sheep's skin, with the wool inside; but some wore good coloured cotton chupkuns. Snuff was more in demand with them than tobacco; but to satisfy the craving desires of such voracious snuff-takers would have required a larger stock of Irish blackguard than we had brought of charcoal. On presenting my box to the chief of the horde, he quietly emptied half its contents into the palm of his hand, then opening his mouth and holding his head back, at two gulps he swallowed the whole. Our boxes were soon emptied, for none of them were contented with a pinch or two for the nose. In this bad habit the Uzbeks likewise indulged, but not to the extent of their relatives the Kirghiz. The latter have invariably bad teeth; many even of their young men are nearly toothless. This they attributed to the coldness of the water they are obliged to drink, but I should imagine that the snuff had a good deal to do with it.

We now asked permission to rest awhile in one of their kirgahs, and were immediately led up to one of the best in the encampment. Its outside covering was formed of coarse dun-coloured felts, held down by two broad white belts about five feet above the ground. To these the dome or roof was secured by diagonal bands, while the felts which formed the walls were strengthened by other bands, which descended in a zig-zag direction between those first mentioned and the ground. Close to the door lay a bag filled with ice—the water of the family. On drawing aside the felt which screened the entrance, the air of tidiness and comfort that met our eyes was a most agreeable surprise. In the middle of the floor, upon a light iron tripod, stood a huge Russian caldron, beneath which glowed a cheerful fire, which a ruddy-cheeked, spruce damsel kept feeding with fuel, and occasionally throwing a lump of ice into her cookery. She modestly beckoned us to be seated, and continued her household duties unembarrassed by the presence of strangers. If unable to praise the men of the Kirghiz for their good looks, I may, without flattery, pronounce the young women pretty. All have the glow of health in their cheeks, and though they have the harsh features of the race, there is a softness about their lineaments, a coyness and maidenly reserve in their demeanour, that contrasts strongly and most agreeably with the uncouth figures and harsh manners of the men.

The kirgah had a diameter of fourteen feet, a height of eight, and was well lighted by a circular hole above the fireplace. Its frame-work was of the willow-tree, but between it and the felt covering, neat mats, made of reeds, the size of wheat-straw, and knitted over with coloured worsted, were inserted. The sides of the tent, lined with variegated mats of this description, not only looked tasteful, but imparted a snug and warm appearance to the interior. Corresponding to the outside belts were two within of a finer description, and adorned with needle-work. From these were suspended various articles appertaining to the tent and to the field, besides those of ornament and the sampler. Saddles, bridles, rings, thimbles, and beads, all had here their appropriate places. One side of the kirgah had the family's spare clothes and bedding. In another, a home-made carpet hung from the roof, making a recess in which the females dressed, and where the matron kept her culinary stores and kitchen apparatus. The opposite segment was allotted to the young lambs of the flock. A string crossed the tent to which fifty nooses, twenty-five of a side, were attached, to each of which a lamb was fastened. While we were present, they were taken outside to their dams, and after a time again brought back into the kirgah.

Three yaks are able to carry the tent and all its contents. One takes the oostakhan, literally the bones or frame-work, another the felts, and a third its furniture; besides which, a seat is found upon them for the feeble or young of the family. In one kirgah which we entered, the children were conning their lessons under the eye of an aged mullah. Some were learning to write, by tracing letters upon a black board with a bit of chalk, while others were humming over the torn leaves of well-thumbed copies of the Koran. Mutilated as was the condition of their books, they were nevertheless highly valued, if we might judge from the strong wooden box appropriated to their preservation. Where the thirst for instruction appeared to be so keen I could not help wishing there had been better means for its gratification and a safer guide than the Koran.

Continuing our march, a ride of twenty-four miles brought us to Kila Panj, where we crossed the Oxus, and then held on along its right bank to Issar, a village within sight of the fort. Kila Pani is so called from five small rocky hillocks in the neighbourhood, upon all of which there were formerly tenements. One of these hillocks rises immediately from the stream, its surface is covered with houses, and it is crested by a fort in tolerable preservation. A murder was committed in this place seven years ago, and although the criminal had up to this time escaped punishment, vengeance, as the sequel of my narrative will show, at length overtook him; but, unfortunately, in a manner more calculated to excite to other atrocities than to satisfy the ends of justice. It appears that the chief ot Wakhan, Mohamed Rahim Khan, had suffered greatly from the exactions of the Badakhshi ruler Kokan Beg, and at length, rendered desperate, refused to pay tribute. Immediately Kokan Beg carried fire and sword into his territories. The Wakhanis were eventually worsted, and took refuge in Chitral; but their chief threw himself into Kila Panj, and defended it until an amicable arrangement was agreed to by the two leaders, on which Kokan Beg, confiding in the honour of his opponent, entered his castle, and was immediately slain. The Badakhshis, disheartened at the loss of their leader, withdrew, and the exiled Wakhanis returned to their homes. From that time the loyalty of Mohamed Rahim Khan was considered more than doubtful, and though nominally tributary to Kunduz, he was virtually independent. Sometimes, indeed, to ward off a threatened visit from Murad Beg, he would send him an inconsiderable tribute. Distance and poverty had hitherto been his security; but even these would not much longer have availed him, had it not been for the military movements of Bakhara on the Kunduz frontier. When Murad Beg placed in the hands of Mirza Baddi, our letter of introduction to Mohamed Rahim, he observed that he would not be answerable for our reception in Wakhan, since its chieftain had for two years discontinued communicating with himself, which looked like rebellion.

The valley of the Oxus continued level, about a mile wide, grassy in some places, and though far from fertile, improved in appearance as we proceeded. By the bank of the river and among the willow copses, there was considerable herbage; but the mountains offered none, nor did the plain in their neighbourhood. The river flowed slowly, its velocity scarcely exceeding three miles and a half an hour. Where we crossed it, the stream was split into two channels, one of which, twenty-seven yards broad, was two feet deep; the other was wider by ten yards, but so shallow that our dog crossed it without swimming. The mountains forming the valley had decreased in height at Issar; those on the Chitral side were, however, still lofty. Before entering Issar, we passed a mineral spring about 800 feet up the mountain on the right bank of the river. The ground over which it ran had a ferruginous appearance, but the water was tasteless—its temperature was 116°.

The valley of the Oxus may be said to terminate at Issar, to which point from Ish-kashm, in latitude 36° 42' 32" N., its direction is E. by N. ½ N. The latitude of Issar is 37° 02' 10" N., and its height above the sea 10,000 feet. Here the main valley divides into two, which, when a little beyond Kila Panj, bore respectively E. 20° S. and N. 40° E. The former, we were told, conducted into Chitral, Gilgit, and Kashmir, and the latter across the table-land of Pamir to Yarkand. I had now to ascertain, if possible, which of the two streams I was to trace. One of them, it was certain, must lead to the source of the Oxus, but which of the two was a question of difficulty. The Kirghiz had unhesitatingly told us that the object of our search was to be found in a lake upon the "Bam-i-duniah," or Roof of the World, in Pamir, and that the road to it was up the durah or Sir-i-kol; but though the northerly direction of that valley and of the countries to which it led was, when compared with the Mastuch, as the Chitral durah is sometimes called, almost sufficient evidence in favour of Sir-i-kol, I thought it prudent to visit the junction of their respective waters. To my eye the stream of Sirhad, as the river from Mastuch is frequently called, appeared the larger, but the Wakhanis held a different opinion. That from Pamir was divided into several channels, and frozen, so that its aggregate volume could not be well ascertained; though from a clearing in its principal stream I inferred its velocity to be double that of the Sirhad, while its temperature was five degrees lower, being 32°, and that of the other 37°. It seemed a singular circumstance, but certainly confirmatory of the superior height of the source of the river of Pamir to that of the other stream, that it should

[240]

be sheeted with ice to the very point of their junction, whilst the Sirhad was unfettered by the frost, and had a slower current and a higher temperature. According to my informant, the Pamir branch in summer brings down much more water than the Sirhad, though the latter has many tributaries and the former but two trifling rills—those of Langer Kish and Zerzumen. Among the rivulets that pay tribute to the Sirhad is Pir-khar, a name of note in the geography of these regions, since Macartney, with his usual discernment, had supposed it to be the fountain head of the Oxus; and we see how closely he approximated to the truth. Indeed, none but those who have travelled in the countries he mapped, almost entirely from native information, can duly appreciate the labours of that talented and deeply to be regretted officer.

Since crossing the pass of Ish-kashm, we had seen the ruins of three Kaffir forts, which the natives believe to have been erected by the Guebers or Fire-worshippers, one called Sumri, in the neighbourhood of Kundut; another in the vicinity of Ishtrakh, named Kakah; and the last, Kila Zanguebar, close to the hamlet of Issar. I have elsewhere mentioned the repugnance with which a Badakhshi blows out a light. Similar lingering remnants of Zoroaster's creed are to be detected here. A Wakhani considers it bad luck to blow out a light by the breath, and will rather wave his hand for several minutes under the flame of his pine-slip, than resort to the sure, but to him disagreeable alternative.

Before reaching Issar, I had sent Abdal Ghani forward to inform Mohamed Rahim Khan of our arrival, and to deliver the Mir's letter, together with sundry trifling presents in my own name. The chief, who lived about ten miles up the Mastuch valley, did not make his appearance till the second day, and when he did, he was equipped for a journey to Kunduz, and not, as we expected, for the purpose of guiding us to Pamir. It appeared, however, that this journey to Kunduz had been contemplated for some time back, and doubts as to the reception he should meet with from Murad Beg had alone kept him from undertaking it before. He had now procured a few Bactrian camels from his new neighbours the Kirghiz; a chuppow on Shakh Durah had enabled him to add a number of slaves to his present, and with this propitiatory offering he was on the eve of starting, when Abdal Ghani reached his residence. On finding Mohamed Rahim Khan had no intention to accompany us, I spoke my mind plainly to him; any affectation of ignorance on my part as to the real state of things would have been perfectly useless, since what had been only whispered in Kunduz was notorious here; and the disaffection of the chief was openly encouraged by his people. It is true the Mir, with proper caution, had made no mention in his letters of the suspicions to which the Wakhan chief's conduct had given rise; but, on the contrary, professed the fullest confidence in his loyalty. He was directed to accompany us in person with twenty horsemen, to protect our party from the Kirghiz, and he was told that his honourable treatment of us would be considered by the Mir as kindness shown to himself, for, said Murad Beg, "they are my guests;' and the Uzbek did not omit to add, that were a hair of our beards injured, he would annihilate his power in Wakhan—"Beikh Mekushum," literally, he would uproot him. I argued the point at great length with the chief, and pointed out to him, that if he really intended a visit to Kunduz, it would be a wiser course first to execute the Mir's commands, and by so doing entitle himself to a favourable reception, rather than by spurning his authority on such an occasion to add to his resentment. The letter, as he saw, described me as an honoured guest of the Mir, and that it therefore behoved him, for his own sake, to be exceedingly careful how he acted in opposition to his wishes. We were, moreover, foreigners, in all transactions with whom, as he must be well aware, the Mir was particularly jealous of his honour, and would be certain deeply to feel and to resent conduct that could not fail to lower him in the estimation of strangers. Mohamed Rahim was on the point of yielding, when Abdal Ghani drew me aside, and declared in the most positive terms, that if the chief accompanied us, he, the Mir's Yesawal, would not. Knowing, as I did, that he had been fully instructed in Murad Beg's wishes on the subject, I was greatly astounded at this announcement, but restraining my indignation, I merely told him that as he was no doubt fatigued, and could not partake of the feelings which actuated me to undertake the journey, I conceived the arrangement he proposed was judicious, and that he had permission to remain. This did not satisfy the Yesawal. He now motioned to the chief to go out of doors with him. What passed between them I know not, but on their re-entering the house the whole affair was arranged—Mohamed Rahim was to go on to Kunduz, and the person who was to be his representative during his absence, was to accompany us. In vain did I try to persuade the chief that this arrangement would highly incense the Mir. Backed by the Yesawal, and urged on by his own dogged resolution, Mohamed Rahim laughed at my admonitions, and with his half savage escort of armed, skin-clad followers, set out for the plains, from which he was doomed never to return. No sooner was he gone than Abdal Ghani stigmatized him as every thing that was vile; said that he had even been so mean as to refuse a feed of barley for his horse, and that he trusted the Mir would not only punish him, but chuppow Wakhan, and make slaves of every soul it contained.

Mohamed Rahim's locum tenens was now called upon for the mounted guard, but he could only furnish two horses and five men on foot. No others would volunteer to be of the party, and the vice governor lacked authority to compel them. In this extremity I turned my thoughts to the Kirghiz, and though these were the very people whose aggression we feared, I resolved to adopt towards them a policy not often unsuccessful with barbarous nations—namely, the reposing implicit confidence in those you dread. I sent a messenger down to their encampment with a letter to their chief, requesting that he would permit a few of his young men to be of our party to Pamir, for that the Wakhanis were not much to be trusted, and were, besides, ignorant of the road. I promised a handsome chupkun to each man, and the letter was backed by the present of a mukhmul, or velvet pelisse, for himself. The arrival next day of five mounted and armed Kirghiz gladdened our hearts; they joined us at Langer Kish, a village at the entrance of the Sir-i-kol-durah, to which in the interim we had removed.

The Kirghiz, like the Kazaks, are a pastoral and nomadic race, inhabiting the steppes of central Asia, and both are termed Mongolian by the writers on the varieties of the human species. The Kazaks range the low-lying plains between the vast empires of Russia and China. The Kirghiz domain is the table-land of Pamir, which, buttressed by Tibet, slopes northward upon Kokan, having the Chinese territories to the east, and the rugged country that feeds the rivers Oxus and Sirr to the west. Their language does not differ, or only in a trifling degree, from that spoken in Kunduz. They acknowledge allegiance to Kokan, and pay tribute to its ruler; but with China and Tibet they are constantly at feud, or, what is much the same thing, rob all parties from either country whom they can overpower. They are, if what we have heard of them in Wakhan be true, notorious plunderers, pusillanimous, and faithless. No one trusts a Kirghiz escort; and they repay this want of confidence by rifling every Yarkand caravan they can master. A horde, at the instigation of the Kokan chief, sometimes migrates to Tibet for the sole purpose of waylaying the Yarkand trader. The Chinese, therefore, as might be expected, detest the race, and their authorities consider them all equally criminal, and put them to death wherever found. The Kirghiz, on the other hand, hold the subjects of the celestial empire in abhorrence, pronouncing them Kaffirs and bad men. Such inveterate thieves are the Kirghiz, that robberies often occur, not only in a horde, but in its smallest sub-divisions. If one man be robbed, he retaliates on his next door neighbour. Their Bais, or chiefs, have little power over them for good or evil. In consideration of their age and blood, some deference to their opinions is shown, but nothing more.

In stature the Kirghiz are under the middle size. Of a Kyl numbering seven men whom I measured, the tallest stood five feet five and a half inches—the shortest five feet two inches. Their countenance is disagreeable: the upper part of the nose sinks into the face, leaving the space between their deep-seated and elongated eyes without the usual dividing ridge; the brow immediately above the eye is protuberant, but slants back more abruptly than in Europeans; their cheeks, large and bloated, look as if pieces of flesh had been daubed upon them; a slender beard covers the chin, and with those individuals who have a more luxuriant growth of hair, both beard and whiskers have a close natural curl; their persons are not muscular, and then complexion is darkened by exposure in all weathers, rather than by the sun. This description does not apply to the Kirghiz women, whom, as I have before said, are rather good looking. They resemble the Hazara females in their small and delicate form, and, like them, too, seem more calculated for a genial clime than for the stern one they inhabit. Though Suni Mohamedans, they go unveiled, and have quite as much liberty as women have with us. They are modest, but like most of their sex, have a prying curiosity and a craving for dress. At our request they took their ornaments off, and permitted us to examine them. Beads of black and red coral were in the highest estimation, though some had them of stained glass. Others wore gems rudely set in silver, brass ornaments and fanciful decorations carved out of the pearl oyster shell. Both sexes wore round hollow brass buttons about their clothes All these articles were obtained from the Chinese. The high head-dress of the women resembles a white paste-board crown, and when the coquette ties a coloured band in front, her look is queenly. They appear to make good wives. All we saw were attentive to the comforts of their domestic circle and if the thimble was not on the finger, it, and the other implements of knitting and sewing, were seen hanging from the walls of the kirgah. Slaves are not common among this people, though they have, like European families, maid servants. With the Kirghiz, a daughter is more desired than a son. Their flocks and herds, though large, do not require many men to manage them; and as they never cultivate the earth, but are continually on the march, an excess of profitless mouths is not desirable where food is not over abundant. But for a daughter a large sum is obtained— often as much as £40, if she be not above fifteen years of age. On a husband's death the wife goes to his brother, and on his decease becomes the property of the next of kin, failing which she returns to her father's kirgah. Should a stranger take the widow to wife, a blood feud is inevitable. Both sexes, but especially the women, suffer from cutaneous disease.

The Kirghiz may be said to subsist chiefly on milk and its various preparations, the produce of their herds and flocks. What flesh they consume is obtained by their matchlocks; and the number of horns that strew Pamir bear evidence to the havoc they make among the wild flocks of the mountain. These horns, being of a remarkably large size, supply shoes for the horses' feet, and are also a good substitute for stirrup irons. The shoes are nothing more than a semi-circular piece of horn placed on the fore part of the hoof. When the horse is in constant work, it requires renewal at least once a week. I had been led to entertain much too high an opinion of Kirghiz horses. They are rough-coated, ill-looking animals, incapable of standing great fatigue. A Kattaghan galloway of Kunduz will do double the work of a Kirghiz pony. The horse of the Kazak is quite another animal. What his useful qualities may be I know not; but for beauty, as far as it consists in his shaggy coat, he is unique. Neither goats nor the common cow are domesticated by the Kirghiz, the continued cold of winter being too severe for them to thrive. I have already mentioned the yaks and camels; the latter is a very handsome animal. In their own native region it may be a question which is the most useful; but, like man, the camel adapts himself to circumstances, and consequently is by far the most valuable, being equally well calculated to move across burning sands or frozen steppes. The Kirghiz, as well as the Uzbeks, keep brood mares, according to their means, and the acidulated milk of these animals yields them in spring the intoxicating liquor called kimiz. If the milk be taken from the mare in the evening, it is churned till sunrise, by which time it is ready for drinking. A spoonful will produce inebrity, but their kashuk or spoon is much more capacious than the largest upon our tables. They assert that when the intoxicating effect has worn off, the appetite is increased and the general health improved. I was told that when this fermented beverage is in season, the encampment of a horde is a scene of the grossest vice and sensuality; that the men give loose to their passions without restraint, and that the barriers of consanguinity are disregarded. The charge is a grave one, and I therefore should add that it was brought against them by men who were not friends to the Kirghiz.

Their principal men affix the title of Bai to their names, as Kurban Kuli Bai, for example. It has the same signification as Khan with the Afghans; that is, a nobleman. Their influence is more patriarchal than despotic, and seldom otherwise exercised than in collecting tribute for the government, and supporting the interests of their respective hordes. The total number of Kirgahs under Kokan is estimated at 100,000.

They were converted from the Shamanian superstition to Mohamedanism early in the seventeenth century. The former belief, if I may credit Abdal Ghani, is not yet thoroughly eradicated; though in our intercourse with the people, they seemed like all proselytes to erring creeds, to be filled with the most abject reverence for their new doctrines.

In summer the hordes split into parties, and fix themselves in the shallow valleys of the Table-land and in the Alpine glens, where pasturage and water are abundant. Lake Sir-i-kol is one of their most favourite haunts; and in that joyous season its waters are margined by groups of kirgahs. As the departure of the water-fowl gives signs of approaching winter, the Kirghiz seek a somewhat lower station; and again and again shifting their ground, as the weather becomes more severe, at length reach the spot destined for their winter's encampment. This is usually a rough valley, partly sheltered by snowy mountains, among which their yaks may roll and trample, while the other less hardy animals pick up a scanty subsistence on the spots of ground in the plain which the wind has cleared of snow, or on the borders of its ice-bound streams. Most of the Kirghiz annually drive their flocks down the inclined plane of Pamir to Kokhan, and camping near that city, procure by barter various articles of use or ornament for their next migratory campaign.

The Kazaks resemble the Kirghiz in personal appearance, if we may give credence to the latter, except that their necks are thicker and their ears more pendant. The same authority gives them a character of great simplicity; and if all the laughable stories which the Kirghiz tell of them be correct, they are in truth the Johnny Raws of Central Asia; though even when so viewed, their ingenuousness and freedom from guile render their character infinitely more winning than that of the people who make merry at their expense. Among the stories told by the Kirghiz of these "children of the desert," is that of a Kazak who, on his first visit to Bokhara, saw a man on the top of a lofty minaret, giving the Azan, and reminding the faithful that the hour of prayer had arrived, and calling upon every one to kneel and pray. The Kazak, ignorant of the language and usages of Mohamedans, pitied the Mullah in his forlorn situation, and remarked as he passed along, "Poor man, why climb up where it is so difficult to come down." Next year the honest Kazak revisited the holy city, and at the same hour again heard the same sound issuing from the tall turret; he looked up, and, espying the identical individual of the bygone year, gave utterance to his astonishment with a vehemence and grotesqueness of expression which has never been forgotten.

Another story is that of a chief, who, with his people, wishing to become children of circumcision, sent a messenger to Kokan to purchase prayers for the horde. Unfortunately for the interests of Mohamedanism, the person to whom this grave commission was entrusted, fell into the hands of a droll, merry fellow, one who well knew the people with whom he had to do. A jar carefully covered, containing a swarm of bees, was delivered to the dull Kazak, with instructions to his chief not to open it till all the head men of the horde were assembled. He was further told to select the largest tent for this purpose, to close it up from the gaze of the vulgar, and when all present were undressed, to place the jar upon a fire and remove its covering. The chief conformed most exactly to the directions, and all the party accordingly suffered as the wag intended. The chief himself, literally stung to madness, swore that never again should a Mussulman's prayer issue from a Kazak kirgah.

Chapter XXI

After mustering our escort before the door of the Aksikhail of Langer Kish, we mounted our sturdy hill poneys, and having received the "God-speed" of the half savage Wakhanis, struck into the durah of Sir-i-kol. While awaiting the Kirghiz arrival, we had made sundry alterations in our dress, which, however expedient, were certainly not to the improvement of our personal appearance; and as we moved out of the village in single file, I could not help smiling at my Esquimaux-looking body-guard. The Munshi, in particular, was so hampered up with worsted cloaks, that his arms were all but useless; and his short legs had scarcely action enough to keep him on his horse. In addition to the load of clothing with which each had burdened his steed, the animals carried eight days' food for their riders and for themselves, as well as some firewood.

The mountains forming the defile were not very lofty, nor were their sides precipitous; they appeared to have been broken down to abrupt declivities, either by frost and the vicissitudes of weather, or by subterranean convulsions; and amid their dislocated fragments ran the snow-wreathed stream we had come so far to trace.

About three hours after starting we arrived on the brink of a deep chasm that crossed our track, in passing over which we met with considerable delay. Its slippery sides constituted the principal difficulty, and it was not without risk that we got the horses across. The Yarkand caravan is frequently interrupted at this place, and its merchandise is obliged to be transferred from the camel's back to that of the yak. After getting clear of the ravine, we pushed on at as rapid a pace as the depth of snow permitted; and some time before the day closed in, selected a spot on which to bivouac for the night. It was the summit of an unsheltered knoll, free from snow, the only place within sight which was so; in return for which exemption it was swept by every breath of wind that moved either up or down the durah. It was, however, calm when we alighted. The wooden saddles of our steeds and the bags of charcoal were disposed in a circle, within which, with our feet to the fire, each man took his station. The kettle soon sang upon the red embers, and the koor-geens having been opened, we had begun to feast and make merry, when an ill-natured gust came howling down the valley, and destroyed at once our fire and our good humour. The latter we soon recovered, but all our coaxing failed for a long time to rekindle the former. The patient labours of the Kirghiz were at length successful, and before long the tea cup had gone its rounds, infusing a warmth into our frames, and a glow into our hearts that made us, I dare say, happier than many a party who were at that moment quaffing their claret, and surrounded with all the luxuries of civilised life. But all happiness is comparative, and I must confess, that when at the best we were not lying upon a bed of roses, nor was the moaning wintry wind particularly soothing to the ear, nor the biting cold very grateful to the person. The feet were the great sufferers; they were like lead, and when it is so with the extremities, it is no use caring for the body. So peeling stocking after stocking, we toasted our feet into a comfortable burning warmth, and having settled the necessary dispositions for the night, each made his own arrangements to pass it as best he could. Thanks to my good horse and his furniture, I got through it tolerably well, but Abdal Ghani and two Afghans suffered so severely that I was compelled to send them back to

Langer Kish in the morning. Our thermometers were only graduated down to +6° of Fahrenheit; and as the mercury had sunk into the bulb, it was not in my power to register the exact degree of cold; it was, however, intense, and the highly rarified state of the atmosphere caused it to be the more severely felt. The height of this halting place was 12,000 feet above the sea.

In the early part of next day, we continued our route through a narrow, rough valley, resembling in its principal features the portion traversed the preceding day; but towards noon, we descended to the river, and, taking to its icy surface, held on till nightfall. The change was indeed agreeable, for though the snow on the elevated table ridges, of which the sides of the river are here formed, rarely exceeded two feet in depth, our horses were frequently engulphed in wading through the drift which was collected on the margins of these plateaux. The river in this day's march held its course for upwards of a mile, through a narrow strait not more than forty yards across in its widest part, and walled throughout the whole distance by perpendicular banks eighty feet high. On emerging from this gut the ravine opened, and resumed its old character.

In the afternoon, a party of men were descried watching us from a height, about a mile in advance. A halt was immediately called, and after the Kirghiz of our party had reconnoitred the strangers attentively, a scout was sent forward to observe them more narrowly, while we dismounted and prepared our fire-arms. Much to our satisfaction, the spy made the signal for friends, on which we pushed forward to meet them. They were a party of Kirghiz, who had left Langer Kish three weeks before us, charged with letters from Mohamed Rahim Khan to their brethren on the Khoord, or Little Pamir. Having executed their commission, they were now on their way to Wakhan. We found that it was to these men we had been indebted for the comparative ease with which we had hitherto journeyed. Their tracks in the snow had been carefully followed by our party, who were thus saved the disheartening toil of forcing a path through an unbroken, though imperfectly, frozen surface. After parting with these strangers, we arrived at a copse of red willows; and as no other opportunity of procuring firewood would offer between it and the head of the Oxus, we halted, and cut down, or rather dug out from under the snow, as much fuel as our already jaded horses could carry. The bushes were stunted, the tallest not much exceeding the height of a man, and they extended for a quarter of a mile along the banks of the river, in a patch of swampy ground. It was dark before we reached the spot which our guides had selected for the night's bivouac; but we were now on the Kirghiz ground, with every inch of which they seemed familiar. Quitting the river, they struck into a lateral defile to our left, and after winding up it for another hour, pointed to a cold, ugly looking spot, buried three feet deep in snow, as our quarters for the night. We remonstrated, at which the Kirghiz laughed, and, seizing their wooden shovels, soon drew from the soil below an ample store of firing, in the shape of sheep's and camel's dung. The eligibility of the place for a night's lodging was now past dispute; no other recommendation was necessary; and what with the fire we were thus enabled to keep up through the night, and the high and warm snow-walls that soon encircled our wintry habitation, we had all great reason to thank our escort for bringing us to such a favoured spot.

The unmounted portion of our party did not reach the camping ground till near midnight, and then so exhausted and wayworn as to render it evident that they would not be able to proceed on the morrow. It was therefore determined that they should be left behind us, to hunt in this neighbourhood till our return, and to look after a cache of provision, which was here formed. The height of this station above the sea was 13,500 feet.

On the following morning we retraced our steps to the river, the icy surface of which offered an admirable road. For a great portion of this day's march, the bottom of the valley was bare of snow, or but partially spotted with it, and this was the more remarkable from its lying so deep, further down the durah. We saw numbers of horns strewed about in every direction, the spoils of the Kirghiz hunter. Some of these were of an astonishingly large size, and belonged to an animal of a species between the goat and sheep, inhabiting the steppes of Pamir. The ends of the horns projecting above the snow, often indicated the direction of the road; and wherever they were heaped in large quantities and disposed in a semi-circle, there our escort recognised the site of a Kirghiz's summer encampment. Our keen-sighted guides again pitched on an old haunt for a resting place, and to their practical sagacity we were indebted for a repetition of the comforts of the preceding night. We here found ourselves to be 14,400 feet above the sea.

When about to resume our journey on the following day, a majority of the escort murmured at proceeding further, and coolly requested to be left behind. I endeavoured in a good-humored tone to reason with the defaulters; failing in this, I next tried the efficacy of upbraiding them with their unmanly conduct; but to such a rascally set shame was unknown, and though I managed to work myself into a towering passion, it produced no corresponding effect on the knaves. The more violent my language, and the more bitter my taunts, the more doggedly did they adhere to their resolution. With those, therefore, of the party who remained true, we were fain to set forward, ere disaffection should have further thinned our ranks. Two of the Kirghiz were among the faithful; and as the object of our search was reported to be only twenty-one miles distant, we cared little about the strength of our party, so that it contained a person qualified to lead us to the goal. The cause of this secession soon became apparent. The snow track which I have mentioned, and in which we had hitherto conveniently enough trodden, struck off, towards the close of the preceding day's march, over the hills on our left to the plain of Khoord Pamir, which lay beyond them, after which we had to force our own way up the main defile, and this labour the coward deserters would not face.

We had no occasion to remark the absence of snow this day, for every step we advanced it lay deeper and deeper; and near as we had now approached to the source of the Oxus, we should not have succeeded in reaching it had not the river been frozen. We were fully two hours in forcing our way through a field of snow not five hundred yards in extent. Each individual of the party by turns took the lead, and forced his horse to struggle onward until exhaustion brought it down in the snow, where it was allowed to lie and recruit whilst the next was urged forward. It was so great a relief when we again got upon the river, that in the elasticity of my spirits I pushed my pony to a trot. This a Wakhani perceiving, seized hold of the bridle, and cautioned me against the wind of the mountain. We had, indeed, felt the effects of a highly rarified atmosphere ever since leaving Wakhan; but the ascent being gradual, they were less than what would be experienced in climbing an abrupt mountain of much less altitude.

As we neared the head waters of the Oxus the ice became weak and brittle. The sudden disappearance of a yabu gave us the first warning of this. Though the water was deep where the accident occurred, there fortunately was little current, and, as the animal was secured by his halter to a companion, he was extricated, but his furniture and lading were lost. The kind-hearted Khirakush to whom the animal belonged wrapped him in felts, took off his own warm posteen, and bound it round the shivering brute. Had it been his son instead of his yabu, he could not have passed a more anxious night as to the effects of this ducking. The next morning, however, the yabu was alive and well, and the good mule-driver was most eloquent in his thanks to Providence for its preservation.

Shortly after this accident we came in sight of a rough-looking building, decked out with horns of the wild sheep, and all but buried amongst the snow. It was a Kirghiz burial-ground. On coming abreast of it, the leading horseman, who chanced to be of that tribe, pulled up and dismounted. His companion followed his example, and wading through the deep drift they reached a tombstone, the top of which was uncovered. Before this they knelt, all cumbered as they were, and with their huge forked matchlocks strapped to their backs; and offered up prayers to the ever-present Jehovah. The whole of the party involuntarily reined in their horses till the two men had concluded their devotions. The stillness of the scene, the wild and wintry aspect of the place, with the absence of all animated nature save these devotees and ourselves, were not unimpressive to a reflecting mind. They forcibly told us that man must have something beyond this life on which to rest his hopes, and that the sight of a brother's grave should remind him of his own fleeting existence; and that, when surrounded with difficulties and perils, he should appeal to that Being in whose hands he believes his destinies to be.

After quitting the surface of the river we travelled about an hour along its right bank, and then ascended a low hill, which apparently bounded the valley to the eastward; on surmounting this, at five o'clock in the afternoon of the 19th of February, 1838, we stood, to use a native expression, upon the Bam-i-Duniah, or "Roof of the World," while before us lay stretched a noble but frozen sheet of water, from whose western end issued the infant river of the Oxus. This fine lake lies in the form of a crescent, about fourteen miles long from east to west, by an average breadth of one mile. On three sides it is bordered by swelling hills, about 500 feet high, whilst along its southern bank they rise into mountains 3,500 feet above the lake, or 19,000 above the sea, and covered with perpetual snow, from which never-failing source the lake is supplied. From observations at the western end I found the latitude to be 37° 27' N. by mer. alt. of the sun, and longitude 73° 40'

E. by protraction from Langer Kish, where the last set of chronometric observations had been obtained; its elevation, measured by the temperature of boiling water, is 15,600 feet as my thermometer marked 184° of Fahrenheit. The temperature of the water below the ice was 32° — the freezing point.

This, then, is the position of the sources of this celebrated river, which, after a course of upwards of a thousand miles in a direction generally northwest, falls into the southern end of the sea of Aral. As I had the good fortune to be the first European who in later times had succeeded in reaching the sources of this river, and as, shortly before setting out on my journey, we had received the news of her gracious Majesty's accession to the throne, I was much tempted to apply the name of Victoria to this, if I may so term it, newly re-discovered lake; but on considering that by thus introducing a new name, however honoured, into our maps, great confusion in geography might arise, I deemed it better to retain the name of Sir-i-kol, the appellation given to it by our guides. The description of this spot given by that good old traveller Marco Polo, nearly six centuries ago, is so correct in all its leading points, that I have deemed it right to subjoin a considerable portion of it.[1]

[1] Leaving the province of Balashan (Badakhshan), and travelling in a direction between N.E. and E., you pass many castles and habitations on the banks of the river belonging to the brother of the king of that place, and after three days' journey reach a province named Vokan (Wakhan). Upon leaving this country and proceeding for three days, still in an E.N.E. course, ascending mountain after mountain, you at length arrive at a point of the road where you might suppose the surrounding summits to be the highest land in the world. Here, between two ranges, you perceive a large lake, from which flows a handsome river that pursues its course along an extensive plain covered with the richest verdure. Such, indeed, is its quality, that the leanest cattle turned upon it would become fat in the course of ten days. In this plain there are wild animals in great numbers, particularly sheep of a large size, having horns three, four, and even six, palms in length. Of

The hills and mountains that encircle Sir-i-kol give rise to some of the principal rivers in Asia. From the ridge at its east end flows a branch of the Yarkand river, one of the largest streams that waters China, while from its low hills on the northern side rises the Sirr or river of Kokan, and from the snowy chain opposite both forks of the Oxus, as well as a branch of the river Kuner, are supplied. When the lake is swollen by the melted snow of summer, the size of the infant river is correspondingly increased, and no great alteration takes place in the level of the lake itself.

The aspect of the landscape was wintry in the extreme. Wherever the eye fell one dazzling sheet of snow carpeted the ground, while the sky overhead was everywhere of a dark and angry hue. Clouds would have been a relief to the eye; but they were wanting. Not a breath moved along the surface of the lake; not a beast, nor even a bird, was visible. The sound of a human voice would have been music to the ear, but no one at this inhospitable season thinks of invading these gelid domains. Silence reigned around—silence so profound that it oppressed the heart, and, as I contemplated the hoary summits of the everlasting mountains, where human foot had never trode, and where lay piled the

these the shepherds form ladles and vessels for holding their victuals; and with the same materials they construct fences for enclosing their cattle and securing them against the wolves, with which they say the country is infested, and which likewise destroy many of the wild sheep or goats. Their horns and bones being found in large quantities, heaps are made of them at the side of the road, for the purpose of guiding the travellers at the season when it is covered with snow. For twelve days the course is along this elevated plain, which is named Pamer. So great is the height of the mountains that no birds are to be seen near their summits; and, however extraordinary it may be thought, it was affirmed that, from the keenness of the air, fires when lighted do not give the same heat as in lower situations, nor produce the same effect in dressing victuals.—"Travels of Marco Polo," translated from the Italian by Wm. Marsden. London, 1818.

snows of ages, my own dear country and all the social blessings it contains passed across my mind with a vividness of recollection that I had never felt before. It is all very well for men in crowded cities to be disgusted with the world and to talk of the delights of solitude. Let them but pass one twenty-four hours on the banks of the Sir-i-kol, and it will do more to make them contented with their lot than a thousand arguments. Man's proper sphere is society; and, let him abuse it as he will, this busy, bustling world is a brave place, in which, thanks to a kind Providence, the happiness enjoyed by the human race far exceeds the misery. So, at least, it has always appeared to me.

In walking over the lake I could not but reflect how many countries owe their importance and their wealth to rivers the sources of which can be traced to the lonely mountains which are piled up on its southern margin. This elevated chain is common to India, China, and Turkistan; and from it, as from a central point, their several streams diverge, each augmenting as it rolls onwards, until the ocean and the lake of Aral receive the swollen tribute, again to be given up, and in a circuit as endless as it is wonderful to be swept back by the winds of Heaven, and showered down in snowy flakes upon the self-same mountains from which it flowed.

How strange and how interesting a group would be formed if an individual from each nation whose rivers have their first source in Pamir were to meet upon its summit; what varieties would there be in person, language, and manners; what contrasts between the rough, untamed, and fierce mountaineer and the more civilized and effeminate dweller on the plain; how much of virtue and of vice, under a thousand different aspects, would be met with among them all; and how strongly would the conviction press upon the mind that the amelioration of the whole could result only from the diffusion of early education and a purer religion!

Pamir is not only a radiating point in the hydrographical system of Central Asia, but it is the focus from which originate its principal mountain-chains. The plain along the southern side of which the lake is situated has a width of about three miles; and viewed from this elevated plateau the mountains seem to have no great elevation. The table-land of Pamir is, as I have already stated, 15,600 feet high, or sixty-two feet lower than the summit of Mont Blanc; but the height of 3,400 feet, which I have assigned to the mountains that rise from this elevated basis, is a matter of assumption only. Where nothing but snow meets the eye it is not easy to appreciate heights and distances correctly; and it is therefore not improbable that the dimensions thus assigned to Sir-i-kol may be subsequently found incorrect. Covered as both the land and water were with snow, it was impossible to tell the exact size; the measurements given were obtained from the Kirghiz, who were familiar with the spot, assisted by my own eye. I regret that I omitted to take the necessary trigonometrical observations for determining the altitude of the southern range of mountains. I estimated their height on the spot, and noted down the impression at the moment; but though I had fully intended to have made the measurements on the morrow, it quite escaped me in my anxiety to fix the geographical position of the lake, nor did I discover the omission until our arrival in Wakhan.

The Wakhanis name this plain Bam-i-Duniah, or "Roof of the World," and it would indeed appear to be the highest table-land in Asia, and probably in any part of our globe. From Pamir the ground sinks in every direction except to the south-east, where similar plateaux extend along the northern face of the Himalaya into Tibet. An individual who had seen the region between Wakhan and Kashmir informed me that the Kunar river had its principal source in a lake resembling that in which the Oxus has its rise, and that the whole of this country, comprehending the districts of Gilgit, Gunjit, and Chitral, is a series of mountain defiles that act as water-courses to drain Pamir.

As early in the morning of Tuesday the 20th February as the cold permitted we walked out about 600 yards upon the lake, and, having cleared the snow from a portion of its surface, commenced breaking the ice to ascertain its depth. This was a matter of greater difficulty than it at first sight appeared, for the water was frozen to the depth of two feet and a half, and, owing to the great rarity of the atmosphere, a few strokes of the pick-axe produced an exhaustion that stretched us upon the snow to recruit our breath. By dint, however, of unwearied exertions and frequent reliefs, we had all but carried the shaft through, when an imprudent stroke fractured its bottom, and up the water jetted to the height of a man, sending us scampering off in all directions. This opening was too small to admit our sounding-lead, and had of necessity to be abandoned; besides, a wet jacket where the thermometer is at zero is a much more serious affair than where it is at summer-heat. We resolved to be more circumspect in our next attempt, and diligent search having revealed to us a large stone upon an islet in the lake, it was forthwith transported to the scene of our labours. When, judging by the depth of the first shaft, we concluded the second to be nearly through, the stone was raised and upheld by four men immediately above the hole. A fifth man continued to ply the axe, and at the first appearance of water the stone was dropped in and went clean through the ice, leaving an aperture its own size, and from this larger orifice there was no rush of water. The sounding-lead was immediately thrown in, when, much to my surprise and disappointment, it struck bottom at nine feet, and we had prepared and brought with us from Langer Kish a hundred fathoms of line for the experiment.

The water emitted a slightly fetid smell and was of a reddish tinge. The bottom was oozy and tangled with grassy weeds. I tried to measure the breadth of the lake by sound, but was baffled by the rarity of the air. A musket, loaded with blank cartridge, sounded as if the charge had been poured into the barrel, and neither wads nor ramrod used. When ball was introduced the report was louder, but possessed none of the sharpness that marks a similar charge in denser atmospheres. The ball, however, could be distinctly heard whizzing through the air. The human voice was sensibly affected, and conversation, especially if in a loud tone, could not be kept up without exhaustion: the slightest muscular exertion was attended with a similar result. Half a dozen strokes with an axe brought the workman to the ground; and though a few minutes' respite sufficed to restore the breath, anything like continued exertion was impossible. A run of fifty yards at full speed made the runner gasp for breath. Indeed, this exercise produced a pain in the lungs and a general prostration of strength which was not got rid of for many hours. Some of the party complained of dizziness and headaches; but, except the effects above described, I neither felt myself, nor perceived in others, any of those painful results of great elevation which travellers have suffered in ascending Mont Blanc. This might have been anticipated, for where the transition from a dense to a highly-rarified atmosphere is so sudden, as in the case of ascending that mountain the circulation cannot be expected to accommodate itself at once to the difference of pressure, and violence must accrue to some of the more sensitive organs of the body. The ascent to Pamir was, on the contrary, so gradual that some extrinsic circumstances were necessary to remind us of the altitude we had attained. The effect of great elevation upon the general system had indeed been proved to me some time before in a manner for which I was not prepared. One evening in Badakhshan, while sitting in a brown study over the fire, I chanced to touch my pulse, and the galloping rate at which it was throbbing roused my attention. I at once took it for granted that I was in a raging fever, and after perusing some hints on the preservation of health which Dr. Lord, at parting, had kindly drawn out for me, I forthwith prescribed for myself most liberally. Next morning my pulse was as brisk as ever, but still my feelings denoted health. I now thought of examining the wrists of all our party, and to my surprise found that the pulses of my companions beat yet faster than my own. The cause of this increased circulation immediately occurred to me; and when we afterwards commenced marching towards Wakhan I felt the pulses of the party whenever I registered the boiling point of water. The motion of the blood is in fact a sort of living barometer by which a man acquainted with his own habit of body can, in great altitudes, roughly calculate his height above the sea. Upon Pamir the pulsations in one minute were as follow:—

	Throbs	Country	Habit of body
My own	110	Scotland	spare
Golam Hussein, Munshi	124	Jasulmeree	fat
Omerallah, mule-driver	112	Afghan	spare
Gaffer, groom	114	Peshawuree	spare
Dowd, do.	124	Kabuli	stout

The danger we incurred in sleeping literally amongst the snow, in the middle of winter, at the great elevation of 15,600 feet, did not occur to me at the time: we were most fortunate in having done so with impunity. Fatal accidents from this very cause are of frequent occurrence in the Himalaya, as we learn from the late Capt. Alexander Gerard's narrative. But, indeed, that drowsiness, which cold engenders, and which ends in death, has been made familiar to us all by the interesting voyages of Capt. Cook. The misfortunes that befel Dr. Solander and his botanising party in Terra-del-Fuego is as touchingly told an incident as any in that attractive work. Our escape is, under Providence, to be attributed to the oceans of tea we drank. The kettle was never off the fire when we were encamped; indeed, throughout the whole of our wanderings, except when feasted in Jerm, the Munshi and myself lived almost entirely upon it. We used the decoction, not the infusion, and always

[263]

brewed it strong. Another preservative was the firing we kept up and the precaution of sleeping with our feet towards it.

The height of the snow-line in this parallel is above 17,000 feet. As I visited Pamir in the winter season I could not myself have ocular demonstration of this interesting fact; but that the ice upon the lake is broken up, and the hills in its neighbourhood clear of snow, by the end of June, are facts in which my informants, the Kirghiz, could not possibly be mistaken. At that season, it is said, the water swarms with aquatic birds, which, as the winter approaches, migrate to warmer regions: many are killed by the cold. The lake is a favourite resort of the Kirghiz, and no sooner is the snow off the ground than its banks are studded with their kirgahs. A spot better adapted to the wants of a pastoral community cannot well be imagined, and the hordes that frequent it seem fully to appreciate its advantages, since they are never weary of expatiating upon them. The grass of Pamir, they tell you, is so rich, that a sorry horse is here brought into good condition in less than twenty days; and its nourishing qualities are evidenced in the productiveness of their ewes, which almost invariably bring forth two lambs at a birth. Their flocks and herds roam over an unlimited extent of swelling grassy hills of the sweetest and richest pasture, while their yaks luxuriate amid the snow at no great distance above their encampment on the plains.

After getting a clear and beautiful meridian altitude of the sun on the 20th, we saddled, and casting a last look at Lake Sir-i-kol, entered the defile leading to Wakhan. As we increased our distance from Pamir, the hillocks on each side gradually rose in altitude, till at the end of twenty-one miles we had descended by an inclined plane 1,200 feet, and the mountains on our left hand were of that height. That which most forcibly strikes a traveller in these regions is the total absence of wood— the nakedness of the country. There are no timber-yielding trees indigenous to the Hindu Kosh, in which appellation I include the range from its first rise in Pamir to its termination at Koh-i-baba, a remarkable mountain to the north-west of Kabul. In making this assertion I should except the Archa, a dwarfish fir, which never equals in size its congeners of the Himalayan forest. It serves, however, for the building purposes of the natives, and is too valuable to be used as fuel. The poplar is seen by the sides of most rivulets, but never in great numbers, and always in localities which indicate that man has placed it there. The same may be said of fruit-bearing trees, except the almond and pistachio-nut, which are evidently natives of the lower portions of the Hindu Kosh, and more especially of the secondary ranges on the northern face of the chain. The willow of many varieties, loving a cold, moist soil, is found margining every stream, and in Durah Sir-i-kol this hardy plant was seen at an altitude of 13,000 feet. There, however, and long before that height was attained, it should be termed a bush rather than a tree. Fruit-bearing trees, of the plum species, were found at Langer Kish at 10,800 feet above the sea. The height to which the ground is cultivated by man I could not ascertain, the snow being upon its surface, though, from the nature of the soil upon Pamir, I can see no reason why a hasty harvest should not be reaped even there. But the Kirghiz abstain from agricultural pursuits; and it is certain the Wakhanis, for such a purpose, would not venture so high. The fuel in use throughout these mountains is a scrubby description of furze-bush, which has but little of woody fibre in it; and in the higher districts the fire-places are adapted solely to this description of fuel. The willow also is used for firing; and when the more affluent burn charcoal, it is prepared either from the archa or the almond-tree. That obtained from the latter is much the best.

In speaking of the Hindu Kosh range of mountains in contradistinction to the Himalaya, it may be well to define both chains. The latter, as is well known, bounds Hindustan on the north, and after crossing the river

Indus extends westward to the valley of Panchshir and the meridian of Kabul. The other chain I have before described. They are connected by numerous lateral ridges, and evidently belong to the same great system of the Himalayan-Tartaric mountains, which extend both to the east and west beyond the limits to which my experience reaches. Hindu Kosh is their northern wall, Himalaya is the southern one. The former, however, would appear to be the superior ridge, since it divides the waters of Central Asia from those which flow south. It is one continuous chain; while, on the contrary, the Himalaya is pierced by both the Kuner and Indus rivers; and no stream that has its rise in this range runs towards the north.

On arriving at the station where we had left the hunters we were agreeably surprised to find they had been successful in the chase, and had slaughtered a Kutch-kar, or wild sheep. It was a noble animal, standing as high as a two-year-old colt, with a venerable beard, and two splendid curling horns, which, with the head, were so heavy as to require a considerable exertion to lift them. Though in poor condition, the carcase, divested of offal, was a load for a baggage-pony. Its flesh was tough and ill-tasted; but we were told that in autumn, when the animal is in prime condition, no venison is better flavoured. The Kutch-kar is gregarious, congregating in herds of several hundreds. They are of a dun colour, the skin more resembling the hide of a cow than the fleece of a sheep. There is another animal peculiar to Pamir, named Rass by the Kirghiz: it differs from the Kutch-kar, having straight spiral horns, and its dun colour being of a redder tinge; but this species we did not meet with. The only other quadrupeds we observed were wolves, foxes, and hares; and of birds we saw but one. It was, however, a regal bird; a fine black eagle, which came sailing over the valley, flapping his huge wings as if they were too heavy for his body.

On the evening of the fourth day after quitting the source of the Oxus we were again housed in Langer Kish, which, considering the nature of the ground, was tolerable travelling, the distance being upwards of seventy miles.

Chapter XXII

The district of Wakhan embraces the main valley of the Oxus, from Ish-kashm upwards, and the durahs of Sirhad and Sir-i-kol. Population is confined to the two first regions, the last, as the preceding narrative will have shown, being, throughout the greater portion of the year, a dreary, uninhabitable waste. The total number of souls ruled by Mir Mohamed Rahim did not exceed one thousand: were its poor soil and scanty pasture turned to the best advantage, it might possibly supply with food five times that number. At present it does not produce sufficient grain for its own consumption, the deficiency being imported from countries lying lower down the valley of the Oxus. In former times, when a considerable trade passed through Wakhan, the Mir drew a small revenue by taxing in kind the Yarkand Kafilas, for which he escorted them from the southern limits of his territories to the east end of lake Sir-i-kol, where the Chinese frontier begins. This was an exaction on the part of Mohamed Rahim, since, for this very protection, the chief of Kunduz previously levied fifteen rupees on each camel-load. However, the allegiance of the mountain chief has always been dubious, and though nominally a feudatory of Kunduz, he is virtually independent. The merchants might indeed have remonstrated against this exaction, but they knew their own interest better.

Another source of income to the ruler of Wakhan is

from his slaves. It is disgusting to see the subterfuges and hypocrisy, to which men resort to circumvent their neighbours.

The laws of their Prophet do not admit the making of slaves, but the Mohamedans get over the difficulty by calling their victims proselytes. The beautiful moral axiom that we must not do evil that good may accrue is quite overlooked, and the Sunis of Tartary affect to have reasoned themselves into the pious belief, that in enslaving their heretical brethren they perform an acceptable service to God and to Mohamed.

Avarice gets the better of controversy, and we find the Wakhanis who are of the Shiah belief assuming, in their intercourse with Kunduz, the tenets of an opposite sect; cursing the son-in-law of the Prophet, and lauding to the skies the three first caliphs. By such detestable means they compound with their conscience, and steel their minds to enslave the natives of the Shakh durah, a mountain defile immediately north of Wakhan, who are of their own creed. With the Uzbeks they are Sunis, at home Shiahs; but as some apology for them, it should be remembered that the detestable doctrines of the latter sect not only pardon but enforce dissimulation. The unhappy wretches who are thus enslaved are bartered with the Uzbeks of Kunduz for horses, and are again sold by them to Shah Kittore, the Chitral ruler, at an advance of fifty per cent.

The chief of Wakhan traced his ancestry to Alexander the Great, a descent, whether fabulous or true, of which he was not a little vain. Mohamed Rahim considered his illustrious lineage a fact which none dare dispute, and indeed his neighbours spoke with equal confidence of his high claim. This honour, as other travellers have remarked, is not confined to Wakhan, but is one to which the rulers of Badakhshan, Darwaz, and Chitral, are also aspirants. The representative of Badakhshan we have already described; but on subsequent inquiry in Jerm, we discovered his only title to Grecian lineage rested on an intermarriage with the royal family of

Chitral, the blood of which is supposed to be particularly noble, and therefore as a matter of course must flow from Hazrat Zekunder, whom, he it observed, the Mohamedans have canonised. Shagnan and Roshan, two mountain districts in the valley of the Oxus immediately south of Darwaz, demand for their rulers the same classic lineage; but the Mullahs, who alone are given to antiquarian research, assert that their right to such a splendid ancestry rests on no better foundation than does that of the fallen house of Badakhshan. Among a rude and half savage people, not given to chronicle their doings, and with whom books and men to read them are equally rare, we would search in vain for valid evidence, either in support or refutation of these pretensions. Being, however, on the spot, I deemed it right to inquire into this prevailing tradition, which the Honourable Mr. Elphinstone, and subsequent travellers, have upon more remote information given to the public; and I will add a few words on the physical appearance of these true or pseudo Greeks. Of fifteen Wakhanis whom we measured, the tallest stood 5 feet 7 ¼ inches; the shortest, 5 feet 1 ¾ inches. The men are much tanned by exposure to all weathers; they have nothing peculiar in their facial line, nor in the colour of their eyes and hair, but in every feature bear a strong resemblance to Tajiks. They wear chupkuns of wool, with posteens of untanned sheep-skins. Those who can afford it have turbans, but the greater number are content with caps fitting close to the head. Their garments being tattered and sadly out of repair, give them a savage, reckless air; nor does their appearance belie their disposition. The women wear long white woollen gowns, and those who can procure it tie a piece of cotton cloth about the head. They are by no means backward in expressing their wishes on the all-important subject of dress. Among the articles which we had brought with us for barter, were a few handkerchiefs made from the silk called lub-i-ab, the produce of worms reared on the banks of the Oxus. These and ornamented chupkuns were intended as presents for the chiefs. But the daughter of a miller with whom we were lodging chanced to espy one of the smart handkerchiefs, and as a matter of course asked for it. She was refused; but next day resumed her suit, and by way of temptation, handed me a lump of sicee or Chinese silver, weighing about a quarter of a pound. The young woman had set her heart upon the handkerchief, but it was not deemed prudent to gratify her taste for finery; and as for the silver, I feigned as great a contempt for the precious metal, as the unsophisticated girl had shown. To these poorly clad mountaineers coarse fabrics were more useful, and of such, both in bartering for our food and in presents, we had occasion to distribute a considerable quantity. The flocks of the Wakhani constitute his riches, or rather enable him to endure the ills to which his bleak high-lying valley exposes him. The skin and fleece of the sheep supply him with every article of dress, in preparing which, both women and men find their winter's employment. The women clean and spin the wool, while the men weave it into cloth. The valuable wool of Tibet, from which the costly shawls of Kashmir are fabricated, or at least a wool that has all its good qualities, is yielded by the goat of Wakhan.

The Wakhan dogs differ much from those of India, and bear a strong resemblance to the Scotch colly. They have long ears, a bushy tail, and a frame somewhat slender, and more calculated for swiftness than strength. They are very fierce, make excellent watchers, and will fight dogs twice their own weight. Their prevailing colours are black, or a reddish brown; the latter often mottled. The breed is from Chitral, and so highly are their game qualities valued, that the Sind Amirs, who are great followers of the chase, have their packs improved by importations from this country. The double-humped camel I had always supposed to be the native of Uzbek Tartary; but we here learned that it is bred only among the Kirghiz of Pamir and Kokan.

The principal crops in Wakhan are peas and barley.

Wheat is likewise grown, but only to a very limited extent. In April the seed is put into the ground, and in July the harvest is reaped. The land requires to be irrigated, and to yield even a moderate crop must be richly manured. The strong wind that blows with little intermission throughout the winter and spring, down the valley of the Oxus, is unfavourable to vegetation.

The houses resemble those in Badakhshan, except that instead of the central fire-place, they have large stoves after the Russian fashion. These occupy an entire side of the house, and throw out so general a warmth, that when once you have fairly domesticated yourself under a Wakhani's humble roof, you are unwilling to quit such comfortable quarters. The smoke is somewhat annoying; but the nearer you lie to the floor, the less of it you inhale. To me a wood-fire is more agreeable than a coal one. I loved to hear its cheerful crackling sound, and to feed it during the long hours that we were compelled to remain in-doors was my delight; not that we needed its warmth, but the sight of its long tongues of flame, frisking and roaring under the good wife's enormous pot, induced a contented and happy state of mind, to which a knowledge of the good things it contained might probably no little contribute. It is not uncommon for six families to live together; not in separate apartments as in Badakhshan, but in one, or at most two rooms. As night draws on, the Wakhani pulls down a dry branch of the willow tree out of the many bundles suspended beneath his rafters, and putting one end of the branch to his breast, while the other is held by his wife's foot, takes his knife from his girdle, and with both hands sheaves from off the rod as many lengths as he conjectures will last through the evening. These resinous slips are then deposited above the lintel of the inner door; and they answer all the purposes of an oil lamp or candle.

By the 1st of March we had reached Ish-kashm on our return to Kunduz, and put up in a house, where we had ample opportunity of learning that the matrimonial state is not all sunshine even among Mohamedans;

upon whom, in such matters, their Prophet's intended kindness has entailed much misery. Of all the trials which assail a human being in his course from infancy to the grave, I should think a good perfect specimen of a scold of a wife must be the greatest. If a man, whose mind is harassed by contact with the world, have a happy fireside of his own, he soon forgets the rubs of the business day in the comfort in store for him at home. But if he comes into a house where a vixen of a wife galls his very soul with bitter taunts and reproaches, what chance is there for him? Of this calamity, the house in which we lodged at Ish-kashm offered a very striking example. Our host, a young, good-looking, merry fellow, was tethered to a perfect termagant of a wife. She was a manumitted slave of Afghan extraction. He knew nothing of her temper before marriage, but on being introduced to the father foolishly agreed to take his daughter to wife; and as the poor fellow dolefully expressed himself, "On that ill-fated day she seized me by the throat, and has held fast ever since." But, added he (in a half whisper, and by the motion of his hand warning us that his better half was not far distant,) "Never mind, never mind, I am making love to a young woman in the next village, a pretty gentle soul, and when the affair is all settled I will break the matter to my wife. If she heard of my intentions now, my life would not be safe. Did she only bite I could live with her, for teeth can be extracted; but, oh the tongue! the tongue! there never was a husband yet could get rid of that. The lady was called Gool dustah, or the nosegay; and with reference to this sweet name, the good-humoured facetious husband gave loose to his wit, till he had almost convulsed us with laughter.

It is a mistake to suppose that with Moslems the women have no power. They have, to the full, as much influence in their own house as our fair countrywomen; and not a few, especially in Afghanistan, have become honourably conspicuous by the wisdom with which they guide their husbands' affairs. The wife of Jabar Khan,

[273]

brother to the late ruler of Kabul, was a well known instance. For a long time she had the entire management of his estates; and since her death the worthy Nawab's exchequer has not been so well filled, nor his influence with Dost Mohamed and the Afghans what it formerly was.

Ish-kashm is the southern entrance to the districts of Roshan, Shagnan, and Darwaz. The season of the year rendered it impossible for me to visit those countries; but I deem it right briefly to give such particulars regarding them as I was enabled to collect. All the three are situated in the valley of the Oxus; and below Wakhan, which, as the reader must already be aware, is the uppermost peopled district on that river. They are passed through by the traveller who descends the stream in the order in which I have named them. They are all strong countries, accessible only at midsummer, and even then the passes are treacherous. Five years ago, during an expedition into Shagnan, Murad Beg in the middle of summer lost nearly one hundred troopers in a snow-fall. When the Oxus is frozen, the best entrance to them is by the river from Ish-kashm, by way of Gharan, and the ruby mines. There is said to be a lake in Shagnan, half a day's journey in circumference, which drains the country on the left bank of the Panj, as the Oxus is here called. A stream sufficient to turn two mills runs from this lake into the river. The three countries abound in stone-fruit, and the mulberry is also plentiful in them all. Their crops are wheat and barley. The Kirghiz camel is the beast of burden; the cow and sheep, both of the usual description, constitute their stock. Horses are not numerous. In Roshan and Shagnan the inhabitants are Shiahs, their dress is similar to that of the Wakhanis, and they occupy the same description of houses. Shagnan now contains about 300 families, but before it was chuppowed by Murad Beg, it could boast of nearly one thousand. Roshan is more populous, and still holds about the last-mentioned number of families. The two districts pay a joint tribute to Kunduz of fifteen slaves, and receive presents in return, of nearly equal value. Their language is a dialect peculiar to themselves. Darwaz is independent of Kunduz, and the intercourse between them is confined to the exchange of presents. This country is exceedingly mountainous, and its dizzy paths can only be traversed by footmen. Cotton is grown on what little soil there is. Made into cloth, it forms an article of export; in return for which they receive grain and gunpowder. All its villages are situated on the banks of the Oxus. The Shah or King keeps up some show of state, and a large force,—large at least when compared with the troops of his weaker neighbours. The natives of Darwaz are Tajiks, and most of them Suni Mohamedans. Their language is Persian. To the north-north-east of this state is the district of Karategein, which vacillates in its allegiance between Kokan and Kunduz.

On the 2nd of March we passed, by the Kotul of Ish-kashm, out of the valley of the Oxus, into that of the Wardodj, a tributary of the Kokcha. Here we met an Indian fakir wending his solitary way to Wakhan, where he intended remaining until the summer sun should open the passes to Shagnan. Scantily clad in the skin of a tiger, or of some other wild beast, these devotees pass unharmed. No one would injure a Callender. He is a welcome guest at every hamlet, and, like the Gaberlunzie of Scotland, in a former age, he is the grand newsvender in regions rarely visited but by himself.

Once again in Badakhshan, Abdal Ghani resumed the authority which he had wisely permitted to lie dormant during our abode in Wakhan. The Aksakal (or elder) was directed to convene the people, and organise a singing entertainment for the amusement of the Mir's Yesawal. We were present, and partook of the festivity. The villagers assembled in a large barn-like tenement, with benches round its four sides: a cheerful fire in the centre of the room illumined the countenances of the audience, whilst, in the open space around it, a Chitral youth exhibited the dance of his country, with great strength and activity, and not without some grace. Four

[275]

men sang in chorus to the sound of the tambourine; and although perhaps the scientific amateur might have discovered a want of taste in the music, the deficiency was compensated for in our opinion by the spirit and correctness with which each performed his part. The hands of the singers were constantly in motion, and their countenances showed that they felt the full force of the words they uttered. Towards the conclusion all present joined in chorus, and the song finished with a sustained shout which somewhat reminded me of the good honest cheer from the one-shilling gods of an English theatre.

As we approached the bottom of the Wardodj valley, everything wore the joyous air of spring. The change was delightful. When we passed up snow lay everywhere. Now the plough was in the field; wild flowers were sparkling amongst the withered herbage of the bygone year; and around the edges of the stones tufts of young grass were everywhere to be seen. The sheep, let loose from their sheds, were remunerating themselves for the dry and scanty fare of their winter's quarters. The streams were all unlocked, and we encamped in the open air. The raven, the jay, the lark, and the bulbul, or Badakhshan nightingale, were all upon the wing. Numerous insects, too, aroused from their long sleep, began to show themselves: among them were butterflies, and a most beautifully painted species of gad-fly.

The effects of winter were evidenced by deep furrows in the bottom of the valley. Now that the snow had thawed we could in many places discern the extensive destruction the frost bad caused on the steep flanks of the mountains. From these "elder born of time" large fragments had been detached, and, judging from their position, the force with which they had been washed into the plain must have been immense. The mountain chains of Badakhshan are formed of the older rocks, but they are largely traversed by immense masses of a very impure limestone. It is in this latter formation that the deposits of lapis-lazuli occur. Bordering the Kokcha, mica slate, richly impregnated with iron ore, abounds; and here also asbestos and antimony are occasionally found. The Kokcha, like every other tributary of the Oxus, is fertile in gold.

On the 5th we debouched into the valley of the Kokcha, at Khyrabad. Here a danger of a new kind arose, and it was well for us that it had not shown itself at an earlier period. Our sojourn in Jerm had been, it seems, fatal to the too tender heart of Abdal Ghani—a damsel in Khyrabad having completely captivated the Mullah. He now proposed marriage, and taking her on with our party to Talikhan. To the union the young lady gave an extremely willing assent; but the very idea of going, as she expressed it, to "the grave of the Badakhshi, the fens of Kunduz, made both her and her parents absolutely shudder. The matter was referred to the Mir of Jerm, and I also was called into council. The Yesawal, in very decisive terms, stated that for him again to leave his adorable mistress was quite out of the question. I was constrained, therefore, to dispense with his further services, which, fortunately, were no longer indispensably necessary to our journey; and as I could not conveniently stand bride's-man on this interesting occasion, I made the blushing fair a present; and leaving Abdal Ghani displaying all the raptures of a successful lover, we continued our journey.

The weather was cloudy, with a drizzling rain. Still the air was delicious, and gentle showers at the opening of the season could not fail of doing much good to the soil, already renovated by the snow with which it had so long been covered. We again passed through Fyzabad,

" Where many a garden flower grows wild,"

and, on entering the beautiful lawn at the gorge of its valley, I was enchanted at the quiet loveliness of the scene. Up to this time, from the day we left Talikhan, we had been moving in snow; but now it had nearly vanished from the valley, and the fine sward was enamelled with crocuses, daffodils, and snowdrops.

[277]

As we pushed briskly along tho Kokcha for the plain of Argu, we could see that the Turk of Badakhshan, true to the habits of his race, had already driven forth his flock, and pitched the kirgah where the pasturage was the sweetest and the best. In one spot several agricultural families had set themselves down, and were employed putting their wheat into the ground. The field they had selected, doubtless for some good reason, was the face of a sloping hill, and not the level arable land in the bottom of the valley. Several donkeys, with salt from Akb-olak, passed us here on their way to Jerm.

The plain of Argu still wore its snowy robe, but the southern side of the pass of Taishkhan, though much higher, was uncovered. Here the entire face of the mountain was studded with almond bushes. The fruit of the past year still clung to many of them, while the beautiful bell-blossoms mingled lilac and purple—the germ of this year's growth—shot through the withered leaves which still partially clothed them. The almond, like the mulberry and the pistachio, flowers before its leaves appear.

The 8th of March was the Edd-Kurbani, or the Sacrifice, the day on which Abraham offered up Isaac, or, according to Mohamedans his brother Ishmael. In Mussulman countries this day is one of great rejoicing; and here the men devote it chiefly to the pleasures of horse-racing. But it is the women who profit most by the Edd-Kurbani. In the valley of Meshid, which we crossed on that day, a large party of females had congregated at one end of the little village, and were in high merriment, enjoying the pleasures of a swing. As we drew near, the principal performer ceased her airy circle, but kept her seat, and from beneath a silk handkerchief eyed the intruders. Seeing that our presence checked their festivity, we turned away, and immediately the young lady was again careering in mid-air, amid the flaunting of kerchiefs and the admiration of her fellows. All household drudgery ceases on this day The husband puts on his best clothes, repeats the fatha, or opening verse of the Koran, and goes to run his horse; whilst the wife has the double gratification, first of putting on her smart things, and next of showing them off to her female friends.

It snowed as we passed along the plain of Kila Afghan; but the flakes became rain-drops as we descended the other side of Latta-band, and we arrived late at night in Talikhan, soaked to the skin Our reception was less cordial than it had formerly been, and I could gather from the altered manner of our host that our influence at court was on the wane.

Saddling next morning long before daybreak, we passed rapidly across the Talikhan plain, and without waiting to bait our horses at Khana-a-bad, pushed on for Kunduz, where we arrived about seven o'clock on the evening of the 11th, just as Dr. Lord was seating himself to his solitary meal.

I had been absent exactly three months; and those only who have been separated for so long a period, in countries as wild as these, from a most kind and valued friend, can appreciate my pleasure at the meeting. We each of us had much to communicate to the other; and it was deep in the morning before our conference ended.

Chapter XXIII

I now learned from my friend, that in addition to the disease in his eyes, the general health of Mohamed Beg had become precarious, and also that his eldest son was alarmingly ill. On the very day of our arrival, Dr. Lord had been summoned to Hazrat Imam on their account; and the arrangements for the journey having been already made, we started next morning, leaving Atma, the Mir's Dewan Begi, to report my safe arrival to Murad Beg, and to inform him that I had travelled not only unmolested, but honoured throughout his wide dominions.

A ride of nearly six miles brought us to the river of Khana-a-bad. It was not here the same rapid stream which had well-nigh unhorsed the Munshi on a former occasion; but, deep and turbid, it moved sluggishly on between low banks of the richest loam. The taller horses were able to ford the river, but the yabus were obliged to swim. Climbing its right bank, we entered a spacious plain, carpeted with the finest grass, over which we continued for the further distance of thirteen miles, and then dismounted at an abdan, or reservoir, where we pitched our tent for the night.

Travelling, as we now did, with the appendages of civilization about us, if a small tent may be so denominated, we bad to pack up before mounting, and were thus detained longer on our camping ground after daybreak than had been usual in my late trip to the eastward. There is something extremely pleasant in our mode of travelling in India: the care with which all the arrangements are made, and the attention which is invariably paid to various items of luxury and comfort, among which not the least important are shade, cool water, and a frothy glass of Hodgson's or Bass's beer. The larger tents and the heavy baggage are sent forward over night, and pitched by sunrise, or a little after; so that the European, after a cool morning's ride, can sit down to breakfast immediately on his arrival—the little tent in which he passed the night being brought up to the ground in the course of the day. In the sultry plains of Hindustan this is a safe and very agreeable mode of journeying; but delightful though it be in summer, it cannot in the winter season bear a comparison with the off-hand, free and easy style of travelling practised by all classes in Afghanistan, where your lodging is under the felts of a Kyl or the roof of a farm-house, and where rude hospitality, a good fire, and friendly converse, make ample amends for poor fare and the total absence of form and ceremony. When once you have seen your horse well provided with corn, and have carried your saddle-bags into the house, there is nothing more to do but chat and eat and be at your ease. You are not only more independent, and more the master of your own actions than the traveller who creeps across the plain encumbered with baggage and attendants, but you escape a thousand causes of worry to yourself and others. If when you are roughing it, hardships do occur, as they sometimes will, the buoyancy of spirits which the keen air and light atmosphere of high lands bestow, enables you to bear them without repining.

Resuming our march, the path for three miles continued along the plain, after which we wound for another five through a ridge of grassy hills, on emerging from which we came in sight of Hazrat Imam, and debouched into the valley of the Oxus. An hour's ride from this point over a rich, well-cultivated country, brought us to the end of our journey.

Hazrat Imam is about the same size as Kunduz; and its fort, though not so large, is more judiciously constructed. The ditch was full of water, and a wooden bridge in good repair kept up the communication with the town. The market-place is an open square, lying immediately under the south-west bastion of the fortress.

Dr. Lord, after seeing his patients, prescribed moderate exercise for the Mir's son, who, poor lad, with little originally the matter with him, had by the unskilful treatment of a native practitioner been brought to the brink of the grave. They had deferred calling in my friend until the time had gone by when his advice would have been useful. The spirits of the young man were much depressed; but it was thought that country air and the excitement of the chase might dissipate the langour which, independent of bodily infirmities, preyed on his mind; and the result was more favourable than could have been anticipated.

A large party of well-mounted horsemen were accordingly assembled next day at the gate of the fort: a mongrel pack of dogs were in attendance. When joined by the sick prince and his younger brother, we struck north over the country for the Oxus, the banks of which were to be the scene of our sport.

Though I have spoken in somewhat disparaging terms of Mohamed Beg's pack of hounds, there were some dogs in it which could not but have found favour even in the eyes of an English sportsman. These were the tazi; a breed which for strength and symmetry, vie with our greyhound, and in beauty surpass it; the spaniel from Kulab, and others of mixed blood, but possessing keen scent, and some of the qualities of our pointers.

On nearing the river the party broke up into small knots, each seeking its own amusement. The objects of our search were pheasants, a goodly number of which were bagged in the course of the day. As soon as a bird was put up, the nearest horseman set off at full speed in the direction of its flight, which was nine times out of ten a straight line. Few escaped us, for we went along at a pelting pace, and two flights are as many as the pheasant can take without a long rest. When the dogs were kept back by the stiff reedy grass, which was generally the case, the bird was struck down by the horse's feet.

While at Hazrat Imam, we were shocked to hear that Mohamed Rahim Khan of Wakhan had been murdered by Murad Beg. Atma, who was present when the crime was committed, gave us, on our return to Kunduz, the following particulars:—

The Wakhan chief on his first arrival at Kunduz was well received; but when, instead of the arrears of tribute, a meagre present was offered, Murad Beg was so enraged, that he instantly placed him in confinement, and he was arraigned in the Mir's durbar on the very day that Abdal Ghani arrived. Murad Beg, who had predetermined the chief's death, inquired of the Yesawal, as if casually, whether his party had been well treated in Wakhan? "No," was the lying reply. "Kaffir," exclaimed the enraged Uzbek, turning to his victim, "and is it thus you set me at defiance: kutta chob bizun, strike him with a club." A courtier present, whose father had been killed in Wakhan, required no second bidding; he darted out of the presence-chamber, and returning with a large wooden billet, felled the unhappy man at a single stroke, bespattering with his brains the dresses of those near him. "Koob kurde! Koob kurde!" "Well done! well done!" shouted the savage ruler from his musnud.

I soon became weary of remaining inactive at Hazrat Imam, and Dr. Lord having obtained permission for me to visit the Oxus, on the 17th of March, accompanied by Gholam Hussein, I started for its fords. The country was so thickly peopled for the first twenty miles, that frequently a dozen villages were in sight from one spot, each marked by its own little clump of trees. These hamlets, seen from a distance, brought to my recollections the Tandas, or farm-steadings of Sind; but the little white mosque with its blue-stained tiles is

[283]

wanting here. The soil is darker in colour, and of a better quality than Sind can boast, where the cracked, sun-glazed surface of the ground is for the most part a poor, alluvial deposit, interspersed occasionally with tracks of richer land.

The Uzbeks, who follow agricultural pursuits, pitch their kirgahs in localities which most people would avoid. Though the green-sodded hills around invite them to encamp where the air is pure and the breeze healthy, they prefer the swamp and its miasma, and will not purchase health at the price of a certain degree of extra labour. It is no doubt convenient to them to reside in the midst of their cultivated fields; but the very circumstances which cause the extreme fertility of those fields render them deadly to man; to those, at least, who have not been gradually seasoned to the region; nor can any advantages which the husbandman obtains by residing on the low grounds be worth the risk which he incurs. Since the year 1830, Badakhshan and the countries subject to or rather "chuppowed" by Murad Beg, on the northern bank of the Oxus, have been depopulated to stock the plains of Kunduz and Hazrat Imam. The aggregate of foreigners thus forcibly planted in these unhealthy marshes from that year to the present time, is estimated by the Uzbeks at 25,000 families, or, in round numbers, 100,000 souls; and I question whether of these 6,000 were alive in 1838; so great had been the mortality in the short space of eight years. Truly may the proverb say, "If you wish to die, go to Kunduz." Twelve months antecedent to our visit, a great portion of the inhabitants of Kulab were brought from their own hilly country down to Hazrat Imam. Dr. Lord and myself walked over the ground which their straw kirgahs had covered, and where some still stood; but silence and the numerous graves around told us the fate of their former inmates.

In the case of these unhappy people, the mind predisposes the body to disease; for a free mountaineer when forcibly transported to labour in these fens, considers himself a doomed man; pines for the cooling breezes of his own Alpine home, and gradually droops. The energy of his character subsides, and is succeeded by a gloomy indifference, that unnerves the frame, and prepares it to receive the germ of maladies so prevalent in this unhealthy region. The Uzbeks, inured to the country, suffer less than others.

As we passed their villages, the women in groups were standing in front of the tents, or walking among the Zird Alu trees, now partially in blossom. It had been raining for several days, and they seemed delighted to catch as much sunshine as the fitful clouds would spare them; none of them wore veils. In appearance they do not differ from the Kirghiz, except that they are of a larger frame.

Leaving to our right the hill of Khaja Tow, a principal feature in the landscape, we came upon the canal of Sharwan, which irrigates the whole district of Hazrat Imam. In crossing it, the water reached up to our horses' girths; its width was forty feet, and the current ran at the rate of about two and a half miles an hour. Two hours afterwards we arrived on the Oxus, at the castle of Sharwan, where the water enters the canal from the river. The fort overlooks the Oxus: upon the opposite bank of which was a party of ten gold seekers, searching its sand for the precious metal. Sharwan is more a castellated dwelling-house than a place of strength, and is fortunate in being exempt from the pestilential climate of Kunduz and Hazrat Imam. Immediately south of it, between Khaja Tow and the still more remarkable mountain of Koh Umber, lay a beautiful tract of the most delicious pasture, over which the flocks of Murad Beg were roaming. The grazing ground comes close up to the Oxus, and on its northern verge stands Sharwan.

After a ride of another twelve miles, we dismounted at Kila Chap. Before we reached it night had set in, and our guide could no longer conceal his fears of the wild tenants of the jungle through which the road led; nor was his anxiety without a cause, for we learned at Kila

Chap that beasts of prey were numerous, and among them the lion.

Kila Chap is faced by a high hill on the opposite bank of the Kokcha, called I-khanam, and the next morning, after fording the river, we ascended it to take the bearings. I could hardly recognise in the muddy banks and soil-tinged stream my old friend of the mountains; so different was its appearance here to that which it presented in Badakhshan.

From the summit of I-khanam we had a glorious view of the surrounding country. At the foot of the hill was the junction of the two rivers. From the point of confluence, the Kokcha could be traced to its exit from the mountains on the south, while the eye followed the Oxus westward, till distance concealed its brick-coloured stream. To the east and south, the pinnacles of snowy mountains shot up into the clouds, whilst a lower ridge, but also snow-clad, encircled the horizon to the north. Immediately below I-khanam, on its east side, the ground is raised into low, swelling ridges. Here, we were informed, stood an ancient city called Barbarrah, and there is a considerable extent of mud-walls standing, which the Tajiks think are vestiges of the old city, but which are evidently of a comparatively modern era. The appearance of the place, however, does indicate the truth of their tradition, that an ancient city once stood here. On the site of the town was an Uzbek encampment; but from its inmates we could glean no information, and to all our inquiries about coins and relics, they only vouchsafed a vacant stare or an idiotic laugh.

The whole of this day's march, a distance of twenty-eight miles, was over a splendid pasture-ground as the eye ever saw. From the river on our left to the mountains on the right, was stretched out one sheet of verdure, dotted over with sheep, herds of horses, and droves of cattle. This plain is named Turghi-i-Tippa. We several times came on the remains of a canal, which though filled up, evinced by the height of its two parallel ridges and their width apart, its truly gigantic proportions. At

[286]

the close of the march, when descending to Jan Kila, which stands down in the bed of the Oxus, and on its left bank, we saw where this canal left the river; and here its depth, to reach the level of the stream at this season, must have been at least eighty feet. Such a work could only be executed under a despotic government, or by a wealthy and civilized people.

On the morning of the 19th, accompanied by seventeen mounted Uzbek spearmen, we forded the Oxus abreast of Jan Kila, and opposite the village of Said, which is on the right bank. On our way down to the water's edge, the dogs of the village were seen, just outside the fort, gnawing the bones of a bullock, which during the night a lion had killed for his own repast. At the ford the stream was divided into three channels, the two first of which were easily passed, but the last, though not dangerous, required some generalship in crossing. In all wide-spread rivers the direct line across is never the best ford. Looking attentively on the surface of the water, a slight ripple of a horse-shoe form may generally be detected stretching from bank to bank. The ford is here, and in passing it you must be careful to keep in the deep still water some distance above the ripple, for where the water is shoal, the current shoots down with a velocity against which no horse could stand. A man on foot could not have forded the river at Jan Kila. Three horses abreast is a safer way of passing than in single file. There was something exciting in crossing the last stream. When we had gained the upward curve or horn of the crescent near the opposite shore, it was doubtful whether the leading horses would hold their own. They could make no way against the stream, which fell to the right and left of the line, like waves thrown from off the bow of a steam-boat. It was an anxious moment, since the slightest indecision on the rider's part or any stumbling of his horse, must have annihilated the line. At length, the well-trained steeds began to step out, and, once in motion, slowly but gallantly did they breast the stream till we gained the bank. This largest channel had a width of 200 yards and a velocity of four miles an hour; the centre one was about half the breadth, and had a current of about three miles; the water in the one which we first entered was almost stagnant. The bottoms of all were pebbly.

The Oxus can be forded in the winter season from Hazrat Imam to the frontiers of Darwaz. Westward, the accession of large tributaries renders the stream too powerful to be crossed on foot, while the mountains to the eastward, by narrowing its bed, are productive of a similar result. Within these limits the best ford, both for permanence and good footing, lies immediately under the castle of Sharwan. Guns have there been conveyed across by the Kunduz Mir. Even in the summer season the Oxus in this neighbourhood has been crossed by a troop of Murad Beg's mounted banditti. The riders swam upon mussuks, and guided their horses across. The chuppow on which they were then bent is said to have been eminently successful. In Darwaz the river is bridged, and between it and Shagnan one or two rude description of boats are in use, but no vessel is employed upon the Oxus for commercial purposes, nor indeed at the ferries above the confluence of the Serai river.

Said stands on the permanent bank of the Oxus, and not in its bed like Jan Kila. To reach it we had a march of five miles through a heavy reed jungle abounding in game of every variety. Deer were numerous, and a splendid pair of antlers were procured from one which a villager shot. Pheasants, also, were plentiful, as they are in many other parts of the valley of the Oxus. The method of taking game is to fire the jangal, and when an animal breaks cover he is speared by the horsemen or pulled down by dogs. Upwards of two hundred head of deer are slaughtered annually at Said. I had intended to have remained a few days to see the sport, but when we were about to take the field on the morning following our arrival, the heavens looked so much like rain, that I deemed it prudent to re-cross the river, lest we should be kept prisoners here longer than was convenient.

Said is the frontier province of Murad Beg's dominions, north of the Oxus. The hills in its neighbourhood afford an inexhaustible supply of mineral salt. The village contains a population of about 100 families.

At Jan Kila I found a note awaiting me from Dr. Lord, the contents of which induced me at once to return to Hazrat Imam; so, crossing the plain of Turghi-i-Tippa, we arrived on the banks of the Kokcha about nine o'clock at night. As it had been raining all day it was not judged prudent to attempt fording the swollen stream until daylight. We now looked about for some shelter, the rain still pouring. The flinty hearts of the Uzbeks, who were here encamped, were assailed in vain. Keeping by the stream for a few miles upwards we reached a considerable village; but there we fared no better. We went the round of nearly every house in the place, were threatened at many, and spurned, abused, and driven from the doors of all. Even a cow-house we were not permitted to enter. Our guide, an officer in the service of Mohamed Beg of Hazrat Imam, told them we were guests of Mohamed Beg, to which the Uzbeks replied, "They were subjects of Talikhan, and cared neither for the blind Mir nor his brother." Towards midnight, when these uncouth and inhospitable boors had gone to rest, we stealthily re-entered the village and took possession of an empty house in its suburbs. There was a deep puddle on its floor, but groping round the walls we discovered raised benches, and upon these we lay till day-dawn. When morning broke we found ourselves in an oil-mill shed, cradled in its seed-bins. Having no one to thank for hospitality we left the village before a kirgah was opened. Fording the river, now considerably swollen, we breakfasted at Kila Chap, and that evening by sunset were again in Hazrat Imam.

Dr. Lord's patients were both improving in health; but this was not enough for the friends of the Mir, who had fondly imagined that a single dose of the firingi's patent medicine would open the eyes of the blind chief, and set the crippled son on his legs again. From the first, Dr. Lord held out no hopes to the Mir that he could restore his sight; but he did not hesitate to tell him that his son only required careful treatment to ensure recovery; adding, however, that if his advice was not strictly followed he would not be responsible for the result. The day after my arrival a deputation waited on the doctor to tell him that a lad, suffering as the Mir's son now did, had been completely cured by immersion in an oil-bath, and that Mohamed Beg wished the young Mir to be similarly treated. As it was vain to reason with them, Dr. Lord peremptorily required implicit obedience to his prescriptions or permission to quit the place. After some little deliberation the native Galen prevailed, and his hot and cold nostrums were preferred to the lights of modern science. The poor youth died; but whether his death was hastened or delayed by the book-bound ignorance of Mohamedanism, let others judge. Thanks to the comfortable doctrine of predestination, Wakhut receed, "his time had come." Neither the firingi Tabeeb nor his rival of Peshawar suffered in Uzbek estimation by this melancholy event.

Among the Uzbeks the temper of a medical man is sadly tried, for he can seldom, if ever, depend on his prescriptions being faithfully followed. The people eat so enormously that to adhere to any course of diet is a task to which very few among them are equal. For instance, we discovered that the Mir of Hazrat Imam, when suffering from indigestion and undergoing a course of medicine for relief, was gorging himself every morning with sour milk, hard-boiled eggs, and rich pillaus. Three times did Dr. Lord put him to rights, and as often did the man's indiscretion bring on a relapse. But the Peshawari physician was more summary in his treatment—kill or cure seems to have been his motto. He does not, however, appear to have been very successful in his practice, for soon after our departure from Turkistan we heard of Mohamed Beg's death.

As on our arrival at Kunduz we were informed that the

Passes of Hindu Kosh were still blocked up with snow, and that none of them could be attempted with safety for at least another fortnight. Dr. Lord asked and obtained permission to visit Khulm in the interim; and on the evening of Saturday, the 24th, we set out for that city. Our first march was a short one; seven miles brought us to the western side of the Kunduz plain, where, on the summit of the high grassy plateau which there forms its boundary, we dismounted and pitched the bechoba. Next day a ride of another five miles in a west-south-west direction, over a plain like a bowling-green, took us to the base of a range of hills, crossed by a path on which a wheeled carriage could travel. At the bottom of their western slope stands a water cistern, a dome-covered building, and a guard-tower—remnants of Mongol munificence, evincing, by their usefulness rather than their beauty, the philanthropic spirit of the monarch who erected them. It is such as these—edifices raised for the wayfaring man's accommodation, water-tanks stored for his use, and canals dug to irrigate lands otherwise infertile, that make us sympathise with the fallen fortunes of this once powerful dynasty, which can boast of many generous and enlightened men. The character of Akbar, for instance, will not suffer by being compared with that of any sovereign in Europe with whom he was contemporary. We slept this night at another of these abdans; for during the palmy days of Baber's line the emperors of Hindustan had post-houses not only

"From Agra to Lahore of Great Moghul,"

but across the India-Tartaric Caucasus to Balkh. Here we found some of Murad Beg's soldiers ou guard, as the road was infested by banditti from Bulgewar, on the opposite bank of the Oxus, headed by Kutty Khan, a relation of the Kunduz chief. The guard sent out patrols and saw us down into the plain of Yang Arekh unmolested by their free-booting relatives. Although thus far attentive to the guests of their prince, these troopers showed us little courtesy, and it was not without difficulty that we succeeded in establishing our right to have quarters in their guard-tower.

A slight rise in the ground hid Khulm from our view until we crested the ridge which is within half a mile of the town. The fields around it were green as emeralds, while all beyond was desert. Entering the eastern gate, or that called Badakhshan, we wound through its suburbs to the bazar, which though inferior to that of Kabul is infinitely superior to the one in Kunduz. The hum of voices, the well-covered stalls, the predominance of Tajik features, and the rosy cheeks of the young, were what we had not of late been accustomed to, and each in turn came in for its share of our commendation. The orchards looked beautiful in their fresh livery of leaves and blossoms; the mulberry plantations for the rearing of silk-worms were kept clean and neat, the trunk of the tree being pruned down to the height of from four to six feet to increase its foliage. The fruit was now (April 6) well-formed, though not a leaf was yet open. Nearly a month before this time the plum-trees in the orchards of Kunduz had begun to blossom.

From a Khaja, a descendant of the former rulers of Kashkar, whom we met at Khulm, we learned that the palaces of Samarcand are still in good preservation; that the halls in which Timur revelled, and the colleges where his grandson, the celebrated Ulug Beg, studied, yet exist. The town is in ruins, but a considerable population, attached to the place, still inhabit the ancient Maracanda. By the Khaja's account, Kokan is little, if at all, inferior in size to Bokhara.

I was surprised at the camel-loads of skins that passed the Khulm custom-house for the Bokhara market. We were told by the Hindu who collects the revenue for Murad Beg that the annual export is nearly 200,000 skins. They are principally those of lambs, wolves, and foxes, but nothing comes amiss. All the fur-yielding animals of the surrounding mountains are eagerly sought after, and even the skins of dogs and cats are not rejected. Lambs'-skins are bought at from twenty-four to thirty shillings per hundred, and bring a profit of about cent. per cent. in Bokhara, the expense of carriage not being deducted. In Khulm the water-spouts in the eaves of the houses are formed of the shoulder-blade bones of sheep, a trifling fact in itself, but one which, taken in connexion with the above, is singularly illustrative of Uzbek commerce.

A very superior and handsome fur, called Dalkhafik, is met with in Kabul. The animal that yields it must be diminutive, for its skin rarely measures more than four inches by ten. It is used to line posteens. One hundred and twenty-two skins are required for one cloak, and the price of each being two shillings, the article is costly, and only worn by rich Soudaghurs (merchants), and wealthy chiefs. The animal is a native of the Hazara and other mountains around Kabul. I believe it to be the marten of commerce.

The old town of Khulm is distant five miles from Tash Kurghan (" stone fort "), or the new town, which was built in the time of Kalich Ali Beg, whose memory is still deservedly celebrated in Turkistan. It stands immediately without the gorge of the Khulm river, up the course of which its orchards extend. The ruins of the old town occupy more ground than the new; but it is now quite forsaken, except its fortress, within which a few Arab families have taken up their abode. The valley of the Oxus here bears a striking resemblance to that of the Indus south of Kalabagh. Both are destitute of verdure— the soil, a whitish clay, fertile when irrigated, but yielding nothing spontaneously except the tamarisk bush and a few dwarfish and useless jungle trees. The beds of both rivers are, however, abundantly productive, and along their margins, when cleared from the wood and gigantic grass which are native to them, every plant may be reared that is adapted to the climate. In fact, wherever their waters reach they carry plenty with them, for whether conducted in canals or diffused by

[293]

inundations, water, assisted by man, will clothe the desert with verdure, and rear an oasis in the wilderness.

One evening, when at dinner in Khulm, a Mohamedan saint introduced himself and was told to be seated. Wine stood upon the table, of which he was requested to partake. He looked highly offended, and said little until the dinner was removed and the servants retired. The Pir's countenance then brightened up at once, and he exclaimed, "Now, hand hither the wine cup! Do you think that I, who have disciples everywhere, from Balkh to Herat, know so little of the world, as to throw away my bread, by indulging in shrab (wine) in the presence of Mussulmans? No, no; between ourselves, such restrictions are unnatural and absurd; but you would not have those who live by them let the people know that they think so."

Mazar, where the last of Moorcroft's party died, is thirty miles west of Khulm, and was now visited by Dr. Lord in the hope of procuring any books or manuscripts of the unfortunate travellers which might still be in existence. Nor were his labours without their reward, since with the aid of the Mutawali, or priest, superintendent of the shrine, he succeeded in getting possession of every book which was in Mazar belonging to the party, even to the daily cash account-book. But among them were no manuscript details of their journey, and it is now pretty certain that none exist independent of those from which Professor Wilson compiled his late work.

Being so near to Maimana and Andhko, in which districts many of the Turkoman horses sent to India are bred, we naturally expected to pick up a few choice animals; but we were disappointed. We purchased the only good horse which was shown us, and though it was generally known that we wanted more, we re-entered Kunduz on the 10th of April, without any furthur addition to our stud. In crossing the plain to the west of Kunduz, herds of antelopes were seen in the distance, gazing at us or scampering off in affright beyond the reach of vision. Throughout this excursion, I was struck with the admirable adaptation of this country to the wants of a pastoral people. West of Khulm, the valley of the Oxus, except on the immediate banks of the stream, appears to be a desert; but in an opposite direction, eastward to the rocky barriers of Darwaz, all the high-lying portion of the valley is at this season a wild prairie of sweets, a verdant carpet enamelled with flowers. Were I asked to state in what respects Kabul and Kunduz most differ from each other, I should say in their mountain scenery. Throughout Kabul the hills are bold and repulsive, naked and bleak, while the low swelling outlines of Kunduz are as soft to the eye as the verdant sod which carpets them is to the foot.

Chapter XXIV

On the 11th of April we attended Durbar and received permission to quit Kunduz. Our arrangements were soon made, and a little after midnight we left, without regret, that metropolis of thieves. Old Mirza Badi saw us some miles on our journey, and then with friendly warmth pressing our hands, he consigned us to the care of God and departed. Poor old man, in the usual course of nature a few years more and the grave would have claimed its own; but life is held cheap in Turkistan, and at no long period after this he fell a victim to animosity and avarice. The circumstances of his murder I have already mentioned.

After getting well clear of Kunduz, we struck south-south-east over an elevated plain, and at the close of an eighteen miles' ride, entered the valley of Shor-ab, or the "Salt-water." This stream drains the mountains of Eshk Meshk, and is strongly impregnated by the salt they contain, from which circumstance it derives its name. After pursuing the course of this rivulet for twelve miles, the yabus of the Kafila were too exhausted to proceed any further, and we accordingly halted. The little valley of Shor-ab is fringed by grass-clad hills rarely exceeding 300 feet in height, along the base of which in every nook stood an Uzbek encampment.

The next day rain delayed us until noon; nevertheless we accomplished by eight o'clock at night one and thirty miles, the general direction of our march being still to the south. Our encamping ground was a sweet spot at the head of the Narin plain, in lat. 36° 5' 13" N. The surface of the country had now roughened. To the eastward the Eshk Meshk (probably Isk-Kimish) mountains reared their snowy crests, whilst in other directions the prospect was bounded by lesser and near-lying ridges. Towards the close of this day's journey, we left the little rivulet, flowing from east-by-north, in which direction lay the mountain whence it came. Soon afterwards we crossed the Baghlan, a tributary of the Kunduz river. Westward the country sometimes opened into plains, having their largest axis in that direction.

The following day we traced the river of Baghlan to its source, on reaching which, the Hindu Kosh, only ten miles distant, met our gaze. At the bottom of the pass lay the secluded valley of Inderab, beyond which the snowy mountains rose like a wall, without any intervening ridge to veil their majesty or detract from their bulk. The eye at a glance caught the mighty buttress, from its blackened base to its hoary summit. The snow-line on its mural face was clear and well defined.

As we descended into Inderab, a horseman overtook us, who proved to be Tora Khan, the chief of the valley. He courteously requested us to make his house our home. He had been to Kunduz on business, and though only a short time absent from his people, it was pleasing to see the affectionate manner in which they greeted his return. Every man we passed ran up to the Mir, and taking him familiarly by the hand inquired after his health. The plough was left standing in the fields, and some individuals, who discovered him from their distant cottage-doors, came at full speed to congratulate him on his safe return. The Tajik chief spoke kindly to all. Of some he inquired how certain fields were looking; of others he asked if the last hunt had been successful. More than once he bawled out, and astonished an honest ploughman who had been too mindful of his furrow to perceive his chieftain's approach. How enviable must his feelings have been! It was delightful to us thus unexpectedly to find ourselves in this small but apparently most happy community, where natural affections had their flow, and where its chief was loved rather than feared. Locked up among mountains, the Inderabis know little of what transpires in the country around them. Changes that rend kingdoms disturb not the tranquillity of this secluded district. Now that Kunduz is all powerful north of the mountains, Tora Khan yields a willing obedience, and pays his tribute to its chief; but should Kabul ever regain the provinces she has lost, not only he, but every Tajik who now feels the iron grasp of Murad Beg, would welcome the change.

It is instructive to remark the difference which climate and circumstances everywhere produce on the character and habits of man. The Mir of Inderab, though verging to corpulency, was active both in mind and body. Had he been brought up in India, he would, instead of leading the bustling life he now does, have been, in all probability, a lazy Patan—one of those portly personages, the retainers of the native princes in Hindustan, who, bristling with arms, seem only to relish life in court, in camp, or on a journey. See them at home when the kammerband is ungirdled, and the showy turban replaced by a dirty skull-cap, and they are the very personification of idleness. For hours will they sit on their carpet, or loll upon charpæ (bedstead) in the open air, in seeming unconsciousness; or, if they do give signs of thought and life, it is only to exclaim, "Tobah! Tobah!" and to change their position.

A small colony of Sauleh-aulengis is settled in Inderab, whom Tora Khan assured us were among the most industrious and well-behaved of his Ryots. In their own valley, on the opposite side of the mountains, they are notorious freebooters. Here, however, there is no opportunity of levying black-mail; and, with the orderly habits of an honest community ever before their eyes, the Sauleh-aulengis have "ceased from evil, and learned to do good!"

Circumstances constrained us to remain four days with the chief, whose residence proved superior to what we had anticipated. The building was a facsimile, on a small scale, of Dost Mohamed Khan's new houses in the Bagh-i-shah at Kabul. Our entertainment was such as left us no grounds for quarrel with Tajik hospitality.

The greater number of the inhabitants of Inderab are agriculturists. A portion are, however, pastoral. In early spring their flocks are driven down upon the Oxus. As that season draws to a close, they range the lower hills. Summer advances, and they move towards Hindu Kosh. When autumn is well through, they have eaten their way up to the neighbourhood of the snow line; but the first fall of snow is the signal for a retrograde movement, and the men at once commence providing fuel and provender for winter consumption.

On the 18th, accompanied by Tora Khan, we left Inderab for the Pass of Khawak, by which, and the Panchshir valley, we had decided on entering Afghanistan. Khawak is at the top of the Panchshir valley, and is the source both of its stream and of that of Inderab. It is the most eastern of the Turkistan passes, and by nature one of the most accessible; but the lawless habits of the Panchshiris have long closed it to both traveller and merchant. The power of Kabul is set at nought, and we could not expect that because we were the guests of its ruler we should fare better than others. Superstition was our only safeguard; and Dr. Lord had accordingly arranged for Mir Baba of Koh Daman, a holy man of great influence in these regions, to meet us at the pass, and escort us down the valley.

Following up the stream which wound, in its stony bed, along the foot of the stupendous wall to our right, we arrived at the foot of Khawak, distant twenty-nine miles from Inderab, on the afternoon of the 22nd. Six miles before reaching this halting-ground, we came on two thermal springs, gushing out from the side of a grassy hill, 400 yards to the left of the path, at a place called Sir-ab. Their temperatures were respectively 108°

and 124° of Fahrenheit.

Preparations were now made to pass the snowy mountains, and that evening a large party of our host's peasantry were sent forward with the baggage. The horses, stripped to their felts, accompanied them. It was a clear frosty night, and we were not without hope of their gaining the other side of Khawak before the next day's sun should have loosened the frozen surface of the snow. In the morning we followed, mounted from Tora Khan's stud. When the snow became too soft for the horses, they were to be sent back. After being about an hour on the road, Ibrahim the Sindi, was seen stealing back among the hills towards our last night's encampment; and, as he had charge of a chronometer, I suspected something was wrong, and went after him. It appeared that he had only forgotten his sword. Vexed at this detention, I now endeavoured to overtake my companions; and, in my anxiety to do so, unluckily lost the road. After blundering on for some time to the right and left, I at length discovered the path, and pushed the pony at a glassy steep to reach it. When near the top, the animal lost its footing and fell. Both of us were soon at the bottom of the hill, though the speed with which the pony descended considerably exceeded mine. He did not wait for his rider; for before I could get upon my legs he was off at an easy trot, but much too fast for me to think of following him. Stripping off my fur-coat, I now slowly and carefully scrambled up the ice-sheeted hill, on surmounting which I found myself upon the track of Dr. Lord's party.

Fatigued with the late adventure, I had trudged wearily on for about half a mile, when a party of Inderabis were espied on their return from the pass, sitting round a fire with their steeds picketed hard by. Exchanging a few civil words with the party, I asked and obtained permission to try the paces of the best looking of their horses; when kicking him under the flanks, I set off along the track of those who preceded me. Chase was forthwith given, but this time I won the race, and distanced my pursuers, who appeared quite at a loss to understand my somewhat suspicious looking procedure. My intention was to return the horse by one of the Mir's attendants, but I did not like to ask for the loan of the animal, being pretty sure that it would have been denied me. Two miles beyond the spot where the horse had been obtained, I encountered Tora Khan, who had seen Dr. Lord well up the pass, and was now returning home. He told me to dismount, as the snow could bear the horse but little further; so making the animal over to one of his attendants, I bade the Mir farewell, with my warmest thanks for the great kindness he had shown us, and parted from him just in time to escape the angry accusation of my pursuers. From this spot the view extended far up the pass, the road to which was one glistening sheet of frozen snow. The rise was remarkably uniform, not a ridge occurring in the whole ascent to vary the sameness of its surface. Far in the distance, towards the summit of the mountain, I discerned sundry little dark spots, each of which was some individual of our party, dragging his weary body upwards. On starting off on foot, I stepped out at a good pace, hut soon learned by experience that short steps were not only the more pleasant method of walking up hill, but the speediest in the end. In the course of a few hours I overtook Dr. Lord, supported between two mountaineers, and in a state of great exhaustion. His plan had been to walk fast, and when tired to sit down and draw breath. I now communicated to him my system, which, though slow, was sure. The effect was surprising, and the doctor and myself were the first of our party to crown the pass.

While the laggards were coming up, we managed to make a fire, and found by the boiling point of water, that the height of Khawak was 13,200 feet. Having seen all the party, both men and horses, over the crest of the pass, we commenced its southern descent; but had not proceeded far when firm footing began to fail the horses. The depth of snow was about four feet; and most of the animals, after floundering till exhausted, sunk in it up to their bellies. It was no use in attempting to move them further that day, but it was necessary to take some precautions to prevent their being frost-bitten during the night. We therefore spread their felts compactly together on the surface of the snow, and with the aid of tent-poles, lifted the animals upon them, and their weight being thus more equally disposed, the snow sufficed to bear them up.

East-by-south, ten miles and a half from the top of the pass, is the fort of Khawak, 9,300 feet above the sea, in latitude 35° 37' 36" N. This place we reached on the same day that we crossed the pass, but three more elapsed before we got the horses to it. Mir Baba, on whose holy protection our safety depended, had not yet arrived, and we felt uncomfortable at his non-appearance. Fifteen miles, however, and a rough road, still separated us from the inhabited part of the valley; and we trusted to gain intelligence of the Pir's locality before his thievish disciples heard of ours.

Between the top of the pass and the fort of Khawak a lead mine was pointed out to us; but the depth of snow upon the ground prevented our visiting it. In the grave-yard of the little fort nine miners are interred, who had been attacked and slain while at work, by a party of the neighbouring Kaffirs. There were ten in all; but one escaped, though badly wounded.

While detained at Khawak snow fell every day; but the cold was not severe. On the 28th a messenger arrived, reporting the near neighbourhood of our protector, on which we quitted the fort, and that evening gave ourselves into the keeping of the holy man. By this messenger we also received letters from Captain Burnes, briefly mentioning that circumstances had constrained him to make arrangements for quitting Kabul, and desiring us to hasten our return.

On the last day of April we cleared the valley of Panchshir, and that night slept at a fort in Koh Daman, the residence of Mir Baba. The length of the Panchshir valley, its sinuosities included, is seventy miles; its general direction being south west and north-east. It is said to contain seven thousand families, all of which, except those at Khawak, are resident within forty-five miles of its entrance. Probably there is no district throughout Kabul better peopled than this; and I certainly have seen none where signs of prosperity were more abundant. The valley in most places is about a mile and a half wide, and it nowhere exceeds twice that breadth. Numerous streams from the north and south join its main river, and it is up the banks of those that the inhabitants have placed their dwellings. The valley is naturally sterile. Everything here is artificial. Panchshir, like all the cultivated valleys of Afghanistan, owes its productiveness and its beauty to man; there being scarcely a tree but what has been planted by his hand. There is little land fit for cultivation, but the whole of that was in crop. The orchard and mulberry plantations furnish the staple support of its inhabitants. Though limited in range, the scenery of Panchshir is soft and beautiful. Its rugged, red-tinged surface is dotted over with castellated dwellings, whose square corner towers and solid walls rising on every knoll are relieved by the smiling foliage of fruit trees, and the lively green of the garden-like fields which surround them.

Yet this fair scene is chiefly peopled by robbers, whose lawless lives and never-ending feuds render it an unfit abode for honest men. It is astonishing how soon, where crime is general, the moral perceptions and the kind feelings of the heart are lost and blunted. In most other countries atrocious crimes are the result of evil passions strongly excited; but in the Kohistan blood is too often shed without provocation, and in the mere wantonness of cruelty. Some time ago a Kasid coming up Panchshir, with letters for Tora Khan, was asked to part with his shoes (kamaches). He refused, and was put to death. One of our own attendants, attempting to come up the valley, was sent back naked. He afterwards arrived under Mir Baba's protection.

In the quarrels which perpetually occur in this region, where blood had been shed, and castles demolished, never, as far as I could learn, has a mulberry plantation been destroyed. Such an act would complete the ruin of a family; and, if often repeated, as it assuredly would be, were the system once introduced, must desolate the valley; mulberry flour being the staff of life in the Kohistan.

Since the reign of Timur Shah, the Panchshiris have been virtually independent of the many rulers who have successively occupied the Kabul ghuddi. Prior to that period they were governed by nine Khans, revered the king's authority, and peaceably paid their taxes. Now every man is for himself, and the valley has consequently become a scene of turbulence and unnatural warfare. They acknowledged Dost Mohamed Khan as their ruler, but added nothing to his exchequer. It is calculated that, in the event of a religious or a national war, this valley could send out 10,000 armed men. On such occasions their domestic feuds lie dormant for the time, to be revived when peace returns. The same unity of action would have shown itself had Dost Mohamed attempted to force a tribute from them; but though able to cope with the limited means of the ex-Amir of Kabul, they will doubtless be coerced into submission by the disciplined battalions of Shah Shuja. It is, however, more than questionable whether, for some years to come, the tribute realised will defray the expense of its collection, either in this region or among any of the hill-tribes in Afghanistan.

The Panchshiris have the reputation of being good soldiers. Their arms are the musket and the long knife-like sword of the Afghans. All the muskets which we examined bore either the King's or the Company's mark on the lock. In Kunduz a matchlock is preferred to a flint-lock; but south of Hindu Kosh it is otherwise. The Uzbeks detest the very sight of pistols; but an Afghan or Tajik covets their possession. Dr. Lord once presented a brace of pistols to one of the young princes in Kunduz.

Next day they were returned by the father, with the remark that if the doctor wished to make his son a present, he should give him something useful. A matchlock from the bazar, about one-tenth of the value of the pistols, gave unbounded satisfaction.

Leagues similar to those existing between the Kaffirs and Badakhshis are formed here. These are in force during the summer, at the close of which season the hostages are returned. Yearly, when the passes open, the leagues are renewed. Sometimes this pacific compact is broken; but this does not happen so frequently as to do away with all confidence between the contracting parties. When the truce ceases hostilities commence. In the stealthy advance and the night attack the cunning of the Kaffir gives him the advantage; but in open day the musket of the Panchshiri is more than a match for the Kaffir spear.

The Panchshiris, like the rest of the Kohistanis, are Tajiks. They are Suni Mohamedans, and not being very old in the faith, are the more violently bigotted to it. Before Baber's time they are said to have been Kaffirs; and it is also stated that the Sauleh-aulengis became Mussulmans about the same era. We saw a few weavers amongst the former people; but their clothing is principally procured from the bazar of Kabul. Amidst the anarchy which prevails in this valley there are two dignified exceptions. These are the brothers Khanjan Khan and Mohamed Shah Khan, who tranquilly rule over about 500 families, at the beautiful village of Barak.

At eleven o'clock at night, on the 1st of May, after a weary ride of upwards of fifty miles, we re-entered Kabul. Finding that Captain Burnes had left the city we called on the Nawab, from whom we received our letters and a hearty welcome. He was in bed when we arrived, but got up at once, and came out to us in déshabille; nor would he, in spite of all we could say, return till he had seen all our wants supplied. Not to disturb his servants, Nawab Jabar Khan placed refreshments before us, with his own hands; and then, having called up a trusty person to wait on us, this truly hospitable and excellent man went back to his zenana.

The non-arrival of the baggage detained us a few days in Kabul, during which we had ample opportunity of observing how far recent events had influenced the public mind. The Kuzilbash, or Persian party, numbering many of the most respectable citizens of Kabul, rejoiced at what had occurred; but the mass of the people, Afghan and Tajik, were at no pains to conceal their discontent. Annoyed at Dost Mohamed's reception of Vikovitch, the Russian emissary, and disquieted by the departure of the British agent, they looked to the Mir as the sole cause of their troubles, and thought of Shah Shuja and redress. The resistance, passive and open, which our army experienced throughout the late campaign, and which, by the last accounts from India, has not yet altogether ceased, shows that we are no longer regarded by the Afghans as their friends. Can it well be otherwise? The conquest and occupation of their country by British troops, not to mention the brilliant affairs of Ghizni and Kelat, will no doubt diffuse a knowledge of our names from the Indus to the Caspian; but in substituting the dread of our arms for the respect which, throughout Asia, was before voluntarily accorded to the British character, I question whether our present gain may not ultimately prove a loss.

Before finally quitting Kabul, we waited on its ruler, who was residing in the house we ourselves had formerly occupied in the Bagh-i-Shah. Dost Mohamed Khan was engaged at chess when we entered the apartment; and while the interview lasted he affected to be more intent upon the chess-board than on the political game, which we well knew was the uppermost in his mind. His manner was at first cold; but this we could perceive was more feigned than real, as he soon assumed his usual tone of cordiality; and after some conversation upon recent events, he uttered, when we arose to depart, a pious ejaculation, and bade us a kind farewell.

From Kabul we marched to Jelalabad. During the few days of our stay at the former place, we had made the acquaintance of a young Frenchman, of pleasing manners, and gentlemanly address. He gave out that he had travelled among the Kaffirs of Hindu Kosh, and was anxious to make another journey through their country. I had long felt a desire to visit these people, and agreed to accompany him, provided I had Captain Burnes's permission. For this I applied, and arranged with the Frenchman that I would remain at Jelalabad till an answer arrived; where, if it were favourable, he was to join me. In the interim I ordered presents for the journey, to the amount of about 10l. These consisted of looking-glasses, beads, needles, thread, &c. At parting, I requested a sight of my new acquaintance's journal; but to this he demurred, and, in lieu of it, presented me with what he called extracts. This was not so satisfactory a document: however, the strange adventures he professed to have met with among the Kaffirs were so plausibly told, that I had no suspicion of his falsehood, until the day before we entered Jelalabad, when Gholam Hussein asked me whether I believed the Frenchman's story,—"Yes, certainly," was my reply: on which the Munshi exclaimed, Tumam durrohg, "it's all a lie," and brought forward a discharged servant of the Frenchman, who satisfactorily proved that his master had never been nearer to Kaffiristan than Jelalabad, at which place he had gathered the strange stories he was in the habit of relating as his own adventures: This man introduced himself to me as a sailor; and among other stories of the sea, related at great length the incidents of a cruise in the Pacific, in a French vessel commanded by an Englishman. Some months afterwards I discovered, that for all he knew of nautical matters he was indebted to Mr. Masson's library, from which he had borrowed a work, entitled "A Whaling voyage in the Pacific." From Jelabalad we embarked on rafts of inflated skins, and dropped down with the stream to Peshawur. Here we rejoined Captain Burnes, now ordered to Lahore, where events soon transpired, the remote tendencies of which, though they cannot yet be defined, must be pregnant with interest to Great Britain and the East.

THE END.